LEARNING BY DOING

A Handbook for Professional Learning Communities at Work™

Richard DuFour

Rebecca DuFour

Robert Eaker

Thomas Many

Solution Tree | Press

a division of
Solution Tree

555 North Morton Street
Bloomington, IN 47404
800.733.6786 (toll free) / 812.336.7700
FAX: 812.336.7790

email: info@solution-tree.com
solution-tree.com

Visit **go.solution-tree.com/PLCbooks** to download the reproducibles in this book.

Printed in the United States of America

16 15 14 13 12   7 8 9 10

MIX
Paper from responsible sources
FSC® C102027

Library of Congress Cataloging-in-Publication Data

Learning by doing : a handbook for professional learning communities at work / Richard DuFour ... [et al.]. -- 2nd ed.
    p. cm.
  Includes bibliographical references and index.
  ISBN 978-1-935542-09-4 (perfect bound) -- ISBN 978-1-935542-10-0 (library binding) 1. School improvement programs--United States. 2. Group work in education--United States. 3. Team learning approach in education--United States. 4. Educational leadership--United States. I. DuFour, Richard, 1947-
  LB2822.82.L427 2010
  371.2'07--dc22
                        2010009757

Solution Tree
Jeffrey C. Jones, CEO & President

Solution Tree Press
President: Douglas M. Rife
Publisher: Robert D. Clouse
Vice President of Production: Gretchen Knapp
Managing Production Editor: Caroline Wise
Proofreader: Rachel Rosolina
Text Designer: Raven Bongiani

Cover Designer: Pamela Rude

We have been avid, ongoing students of the research regarding professional learning communities (PLCs) and the leadership necessary to bring the PLC concept to life. Our deepest learning, however, has come from our own work in schools that have embodied the PLC concept and from our association with colleagues who have initiated and sustained PLC processes in their own schools and districts. These men and women come from varied backgrounds throughout North America and from schools and districts that represent a broad spectrum of sizes and circumstances. More importantly, these colleagues share certain characteristics. First, they are passionate about the potential for PLCs to have an impact on the lives of the students they serve. Second, they have learned by doing: they have developed their expertise by leading through the rough and tumble of PLC initiatives. Third, they are skillful at sharing their insights with other practitioners. Our own understanding of the PLC concept has been enriched by their efforts and deepened by their insights. We are proud to call them colleagues and friends, and we dedicate *Learning by Doing* to them, our PLC associates.

—Richard DuFour, Rebecca DuFour, and Robert Eaker

To Rick, my friend and mentor, and to Becky and Bob, thank you for inviting me to be a part of creating and sustaining professional learning communities. And to my father, Dr. Wesley A. Many, I thank you for sharing Willie's story. I am a living legacy to the lessons so beautifully illustrated by that simple tale.

—Thomas Many

Acknowledgments

Our work and our thinking have been shaped and influenced by some of the greatest contemporary educational thinkers in North America. We have benefited immensely from the wisdom of Larry Lezotte, Michael Fullan, Doug Reeves, Rick Stiggins, Roland Barth, Mike Schmoker, Jonathon Saphier, Dennis Sparks, Bob Marzano, and Tom Sergiovanni. Like so many educators, we are indebted to them, and we acknowledge the enormous contribution each has made to our practice, our ideas, and our writing.

We also acknowledge the tremendous support we have received for this project from the Solution Tree family. Gretchen Knapp is a skillful editor who polished our prose and designed layouts for the book that greatly enhanced its readability. We are grateful for the enthusiasm and energy she devoted to this endeavor.

Finally, each of us owes a tremendous debt of gratitude to Jeff Jones, the president of Solution Tree. Jeff is more than a publisher. He is one of the most ethical, service-oriented business leaders we know. He has been an ardent advocate for spreading the PLC concept across North America, and his passion and his skill have given our ideas a platform we could not have achieved on our own. Finally, he is a friend in every sense of the word. Every author should have the opportunity to work with a publisher like Jeff Jones. More importantly, everyone should know the joy of having someone like him for a friend.

Visit **go.solution-tree.com/PLCbooks** to download the reproducibles in this book.

Table of Contents

Chapter 3

Chapter 4

Chapter 5

Chapter 6

Chapter 7

Using Relevant Information to Improve Results **181**

Chapter 8

Implementing the PLC Process Districtwide **205**

Chapter 9

Consensus and Conflict in a Professional Learning Community **225**

About the Authors

Richard DuFour, EdD, was a public school educator for thirty-four years, serving as a teacher, principal, and superintendent. He served as the principal of Adlai Stevenson High School in Lincolnshire, Illinois, from 1983 to 1991 and as superintendent of the district from 1991 to 2002. During his tenure, Stevenson became what the United States Department of Education (USDE) has described as "the most recognized and celebrated school in America." It is one of three schools in the nation to win the USDE Blue Ribbon Award on four occasions and one of the first comprehensive schools designated a New America High School by USDE as a model of successful school reform. Stevenson has been repeatedly cited in the popular press as one of America's best schools and referenced in professional literature as an exemplar of best practices in education.

Dr. DuFour is the author of many books and has written numerous professional articles. He wrote a quarterly column for the *Journal of Staff Development* for nearly a decade. Dr. DuFour was the lead consultant and author of the Association for Supervision and Curriculum Development's seven-part video series on principalship and the author of several other videos, including *Passion and Persistence, Through New Eyes, The Power of Professional Learning Communities at Work™, Collaborative Teams in Professional Learning Communities at Work™,* and *Leadership in Professional Learning Communities at Work™.* He was the first principal in Illinois to receive the state's Distinguished Educator Award, was presented the Distinguished Scholar Practitioner Award from the University of Illinois, and was the 2004 recipient of the National Staff Development Council's Distinguished Service Award. He consults with school districts, state departments, and professional organizations throughout North America on strategies for improving schools.

Rebecca DuFour, MEd, has served as a teacher, school administrator, and central office coordinator. As a former elementary principal, Becky helped her school earn state and national recognition as a model professional learning community. She is one of the featured principals in the *Video Journal of Education* program "Leadership in an Age of Standards and High Stakes" (2001). She is also the lead consultant and featured principal for the *Video Journal of Education* program

"Elementary Principals as Leaders of Learning" (2003). Becky is coauthor of many books and video series on the topic of professional learning communities.

She has written for numerous professional journals, including a quarterly column for the National Association of Elementary School Principals publication *Leadership Compass*. She has also served as a book reviewer for the *Journal of Staff Development*.

Becky is the recipient of the Distinguished Alumni Award of Lynchburg College. She consults with and works for professional organizations, school districts, universities, and state departments of education throughout North America.

Robert Eaker, EdD, is a professor in the Department of Educational Leadership at Middle Tennessee State University, where he also served as dean of the College of Education and interim vice president and provost. Dr. Eaker is a former fellow with the National Center for Effective Schools Research and Development. He has written widely on the issues of effective teaching, effective schools, helping teachers use research findings, and high expectations for student achievement. He was cited by the *Kappan* as one of the nation's leaders in helping public school educators translate research into practice. Dr. Eaker was instrumental in the founding of the Tennessee Teachers Hall of Fame and was a regular contributor to the Effective Schools Research Abstracts series.

Thomas Many, EdD, is superintendent of Kildeer Countryside Community Consolidated School District 96 in Buffalo Grove, Illinois. He uses the tenets of the Professional Learning Communities at Work™ model to ensure students from his district are prepared to enter Adlai E. Stevenson High School, a nationally recognized PLC. In each of his roles—superintendent, public speaker, and author—he has worked closely with Dr. Richard DuFour, former superintendent of Stevenson and national authority on PLCs.

In addition to his extensive experience as superintendent, Dr. Many has served as a classroom teacher, learning center director, curriculum supervisor, principal, and assistant superintendent. A dedicated PLC practitioner, he has been involved in local- and state-level initiatives to achieve school improvement. Under his direction, District 96 has been recognized as one of the highest-achieving and lowest-spending elementary districts in Illinois.

Dr. Many has published numerous articles that have received national attention. He is a contributor to *The Collaborative Teacher: Working Together as a Professional Learning Community*.

Other Resources By or Featuring the Authors

Print

The Collaborative Administrator: Working Together as a Professional Learning Community

The Collaborative Teacher: Working Together as a Professional Learning Community

Getting Started: Reculturing Schools to Become Professional Learning Communities

A Leader's Companion: Inspiration for Professional Learning Communities at Work™

On Common Ground: The Power of Professional Learning Communities

Professional Learning Communities at Work™: Best Practices for Enhancing Student Achievement

Professional Learning Communities at Work™ Plan Book

Raising the Bar and Closing the Gap: Whatever It Takes

Revisiting Professional Learning Communities at Work™: New Insights for Improving Schools

21st Century Skills: Rethinking How Students Learn

Video

Collaborative Teams in Professional Learning Communities at Work™

Leadership in Professional Learning Communities at Work™

Passion and Persistence: How to Develop a Professional Learning Community

The Power of Professional Learning Communities at Work™: Bringing the Big Ideas to Life

Through New Eyes: Examining the Culture of Your School

Introduction to the Second Edition

We began the first edition of this book with a simple sentence: "We learn best by doing." This axiom certainly applies to our own work. Since the publication of the first edition, we have made presentations to tens of thousands of educators, served on dozens of panels to answer their questions, worked with several districts on a long-term ongoing basis to assist with their implementation of the professional learning community (PLC) concept, and participated in ongoing dialogue with educators online at www.allthingsplc.info. This continuing work with teachers, principals, and central office staff from schools and districts throughout North America has given us a deeper understanding of the challenges they face as they attempt to implement the professional learning community process in their organizations. This second edition attempts to draw upon that deeper understanding to provide educators with a more powerful tool for moving forward.

What's New

This edition makes editorial revisions throughout the book and offers several substantive changes as well, including those that follow.

1. A Focused Exploration of Reciprocal Accountability

Leaders who call upon others to engage in new work, achieve new standards, and accomplish new goals have a responsibility to develop the capacity of those they lead to be successful in meeting these challenges. Richard Elmore (2006) refers to this relationship as "reciprocal accountability—For every increment of performance I demand from you, I have an equal responsibility to provide you with the capacity to meet that expectation. Likewise, for every investment you make in my skill and knowledge, I have a reciprocal responsibility to demonstrate some new increment in performance" (p. 93).

Effective implementation of the concept of reciprocal accountability is vital to the PLC process. Superintendents cannot implement the process throughout a district unless they build the capacity of principals to lead it in their schools. Principals will not develop their schools as high-performing PLCs unless they develop the knowledge and skills of key staff members

Leaders who call upon others to engage in new work, achieve new standards, and accomplish new goals have a responsibility to develop the capacity of those they lead to be successful in meeting these challenges.

to lead the collaborative work essential to PLCs. Every leader must consider the questions: "How can I fulfill my responsibility to support others? What support can I provide that will help them accomplish what needs to be accomplished?"

In the first edition, we implied that those who lead the PLC process at any level have an obligation to provide others with the rationale, resources, training, and support to increase their likelihood of success. This edition is specifically intended to *equip* school and district leaders with the knowledge and tools to model effective reciprocal accountability in their own settings.

Very predictable questions arise when thinking people are asked to engage in new work. Those questions are likely to include:

1. **Why questions.** *Why should we do this? Can you present a rationale as to why we should engage in this work? Is there evidence that suggests the outcome of this work is desirable, feasible, and more effective than what we have traditionally done?*

2. **What questions.** *What are the exact meanings of key terms? What resources, tools, templates, materials, and examples can you provide to assist in our work?*

3. **How questions.** *How do we proceed? How do you propose we do this? Is there a preferred process?*

4. **When questions.** *When will we find time to do this? When do you expect us to complete the task? What is the timeline?*

5. **Guiding questions.** *Which questions are we attempting to answer? Which questions will help us stay focused on the right work?*

6. **Quality questions.** *What criteria will be used to judge the quality of our work? What criteria can we use to assess our own work?*

7. **Assurance questions.** *What suggestions can you offer to increase the likelihood of our success? What cautions can you alert us to? Where do we turn when we struggle?*

This book is specifically designed to provide leaders with the information and resources that they need to answer these questions for each element of the essential work of PLCs. We hope it will serve as an important tool that benefits educators at all levels who engage in the PLC process.

2. An Examination of How the Central Office Can Facilitate the PLC Process

The case studies and lessons of the first edition focused almost exclusively on the school site, and certainly the individual school is the primary venue for the structural and cultural changes that occur in the PLC process. It has become increasingly evident, however, that effective leadership in the central office can contribute to successful implementation of the process throughout an entire district rather than in isolated schools. In this edition, we reference the role of the central office in several chapters. We consider some of the common challenges leaders at this level will face and strategies and tools for overcoming those challenges.

3. Explicit Advice on Dangerous Detours and Seductive Shortcuts

The PLC journey is filled with dangerous detours and seductive shortcuts at almost every step of the way. There is no guarantee of a successful outcome, and we have witnessed many schools that fail to make progress—typically because they avoid *doing* the work. Every time a district or school takes a shortcut to circumvent doing the real work of PLC process, the likelihood of building the collective capacity to create a strong professional learning community is diminished. A study that monitored the impact of the PLC process in schools found that partial implementation of the process produced no gains in student achievement. But when those same schools engaged in the process *fully*, they experienced dramatic gains (Gallimore, Ermeling, Saunders, & Goldenberg, 2009). Research conducted by Doug Reeves (in press) came to a similar conclusion. So in this edition, we are as specific as possible regarding the work that must be done, and we alert readers in each chapter to the tempting shortcuts that are often taken to avoid doing the work.

4. Specific Protocols for Team Analysis of Student Achievement Data

The idea that evidence of student achievement should be transparent and openly shared among members of a collaborative team seems very foreign to teachers who have spent their lives working in isolation. A common question we hear is, "What does it look like?" This edition offers several protocols to help teams engaged in this aspect of the PLC process focus their collective inquiry on the right questions.

5. A Revised Continuum of Progress on the PLC Journey

We received considerable feedback on the four-step continuum we offered in the first edition. Many educators felt that none of the points on the continuum captured their position because a step was missing. Others felt that the terminology we used slighted their commitment to the process prior to reaching the "sustaining level." We have attempted to address both of these concerns by adding a fifth level and revising the descriptions to provide more specific indicators of progress on the journey.

6. An Updated Research Base

Several important studies have been done, inside and outside of education, that further support the big ideas of the PLC process. This edition provides the most current research.

7. Online Delivery of the Team Tools

The first edition supported schools and teams engaged in the PLC process by providing helpful tools and templates in two formats—in the hard copy of the book and a compact disc that was included with the book. In this edition, we have opted to move many of the tools and templates online so that we can revise, update, and add to them on an ongoing basis. Please visit **go.solution-tree.com/PLCbooks** to download materials related to this book. We will also invite educators to share materials they have created to help them in their work.

The Format

Each chapter of this handbook includes seven parts:

- Part One: The Case Study

- Part Two: Here's How

- Part Three: Here's Why

- Part Four: Assessing Your Place on the PLC Journey

- Part Five: Tips for Moving Forward

- Part Six: Questions to Guide the Work of Your Professional Learning Community

- Part Seven: Dangerous Detours and Seductive Shortcuts

Part One: The Case Study

Each chapter opens with a case study describing some of the issues and challenges that have arisen in a school or district that is attempting to implement the PLC concept. The names of schools and people described in the case studies are fictional, but the situations presented are neither fictional nor hypothetical. They represent the very real issues educators must grapple with and resolve if they are to bring the PLC concept to life in their schools and districts. Readers may be tempted to skip the case studies and move quickly to solutions; we urge you to resist that temptation. A critical step in assessing alternative solutions to any problem is to come to an understanding and appreciation of the problem itself. We hope you will take the time to consider each case study carefully, reflect upon the issues it presents, and generate possible strategies for addressing those issues prior to studying the rest of the chapter. Engaging in this reflective process with your colleagues will further strengthen your learning.

Part Two: Here's How

In our work with schools, we have found that "how" questions come in at least two varieties: one type represents a sincere and genuine solicitation of guidance from inquirers who are willing to act, and the other typically comes in waves as a series of "yeah, but . . ." questions. For example, after listening to an explanation of the PLC process, a teacher or administrator responds:

- "Yeah, but . . . how are we supposed to find time to collaborate?"

- "Yeah, but . . . how can we give students extra time and support for learning when our schedule will not allow it?"

- "Yeah, but . . . how can this work in a school this big [or small, or poor, or urban, or rural, or suburban, or low achieving and therefore too despondent, or high achieving and therefore too complacent]?"

- "Yeah, but . . . how can we make this happen with our ineffective principal [or unsupportive central office, or adversarial teacher union]?"

These questions are less of a search for answers on how to implement the PLC process successfully and more of a search for a reason to avoid implementation. As Peter Block (2003) says, "Asking 'How?' is a favorite defense against taking action" (p. 11). Block goes on to say, "We act like we are confused, like we don't understand. The reality is that we *do* understand—we get it, but we don't like it" (pp. 47–48). Our own work with schools has confirmed that a group that is determined not to act can always find a justification for inaction. Questions about "how" can have a positive impact only if those asking are willing to act on the answers.

Therefore, the "Here's How" sections in this book are written for those who seek ideas, insights, and information regarding how the PLC concept comes alive in the real world of schools. Part Two of each chapter describes how educators bring a particular PLC element to life in their school. It presents exemplars for schools to use as a model as they work through the challenges of moving from concept to action.

We fully recognize that there is no precise recipe for school improvement (blending two parts collaboration with one part formative assessment does not work). We also understand that even the most promising strategies must be customized for the specific context of each district and each school. The most effective improvement models are those that staff have *adapted* to fit the situation in their schools and communities (Hall & Hord, 1987; Hord, Rutherford, Huling-Austin, & Hall, 1987; Marzano, Waters,

Even the most promising strategies must be customized for the specific context of each district and each school.

& McNulty, 2005). Therefore, the "Here's How" sections do not presume to present "The Answer" to problems posed in the case study, because it is the dialogue about and the struggle with those problems at the school and district level that result in the deepest learning and greatest commitment for teachers and administrators. Our hope is that this book can serve as a tool educators can use to initiate the dialogue and to engage in the struggle.

Part Three: Here's Why

Informing others about how something can be done does not ensure they will be persuaded to do it. In fact, we are convinced that one of the most common mistakes school administrators make in the implementation of improvement initiatives is to focus exclusively on "how" while being inattentive to "why." Leaders at all levels must be prepared to anticipate and respond to the inevitable questions and concerns that arise when educators are called upon to engage in new practices. We have included Part Three in each chapter to offer useful tools—research, reasoning, and rationale—to help clarify why the initiative should be undertaken.

Part Three draws upon, but is not limited to, the research base on education. We examine findings from studies in organizational development, change processes, leadership, effective communication, and psychology because the challenges facing contemporary leaders demand that they look outside the narrow scope of their professional field for answers.

Part Four: Assessing Your Place on the PLC Journey

This section calls upon readers to assess the current reality in their own schools as it relates to a particular element of PLC practices. Readers will do hands-on work as they use the charts in this section to assess their policies and practices. They are then asked to present evidence and arguments in support of their assessments.

Part Five: Tips for Moving Forward

Each chapter includes specific suggestions and strategies to assist with the implementation of particular PLC processes. The primary purpose of this handbook is to encourage people to act, to learn by doing. Random actions, however, do nothing to enhance the capacity of a staff to function as a PLC. The challenge facing leaders is to identify purposeful and focused actions that contribute to the goal of improved learning for students and staff alike. Part Five offers insight regarding which actions to take and which to avoid. It identifies tactics that offer the greatest leverage for implementing PLC processes and presents research-based and practitioner-proven tips for pursuing those tactics effectively.

Part Six: Questions to Guide the Work of Your Professional Learning Community

Members of PLCs engage in *collective* inquiry: they learn how to learn together. But only when they focus this collective inquiry on the right questions do they develop their capacity to improve student and adult learning.

It has been said that the leader of the past knew how to tell. The leader of the future, however, will have to know how to ask. Those who lead the PLC process should not be expected to have all the answers and tell others what they must do. Leaders should instead be prepared to ask the right questions, facilitate the dialogue, and help build shared knowledge. Part Six offers some of the "right" questions educators should consider as they work to drive the PLC concept deeper into the culture of their schools and districts.

Part Seven: Dangerous Detours and Seductive Shortcuts

It is the *process* of learning together that helps educators build their capacity to create a powerful professional learning community. One of the most common mistakes that they make on the journey is to seek ways to circumvent that process. This section alerts readers to the some of the most common ways educators have attempted to avoid actually doing the work of a PLC so they can avoid those mistakes.

A Journey Worth Taking

Despite the popularity of the term *professional learning community*, the *practices* of a PLC continue to represent "the road less traveled" in public education. Many teachers and administrators prefer the familiarity of their current path, even when it becomes apparent that it will not take them to their desired destination. We recognize it is difficult to pursue an uncharted path, particularly when it is certain to include inevitable bumps and potholes along the way. We do not argue that the PLC journey is an easy one, but we know with certainty that it is a journey worth taking. We have seen the evidence of improved learning and heard the testimonials of teachers and principals who have been renewed by establishing common ground, clear purpose, effective monitoring, and collaborative processes that lead to better results. They describe a heightened sense of professionalism and a resurgence of energy and enthusiasm generated by committed people working together to accomplish what could not be done alone. As Robert Evans (2001) writes:

We do not argue that the PLC journey is an easy one, but we know with certainty that it is a journey worth taking.

> Anyone part of such a process, or anyone who has seen first-rate teachers engage in reflective practice together, knows its power and excitement. Opportunities to collaborate and to build knowledge can enhance job satisfaction and performance. At their best, they help schools create a self-reflective, self-renewing capacity as learning organizations. (p. 232)

The following chapters will not eliminate the bumps and potholes of the PLC journey, but they will offer some guidance as to how educators can maneuver their way around and through the rough spots on the road. It has been said that the journey of a thousand miles begins with a single step. We urge readers to take that step. Let us begin together.

Chapter 1

A Guide to Action for Professional Learning Communities at Work

We learn best by doing. We have known this to be true for quite some time. More than 2,500 years ago Confucius observed, "I hear and I forget. I see and I remember. I do and I understand." Most educators acknowledge that our deepest insights and understandings come from action, followed by reflection and the search for improvement. After all, most educators have spent four or five years *preparing* to enter the profession—taking courses on content and pedagogy, observing students and teachers in classrooms, completing student teaching under the tutelage of a veteran teacher, and so on. Yet almost without exception, they admit that they learned more in their first semester of *teaching* than they did in the four or five years they spent *preparing* to enter the profession. This is not an indictment of higher education; it is merely evidence of the power of learning that is embedded in the work.

Our profession also attests to the importance and power of learning by doing when it comes to educating our students. We want students to be *actively engaged* in *hands-on authentic exercises* that promote *experiential learning*. How odd, then, that a profession that pays such homage to the importance of learning by doing is so reluctant to apply that principle when it comes to developing its collective capacity to meet the needs of students. Why do institutions created for and devoted to learning not call upon the professionals within them to become more proficient in improving the effectiveness of schools by actually doing the work of school improvement? Why have we been so reluctant to learn by doing?

What Are Professional Learning Communities?

Since 1998, we have published multiple books and videos with the same two goals in mind: (1) to persuade educators that the most promising strategy for meeting the challenge of helping all students learn at high levels is to develop their capacity to function as a professional learning community and (2) to offer specific strategies and structures to help them create PLCs in their own schools.

It has been interesting to observe the growing popularity of the term *professional learning community.* In fact, the term has become so commonplace and has been used so ambiguously to describe virtually any loose coupling of individuals who share a common interest in education that it is in danger of losing all meaning. This lack of precision is an obstacle to implementing PLC processes because, as Mike Schmoker observes, "clarity precedes competence" (2004a, p. 85). Thus, we begin this handbook with an attempt to clarify our meaning of the term. To those familiar with our past work, this step may seem redundant, but we are convinced that redundancy can be a powerful tool in effective communication, and we prefer redundancy to ambiguity.

We have seen many instances in which educators assume that a PLC is a program. For example, one faculty told us that each year they implemented a new program in their school. In the previous year it had been PLC, the year prior to that it had been "understanding by design," and the current year it was "differentiated instruction." They had converted the names of the various programs into verbs, and the joke on the faculty was that they had been "UBDed, PLCed, and DIed." The PLC process is not a program. It cannot be purchased, nor can it be implemented by anyone other than the staff itself. Most importantly, it is ongoing—a continuous, never-ending process of conducting schooling that has a profound impact on the structure and culture of the school and the assumptions and practices of the professionals within it.

We have seen other instances in which educators assume that a PLC is a meeting—an occasional event when they meet with colleagues to complete a task. It is not uncommon for us to hear, "My PLC meets Wednesdays from 9:00 a.m. to 10:00 a.m." This perception of a PLC is wrong on two counts. First, the PLC is the larger organization and not the individual teams that comprise it. While collaborative teams are an essential part of the PLC process, the sum is greater than the individual parts. Much of the work of a PLC cannot be done by a team but instead requires a schoolwide or district-wide effort. So we believe it is helpful to think of the school or district as the PLC and the various collaborative teams as the building blocks of the PLC. Second, once again, the PLC process has a pervasive and ongoing impact on the structure and culture of the school. If educators meet with peers on a regular basis only to return to business as usual, they are not functioning as a PLC. So the PLC process is much more than a meeting.

Other educators have claimed they are members of a PLC because they engage in dialogue based on common readings. The entire staff reads the same book or article, and then members meet to share their individual impressions of what they have read. But a PLC is more than a book club. Although collective study and dialogue are crucial elements of the PLC process, the process requires people to *act* on the new information.

So, what is a PLC? We argue that it is an *ongoing process in which educators work collaboratively in recurring cycles of collective inquiry and action research to achieve better results for the students they serve.* Professional learning communities operate under the assumption that the key to improved learning for students is continuous job-embedded learning for educators. The following section examines the elements of the PLC process more closely.

A Focus on Learning

The very essence of a *learning* community is a focus on and a commitment to the learning of each student. When a school or district functions as a PLC, educators within the organization embrace high levels of learning for all students as both the reason the organization exists and the fundamental responsibility of those who work within it. In order to achieve this purpose, the members of a PLC create and are guided by a clear and compelling vision of what the organization must become in order to help all students learn. They make collective commitments clarifying what each member will do to create such an organization, and they use results-oriented goals to mark their progress. Members work together to clarify exactly what each student must learn, monitor each student's learning on a timely basis, provide systematic interventions that ensure students receive additional time and support for learning when they struggle, and extend and enrich learning when students have already mastered the intended outcomes.

The very essence of a learning community is a focus on and a commitment to the learning of each student.

A corollary assumption is that if the organization is to become more effective in helping all students learn, the adults in the organization must also be continually learning. Therefore, structures are created to ensure staff members engage in job-embedded learning as part of their routine work practices.

There is no ambiguity or hedging regarding this commitment to learning. Whereas many schools operate as if their primary purpose is to ensure that children are taught, PLCs are dedicated to the idea that their organization exists to ensure that all students *learn* essential knowledge, skills, and dispositions. All the other characteristics of a PLC flow directly from this epic shift in assumptions about the purpose of the school.

A Collaborative Culture With a Focus on Learning for All

A PLC is composed of collaborative teams whose members work *interdependently* to achieve *common goals* for which members are mutually accountable. These common goals are directly linked to the purpose of learning for all. The team is the engine that drives the PLC effort and the fundamental building block of the organization. It is difficult to overstate the importance of collaborative teams in the improvement process. It is even more important, however, to emphasize that collaboration does not lead to improved results unless people are focused on the right issues.

A PLC is composed of collaborative teams whose members work interdependently to achieve common goals for which members are mutually accountable.

Collaboration is a means to an end, not the end itself. In many schools, staff members are willing to collaborate on a variety of topics as long as the focus of the conversation stops at their classroom door. In a PLC, *collaboration* represents a systematic process in which teachers work together interdependently in order to *impact* their classroom practice in ways that will lead to better results for their students, for their team, and for their school.

Collective Inquiry Into Best Practice and Current Reality

The teams in a PLC engage in collective inquiry into both best practices in teaching and best practices in learning. They also inquire about their current reality—including their present practices and the levels of achievement of their students. They attempt to arrive at consensus on vital questions by building shared knowledge rather than pooling opinions. They have an acute sense of curiosity and openness to new possibilities.

Collective inquiry enables team members to develop new skills and capabilities that in turn lead to new experiences and awareness. Gradually, this heightened awareness transforms into fundamental shifts in attitudes, beliefs, and habits that, over time, transform the culture of the school.

Working together to build shared knowledge on the best way to achieve goals and meet the needs of clients is exactly what *professionals* in any field are expected to do, whether it is curing the patient, winning the lawsuit, or helping all students learn. Members of a *professional* learning community are expected to work and learn together.

Action Orientation: Learning by Doing

Members of PLCs are action oriented: they move quickly to turn aspirations into action and visions into reality.

Members of PLCs are action oriented: they move quickly to turn aspirations into action and visions into reality. They understand that the most powerful learning always occurs in a context of taking action, and they value engagement and experience as the most effective teachers. Henry Mintzberg's (2005) observation about training leaders applies here: deep learning requires experience, which requires taking action. It "is as much about doing in order to think as thinking in order to do" (p. 10.) In fact, the very reason that teachers work together in teams and engage in collective inquiry is to serve as catalysts for action.

Members of PLCs recognize that learning by doing develops a deeper and more profound knowledge and greater commitment than learning by reading, listening, planning, or thinking. Traditional schools have developed a variety of strategies to resist taking meaningful action, preferring the comfort of the familiar. Professional learning communities recognize that until members of the organization "do" differently, there is no reason to anticipate different results. They avoid paralysis by analysis and overcome inertia with action.

A Commitment to Continuous Improvement

Inherent to a PLC are a persistent disquiet with the status quo and a constant search for a better way to achieve goals and accomplish the purpose of the organization. Systematic processes engage each member of the organization in an ongoing cycle of the following:

- Gathering evidence of current levels of student learning

- Developing strategies and ideas to build on strengths and address weaknesses in that learning

- Implementing those strategies and ideas

- Analyzing the impact of the changes to discover what was effective and what was not

- Applying new knowledge in the next cycle of continuous improvement

The goal is not simply to learn a new strategy, but instead to create conditions for perpetual learning—an environment in which innovation and experimentation are viewed not as tasks to be accomplished or projects to be completed but as ways of conducting day-to-day business, *forever*. Furthermore, participation in this process is not reserved for those designated as leaders; rather, it is a responsibility of every member of the organization.

Results Orientation

Finally, members of a PLC realize that all of their efforts in these areas—a focus on learning, collaborative teams, collective inquiry, action orientation, and continuous improvement—must be assessed on the basis of results rather than intentions. Unless initiatives are subjected to ongoing assessment on the basis of tangible results, they represent random groping in the dark rather than purposeful improvement. As Peter Senge and colleagues conclude, "The rationale for any strategy for building a learning organization revolves around the premise that such organizations will produce dramatically improved results" (1994, p. 44).

This focus on results leads each team to develop and pursue measurable improvement goals that align with school and district goals for learning. It also drives teams to create a series of common formative assessments that are administered to students multiple times throughout the year to gather ongoing evidence of student learning. Team members review the results from these assessments in an effort to identify and address program concerns (areas of learning where many students are experiencing difficulty). They also examine the results to discover strengths and weaknesses in their individual teaching in order to learn from one another. Most importantly, the assessments are used to identify students who need additional time and

Inherent to a PLC are a persistent disquiet with the status quo and a constant search for a better way to achieve goals and accomplish the purpose of the organization.

Members of a PLC realize that all of their efforts must be assessed on the basis of results rather than intentions.

support for learning. Frequent common formative assessments represent one of the most powerful tools in the PLC arsenal, and we will examine them in detail.

> ## Three Big Ideas That Drive the Work of a PLC
>
> The essence of the PLC process is captured in three big ideas:
>
> 1. The purpose of our school is to ensure all students learn at high levels.
> 2. Helping all students learn requires a collaborative and collective effort.
> 3. To assess our effectiveness in helping all students learn we must focus on results—evidence of student learning—and use results to inform and improve our professional practice and respond to students who need intervention or enrichment.

Why Don't We Apply What We Know?

As we have shared our work in support of PLCs with educators in every state in the U.S. and every province of Canada, we have become accustomed to hearing the same response: "This just makes sense." It just makes sense that a school committed to helping all students learn at high levels would focus on *learning* rather than teaching, would ensure students had access to the same curriculum, would assess each student's learning on a timely basis using consistent standards for proficiency, and would create systematic interventions that provide students with additional time and support for learning. It just makes sense that we accomplish more working collaboratively than we do working in isolation. It just makes sense that we would assess our effectiveness in helping all students learn on the basis of results—tangible evidence that they have actually learned. It just makes sense! In fact, we have found little overt opposition to the characteristics of a PLC.

So why don't schools *do* what they already *know* makes sense? In *The Knowing-Doing Gap,* Jeffrey Pfeffer and Robert Sutton (2000) explore what they regard as one of the great mysteries of organizational management: the disconnect between knowledge and action. They ask, "Why does knowledge of what needs to be done so frequently fail to result in action or behavior that is consistent with that knowledge?" (p. 4).

Learning by Doing is intended to help educators close the knowing-doing gap by transforming their schools into PLCs. More specifically, it is designed to accomplish the following four objectives:

1. To help educators develop a common vocabulary and a consistent understanding of key PLC processes

2. To present a compelling argument that the implementation of the PLC process will benefit students and educators alike

3. To help educators assess the current reality in their own schools and districts

4. To convince educators to take purposeful steps to develop their capacity to function as a PLC and offer strategies and tools to help them on their journey

Helping Educators Develop a Common Vocabulary and a Consistent Understanding of Key PLC Processes

Michael Fullan observes that "terms travel easily . . . but the meaning of the underlying concepts does not" (2005, p. 67). Terms such as *professional learning community, collaborative teams, goals, formative assessments*, and scores of others have indeed traveled widely in educational circles. They are prevalent in the lexicon of contemporary "educationese." If pressed for a specific definition, however, many educators would be stumped. It is difficult enough to bring these concepts to life in a school or district when there *is* a shared understanding of their meaning. It is impossible when there is no common understanding and the terms mean very different things to different people within the same organization.

Developmental psychologists Robert Kegan and Lisa Laskow Lahey (2001) contend that the transformation of both individuals and organizations requires new language. They write, "The places where we work and live are, among other things, places where certain forms of speech are promoted and encouraged, and places where other ways of talking are discouraged or made impossible" (p. 7). As educators make the cultural shift from traditional schools and districts to PLCs, a new language emerges. Therefore, we have highlighted and defined key terms used in implementing PLC processes to assist in building shared knowledge of both critical vocabulary and the concepts underlying the terms. We have also included an online glossary at **go.solution-tree.com/PLCbooks** that readers can download and distribute. We hope it will add to the precision and clarity of the emerging language that accompanies the creation of PLCs.

We have included an online glossary at **go.solution-tree .com/PLCbooks**

Presenting a Compelling Argument That the Implementation of PLC Processes Will Benefit Students and Educators Alike

Jim Collins (2001) begins his best-selling book *Good to Great* with a provocative observation: "Good is the enemy of great." "Good" organizational performance can cause complacency and inertia instead of inspiring the pursuit of continuous improvement essential to sustained greatness. Despite the persistent attacks on public schools throughout North America by politicians insisting on greater accountability, business leaders demanding better-trained workers, and members of the media lamenting the failure of public education, most parents believe their children go to "good" schools. While they may be concerned about the quality of education throughout the country, in 2009, 74 percent of parents gave the schools their oldest child attends a grade of A or B, the highest approval rating since this annual poll was first administered in 1969 (Bushaw & McNee, 2009). So what would cause educators to explore more powerful models for learning if the general perception in the community they serve indicates they are already doing a good job? One strategy, increasingly popular in contemporary North America, is to apply sanctions and punishment for schools that fail to demonstrate improvement. The effectiveness of this strategy remains very much in question.

Another approach for motivating a faculty to initiate new practices and procedures is to present a persuasive case that there is a better, more effective, more gratifying way to approach the work. We are convinced that the PLC model makes that compelling case for any educator willing to give it meaningful consideration. The model offers a tangible, realistic, compelling vision of what schools might become. We hope to bring the PLC concept to life in ways that resonate with educators because, after all, "It just makes sense."

Helping Educators Assess the Current Reality in Their Own Schools and Districts

More than a quarter century ago, John Naisbitt and Patricia Aburdene (1985) offered the common-sense conclusion that people find it a lot easier to get from point A to point B if they know where point B is and how to recognize it once they arrive. For many educators, however, school improvement initiatives have been plagued by uncertainty and confusion regarding both points A and B. They have not taken the time to clarify either the current status of their school or what they hope it will become. As a result, efforts to reform their schools have too often been characterized by random stops and starts, rather than by purposeful progression on a path of improvement. A key step in any effective improvement process is an honest assessment of the current reality—a diligent effort to determine the truth. Educators will find it easier to move forward to where they want to go if they first agree on where they are.

A key step in any effective improvement process is an honest assessment of the current reality.

Even when teachers and administrators make a good faith effort to assess their schools, they face significant obstacles. All schools have cultures: the assumptions, beliefs, expectations, and habits that constitute the norm for a school and guide the work of the educators within it. Perhaps it is more accurate to say that educators *do not* have school cultures, but rather that the school cultures have *them*. Teachers and administrators are typically so immersed in their traditional ways of doing things that they find it difficult to step outside of those traditions to examine conventional practices from a fresh, critical perspective. Therefore, this handbook is designed not only to offer specific examples of PLC practices (to help paint a picture of point B), but also to help educators make a frank and honest assessment of current conditions in their schools (to clarify point A).

Convincing Educators to Take Purposeful Steps to Develop Their Capacity to Function as a PLC

Our greatest hope in developing this handbook is that it will help educators take immediate and specific steps to close the knowing-doing gap in education by implementing PLC processes in their own schools and districts. Once again, it will take action on the part of educators to accomplish this objective. The research on what it takes to improve schools has been very consistent over a number of years. Most educators already know what they should do to help students achieve at higher levels, and if they don't have the necessary knowledge, it is easily accessible to them in a variety of forms. The question confronting most schools and districts is not, "What do we need to know in order to improve?" but rather, "Will we turn what we already know into action?"

The question confronting most schools and districts is not, "What do we need to know in order to improve?" but rather, "Will we turn what we already know into action?"

In the past we have provided study guides for our books because we discovered that many faculties use our resources in their book study groups. We call the study guide that accompanies this book an "Action Guide" (available at **go.solution-tree.com/PLCbooks**); we cannot stress enough that this resource is not designed for study, but rather for *action*—to help educators take the essential action steps for building their capacity to create and sustain PLCs.

Taking Action

Perhaps the greatest insight we have gained in our work with school districts across the continent is that organizations that take the plunge and actually begin *doing* the work of a PLC develop their capacity to help all students learn at high levels far more effectively than schools that spend years *preparing* to become PLCs through reading or even training. Developing the collective capacity of educators to create high-performing PLCs demands more than "workshops and professional development for all. It is the daily habit of *working together*, and you can't learn this from a workshop or course. You need to learn by doing it and having mechanisms for getting better at it on purpose" (Fullan, 2005, p. 69). So let's examine some of the challenges of working together and consider mechanisms for getting better at it.

Chapter 2

A Clear and Compelling Purpose

Part One

The Case Study: Clarifying Our Purpose

Principal Cynthia Dion left the Professional Learning Communities Institute with the zeal and fervor of a recent convert. She was convinced that the PLC concept was the best strategy for improving student achievement in her school, and she was eager to introduce the concept to her faculty at the Siegfried and Roy Middle School (nickname: the Tigers).

On the opening day of school she assembled the entire staff to share both her enthusiasm for PLCs and her plans for bringing the concept to the school. She emphasized that she was committed to transforming the school into a PLC and that the first step in the process was to develop a new mission statement that captured the new focus of the school. She presented the following draft to the staff and invited their reaction:

> It is our mission to ensure all our students acquire the knowledge and skills essential to achieving their full potential and becoming productive citizens.

The moment Principal Dion presented the statement a teacher challenged it, arguing that any mission statement should acknowledge that the extent of student learning was dependent upon students' ability and effort. Another teacher disagreed with the reference to "ensuring" all students would learn because it placed too much accountability on teachers and not enough on students. A counselor felt the proposed mission statement placed too much emphasis on academics and not enough on the emotional well-being of students. Soon it became difficult to engage the entire staff in the dialogue as pockets of conversation began to break out throughout the room. Principal Dion decided to adjourn the meeting to give staff members more time to reflect on her mission statement and promised to return to the topic at the after-school faculty meeting scheduled for the next month.

In the intervening weeks, teachers fiercely lobbied for and against different variations of a mission statement. When the staff convened for their next faculty meeting, a group of teachers proposed a compromise, a mission statement they felt would be more acceptable to the staff. It stated:

> It is our mission to give each student the opportunity to learn according to his or her ability and to create a school that is attentive to the emotional needs of every student.

Principal Dion expressed concern that the statement did not convey a commitment to helping all students learn; instead, it merely promised to give them the *chance* to learn. The ensuing discussion revealed significant differences of opinion, and the respective parties became more entrenched in the defense of their positions. Finally, as the time to end the meeting approached, an impatient staff member proposed a show of hands to determine support for the two different mission statements. Fifty-five percent of the staff preferred the compromise statement, 25 percent supported the mission presented by the principal, and 20 percent were indifferent. Principal Dion acknowledged the decision of the majority and said the compromise statement would become the new mission statement of the school.

Principal Dion remained hopeful that this mission statement would inspire new effort and commitment from the staff. As the year wore on, however, she was disappointed to see the staff had returned to business as usual. She became increasingly disenchanted with the PLC concept. After all, she had engaged the staff in clarifying the mission of the school, just as she had been advised to do at the PLC Institute. There was virtually no evidence, however, that this new mission had impacted either teacher practice or student achievement. She resolved to find another improvement model during the summer.

Reflection

Consider Principal Dion's efforts to develop a clear and compelling purpose for the school with her staff. What advice would you give Principal Dion if you were called upon to mentor her as she was beginning to initiate this process with her staff?

As we mentioned in the introduction, to demonstrate the reciprocal accountability required in a professional learning community, leaders must be prepared to address the very predictable and appropriate questions that will arise on each step of the journey. It is reasonable for staff members to seek clarity regarding how they are to engage in the work, what is the nature of the work, why the work is significant, the criteria that might be used to assess their progress, strategies that will increase the likelihood of their success, critical issues they must consider to ensure they are focused on the right work, and common mistakes to avoid. Chapters 2 through 8 are designed to address each of these areas so that leaders have the information and tools that they need to provide clarity and direction to a staff engaged in the challenging work of implementing the PLC process. Let's begin.

Part Two

Here's How

Despite her good intentions and initial enthusiasm, Principal Dion struggled with two significant factors that adversely impacted her efforts:

1. The process she utilized in attempting to build consensus

2. Her failure to move the dialogue beyond the philosophical debate about the mission of the school

A Failure to Build Consensus

How would a PLC work to build consensus, and what steps would it take to move from dialogue to action? Leaders of a PLC recognize it is a mistake to launch an improvement initiative without the support of a guiding coalition. As John Kotter (1996) of the Harvard Business School concluded in his definitive study of the change process:

> No one individual is ever able to develop the right vision, communicate it to large numbers of people, eliminate all obstacles, generate short-term wins, lead and manage dozens of change projects and anchor new approaches deep in an organization's culture. A strong, guiding coalition is always needed—one with a high level of trust and shared objectives that appeal to both head and heart. Building such a team is always an essential part of the early stages of any effort to restructure a set of strategies. (p. 52)

The challenge Principal Dion faced was not "selling" staff on *her* version of the school's mission, but rather engaging in a process that would help the staff co-create a mission (Senge, Kleiner, Roberts, Ross, & Smith, 1994). A guiding coalition is a powerful tool in that process. It could be composed of existing structures in the school such as a school improvement committee, department chairpeople, or representatives of the teacher's association. Alternatively, she could create a new structure such as a task force convened for the specific purpose of leading an improvement process. In any case, a principal benefits by working through the issues with a small group of key staff members and securing them as allies before engaging the entire faculty. In fact, a comprehensive study of effective school leadership

A principal benefits by working through the issues with a small group of key staff members and securing them as allies before engaging the entire faculty.

concluded the creation of a guiding coalition or leadership team is a critical first step in the complex task of leading a school (Marzano et al., 2005).

In presenting the proposal to the entire staff at one time, Principal Dion used a forum—a large group—that was ill suited to the dialogue that facilitates consensus. Most people will have questions when significant change is proposed, and they will want those questions answered before they are willing to give their consent for moving forward. The large-group forum she used in the case study allowed those skeptical of the proposal to dominate the discussion before the idea had been fully considered. A more intimate venue with a small number of staff would have been more effective. Principal Dion might have asked teachers to meet with her in small groups during a preparation period to engage in this dialogue, particularly if she was willing to cancel an after-school faculty meeting to compensate teachers for their lost time. She might have hired enough substitute teachers to free small groups of teachers to meet with her during the school day. Had she done so, she would have found it easier to build consensus one small group at a time rather than in an entire faculty.

When a school functions as a PLC, staff members attempt to answer questions and resolve issues by building shared knowledge.

The biggest *process* mistake principal Dion made was her failure to build shared knowledge among the staff. Although she had apparently learned of concepts and strategies at the PLC Institute that convinced her of the benefits of a PLC, she did nothing to share that learning with her colleagues in the school. When a school functions as a PLC, staff members attempt to answer questions and resolve issues by building shared knowledge. Members of a *learning* community learn together. When all staff members have access to the same information, it increases the likelihood that they will arrive at similar conclusions. Without access to pertinent information, they resort to debating opinions or retreating to a muddied middle ground.

What Questions

Principal Dion and her guiding coalition must consider the following questions:

- What information will our staff require to come to a better understanding of the current reality regarding student achievement in our school?

- What information will our staff require to come to a better understanding of the practices of highly effective schools?

- What steps must we take to move beyond the debate regarding school purpose to help staff clarify the school we are seeking to create, the commitments necessary to move the school in that direction, and the indicators we can track to monitor our progress?

Working with her guiding coalition, Dion might have presented information to help the staff assess the current reality of the school. For example, she could have presented data to help paint a picture of the school's current reality. The data picture worksheet (A Data Picture of Our School, pages 24–26) assists in the gathering and presentation of information to help clarify the existing conditions of the school. Anecdotes and stories about students who were not being successful could also have helped establish what the school experience was like for some students. In addition, the coalition could have presented staff with a synthesis of research on topics such as professional learning communities, improving schools, clear academic goals for every student, and high expectations for student achievement to support the premise that schools are most effective when staff members define their purpose as helping students learn rather than ensuring they are taught. The staff might have heard testimonials from other schools that had adopted PLC processes or conducted site visits to see a PLC in action. Time spent up front building shared knowledge results in faster, more effective, and most importantly, more committed action later in the improvement process (Patterson, Grenny, McMillan, & Switzler, 2002).

Confusing Mission With Action

The biggest mistake Principal Dion and her staff made was confusing *writing* a mission statement with *living* a mission. No school has ever improved simply because the staff wrote a mission statement. In fact, we have found no correlation between the presence of a written mission statement, or even the wording of a mission statement, and a school's effectiveness as a PLC. The words of a mission statement are not worth the paper they are written on unless people begin to *do* differently.

The words of a mission statement are not worth the paper they are written on unless people begin to do differently.

What could Principal Dion have done to bring the mission to life in her school? First, after engaging staff in building shared knowledge on the specific practices and characteristics of schools where all students were learning at high levels, she might have asked them to describe in vivid detail the school they hoped to create. Once the staff could describe that school, the principal and her guiding coalition could have then led the staff in a discussion of the specific commitments each member would need to honor in order to become the school they had envisioned. Principal Dion might have modeled a willingness to make commitments by identifying the specific things she was prepared to do to support the effort to transform the school. She could have shared her commitments with the staff and asked for their reactions, revisions, and additions. Members of the guiding coalition could have then led the staff in a process to clarify their collective commitments.

Principal Dion might also have asked the faculty to identify the indicators that should be monitored to assess the progress they made in creating their agreed-upon school. Benchmarks could have been established for what they hoped to achieve in the first six months, the first year, and the first three years. Each team of teachers could have been asked to establish specific team goals that, if accomplished, would have contributed to achieving schoolwide goals and to moving the school toward the ideal the staff had described.

A Data Picture of Our School

School Name:

Indicator	Student Achievement Results			Facts About Our Data
	Year 20___–20___	Year 20___–20___	Year 20___–20___	
Based on Our School Assessment Data				
Based on Our District Assessment Data				
Based on Our State or Provincial Assessment Data				
Based on Our National Assessment Data				
Student Engagement Data				
Average Daily Attendance				
Percentage of Students in Extracurricular Activities				
Percentage of Students Using School's Tutoring Services				
Percentage of Students Enrolled in Most Rigorous Courses Offered				
Percentage of Students Graduating Without Retention				
Percentage of Students Who Drop Out of School				

A Data Picture of Our School

Student Engagement Data (continued)

Indicator	Year 20__–20__	Year 20__–20__	Year 20__–20__	Facts About Our Data
Other Areas in Which We Hope to Engage Students, Such as Community Service				

Discipline

Number of Referrals/Top Three Reasons for Referrals				
Number of Parent Conferences Regarding Discipline				
Number of In-School Suspensions				
Number of Detentions/Saturday School				
Number of Out-of-School Suspensions				
Number of Expulsions				
Other				

Survey Data

Student Satisfaction or Perception Assessment				
Alumni Satisfaction or Perception Assessment				

A Data Picture of Our School

Survey Data

Indicator	Year 20__–20__	Year 20__–20__	Year 20__–20__	Facts About Our Data
Parent Satisfaction or Perception Assessment				
Teacher Satisfaction or Perception Assessment				
Administration Satisfaction or Perception Assessment				
Community Satisfaction or Perception Assessment				

Demographic Data

Indicator				Facts About Our Data
Percent Free and Reduced Lunch				
Percent Mobility				
Percent Special Education				
Percent English as a Second Language				
Percent White (Not of Hispanic Origin)				
Percent Black				
Percent Hispanic				
Percent Asian				
Percent Native American				

Of course, all of this dialogue would impact the school only if purposeful steps were taken to demonstrate that creating the school of their hopes, honoring their commitments, and achieving their goals were the collective responsibility of every member of the staff. How is that message best communicated? The most powerful communication is not a function of what is written or said, but rather, once again, what is *done*. As James Autry (2001), author of *The Servant Leader*, wrote, "Those around you in the workplace—colleagues and employees—can determine who you are only by observing what you do . . . the only way you can manifest your character, your personhood, and your spirit in the workplace is through your behavior" (p. 1). Or to paraphrase Ralph Waldo Emerson, what you do stands over you all the while and thunders so loudly that we cannot hear what you say to the contrary.

Consider some of the specific actions the principal and staff might have taken to convey their commitment to improving their school:

1. **Initiating structures and systems to foster qualities and characteristics consistent with the school they are trying to create.** When something is truly a priority in an organization, people do not hope it happens; they develop and implement systematic plans to ensure that it happens. For example, if the staff committed to creating a collaborative culture, steps could be taken to organize teachers into teams, build time for collaboration into the contractual workday, develop protocols and parameters to guide the work of teams, and so on. True priorities are not left to chance but are carefully and systematically addressed.

2. **Creating processes to monitor critical conditions and important goals.** In most organizations, what gets monitored gets done. A critical step in moving an organization from rhetoric to reality is to establish the indicators of progress to be monitored, the process for monitoring them, and the means of sharing results with people throughout the organization. For example, if the staff agreed student learning was the priority in their school, creating procedures to monitor each student's learning on a timely and systematic basis would be imperative.

3. **Reallocating resources to support the proclaimed priorities.** Marshall McLuhan observed, "Money talks because money is a metaphor." The actual legal tender may have little intrinsic value, but how it is expended, particularly in times of scarcity, reveals a great deal about what is valued. Money, however, is not the only significant resource in an organization, and in contemporary public education, time is even scarcer than money. As Phil Schlechty (1990) wrote:

    > The one commodity that teachers and administrators say they do not have enough of, even more than money, is time; time to teach, time to converse, time to think, time

A critical step in moving an organization from rhetoric to reality is to establish the indicators of progress to be monitored, the process for monitoring them, and the means of sharing results with people throughout the organization.

to plan, time to talk, time to go to the restroom or have a cup of coffee. Time is indeed precious in schools. (p. 73)

Decisions about the spending of precious resources are some of the most unequivocal ways organizations communicate what is important. Had Principal Dion created a schedule that provided teachers with time to collaborate and students with time for additional support for learning when they experienced difficulty, she would have sent the message that teacher collaboration and student learning were viewed as priorities in the school.

4. **Posing the right questions.** The questions posed by an organization—and the effort and energy spent in the pursuit of answers—not only communicate priorities but also direct members in a particular direction. In too many schools the prevalent question is, "What is wrong with these kids?"—a question that typically has little impact on improving student achievement. Principal Dion and her staff could have conveyed their commitment to student learning by devoting time to the pursuit of critical questions aligned with that goal, questions such as:

The questions posed by an organization— and the effort and energy spent in the pursuit of answers—not only communicate priorities but also direct members in a particular direction.

- What knowledge and skills should every student acquire as a result of this unit of instruction?

- How will we know when each student has acquired the essential knowledge and skills?

- How will we respond when some students do not learn?

- How will we extend and enrich the learning for students who are already proficient?

5. **Modeling what is valued.** Example is still the most powerful teacher. If Principal Dion hopes the staff will make a commitment to high levels of learning for all students, she must demonstrate her own commitment by focusing on learning with laser-like intensity and keeping the issue constantly before the faculty. If she hopes to build a culture in which teachers collaborate, she must engage the staff in collaborative decision making and provide the time and support essential for effective collaboration. As one study concluded, "The single most powerful mechanism for creating a learning environment is that the leadership of the organization be willing to model the approach to learning they want others to embrace" (Thompson, 1995, p. 96).

6. **Celebrating progress.** When an organization makes a concerted effort to call attention to and celebrate progress toward its goals, the commitments it demonstrates in day-to-day work, and evidence of improved results, people within the organization are continually reminded of the priorities and what it takes to achieve them. Furthermore, this celebration provides real-life

models by which they can assess their own efforts and commitment. If Principal Dion devoted a part of every staff meeting to a celebration of steps forward on the journey of school improvement, the faculty would soon learn what was noted, appreciated, and valued in their school.

7. **Confronting violations of commitments.** If Principal Dion hopes to convey what is important and valued, she must be prepared to confront those who act in ways that are contrary to the priorities of the school and the commitments of the staff. Leaders who are unwilling to promote and defend improvement initiatives put those initiatives at risk.

Part Three

Here's Why

Engaging members of an organization in reflective dialogue about the fundamental purpose of the organization, as Principal Dion attempted to do, can be a powerful strategy for improvement. In fact, the first question any organization must consider if it hopes to improve results is the question of purpose (Drucker, 1992). Why does our organization exist? What are we here to do together? What exactly do we hope to accomplish? What is the business of our business? (Bardwick, 1996; Champy, 1995; Senge et al., 1994) As a study of organizations that sustained high performance over an extended period of time concluded:

> Contrary to popular wisdom, the proper first response to a changing world is NOT to ask, "How should we change," but rather, "What do we stand for and why do we exist?" This should never change. And then feel free to change everything else. Put another way, visionary companies distinguish between their core values and enduring purpose (which should never change) from their operating practices and business strategies (which should be changing constantly in response to an ever-changing world). (Collins & Porras, 1997, p. xiv)

The correlation between clarity of purpose and effectiveness has also been established in educational research. The effective schools research has cited the correlation between clarity of purpose and higher levels of student achievement (Lezotte, 1991). A comprehensive study on school restructuring concluded, "There is no point in thinking about changes in structure until the school achieves reasonable consensus about its intellectual mission for children" (Newmann & Wehlage, 1996, p. 295). A synthesis of effective school leadership concluded that a key leadership responsibility was creating a "purposeful community" that was clear on its purpose and goals (Marzano et al., 2005). Effective districts build a collective sense of efficacy throughout the organization by establishing a clear purpose, widely shared (Louis & Leithwood, 2009). Thomas Lickona and Matthew Davidson (2005) found:

> The best schools we visited were tightly aligned communities marked by a palpable sense of common purpose and shared identity among staff—a clear sense of "we." By contrast, struggling schools feel fractured; there is a sense that people work in the same school but not toward the same goals. (p. 65)

Educators who believe that merely clarifying or reaffirming their mission will somehow improve results are certain to be disappointed. In fact, in many schools, developing a mission statement has served as a substitute, rather than a catalyst, for meaningful action. Merely drafting a new mission statement does not automatically change how people act, and therefore writing a mission statement does nothing to close the knowing-doing gap (Pfeffer & Sutton, 2000). To close that gap educators must move beyond writing mission statements to first, clarifying the vision, values (that is, collective commitments), and goals that drive the daily workings of the school and second, align all their practices accordingly.

Merely drafting a new mission statement does not automatically change how people act.

The Foundation of a PLC

Imagine that the foundation of a PLC rests upon the four pillars of mission, vision, values, and goals. Each of these pillars asks a different question of the educators within the school. When teachers and administrators have worked together to consider those questions and reach consensus regarding their collective positions on each question, they have built a solid foundation for a PLC. Much work remains to be done, for these are just a few of the thousands of steps that must be taken in the never-ending process of continuous improvement. But addressing these questions increases the likelihood that all subsequent work will have the benefit of firm underpinnings. If staff members have not considered the questions, have done so only superficially, or are unable to establish common ground regarding their positions on the questions, any and all future efforts to improve the school will stand on shaky ground.

Mission

"Why do we exist?"

The mission pillar asks the question, "Why?" More specifically, it asks, "Why do we exist?" The intent of this question is to help reach agreement regarding the fundamental purpose of the school. This clarity of purpose can help establish priorities and becomes an important factor in guiding decisions.

Vision

The vision pillar asks "What?"—that is, "What must we become in order to accomplish our fundamental purpose?" In pursuing this question, a staff attempts to create a compelling, attractive, realistic future that describes what they hope their school will become. Vision provides a sense of direction and a basis for assessing both the current reality of the school and potential strategies, programs, and procedures to improve upon that reality. Researchers within and outside of education have routinely cited the importance of developing shared vision. The conclusion of Burt Nanus (1992) is typical: "There is no more powerful engine driving an organization toward excellence and long-range success than an attractive, worthwhile and achievable vision of the future, widely shared" (p. 3). The very first standard for school administrators drafted by the Interstate School Leaders Licensure Consortium (1996) calls upon educational leaders to "promote the success of all students by facilitating the development, articulation, implementation and stewardship of a vision of learning that is shared and supported by the school community" (p. 10).

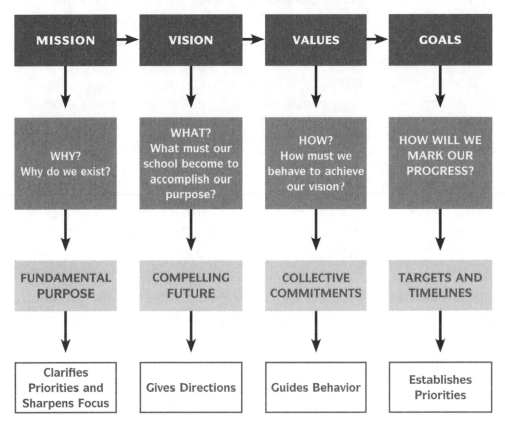

Once again, an important aspect of reciprocal accountability is addressing the "Why" question to offer people a rationale for working in new ways. Therefore, throughout this book, we have provided a concise compilation of research to assist in presenting that rationale. We recommend that staff members be encouraged both to review the summary of research and to look for studies that refute or contradict it. Remember that if people are going to make informed decisions on the basis of evidence rather than opinion, leaders must engage in a good-faith effort to gather evidence and make it easily accessible to all staff. The first of these compilations, Why Should We Describe the School or District We Are Trying to Create? follows on page 32.

"What must we become in order to accomplish our fundamental purpose?"

Why Should We Describe the School or District We Are Trying To Create?

"A vision is a picture of the future you seek to create described in the present tense, as if it were happening now. Vision statement shows where we want to go and what we will be like when we get there. Vision gives shape and direction to the organization's future. It helps people set goals to take the organization closer to its desired future." (Senge et al., 1994, p. 302)

"In a change process, vision serves three important purposes. First, by clarifying general direction for change it simplifies hundreds of more detailed decisions. People can figure out for themselves what to do without constantly checking with bosses. Second, it motivates people to take action in the right direction. Third, it helps coordinate the actions of different people in an efficient way. One question —'is this in line with the vision'—can help eliminate hours of torturous discussion." (Kotter, 1996, pp. 68–69)

"A vision builds trust, collaboration, interdependence, motivation, and mutual responsibility for success. Vision helps people make smart choices, because their decisions are made with the end result in mind. . . . Vision allows us to act from a proactive stance, moving toward what we want. . . . Vision empowers and excites us to reach for what we truly desire." (Blanchard, 2007, p. 22)

An effective school system and its leaders build a shared sense of purpose and a shared vision of what schools and the school system would look like if that shared purpose was acted on, and develop a bias toward action relevant to the vision (Schlechty, 2005).

Shared vision and shared covenants make up the leadership dimension of purposing, which is "key to helping schools become communities of collective responsibility" (Sergiovanni, 2005, p. 8).

"At both school and district levels, administrative tasks essential to teachers' learning and learning communities include building a shared vision and common language about practice." (McLaughlin & Talbert, 2006, p. 80)

Collective Commitments (Values)

In their study of high-performing organizations, Jim Collins and Jerry Porras (1997) found that although creating a vision can be a helpful step in the improvement process, it is never sufficient. Teachers and administrators must also tackle the collective commitments they must make and honor in order to achieve the shared vision for their school or district. The third pillar of the foundation, the values pillar, clarifies these collective commitments. It does not ask, "Why do we exist?" or "What do we hope to become?" Rather, it asks, "How must we behave to create the school that will achieve our purpose?" In answering this question, educators shift from offering philosophical musings on mission or the shared hopes for the school of the future to making commitments to act in certain ways—starting today. Clarity on this topic guides the individual work of each member of the staff and outlines how each person can contribute to the improvement initiative. When members of an organization understand the purpose of their organization, know where it is headed, and then pledge to act in certain ways to move it in the right direction, they don't need prescriptive rules and regulations to guide their daily work. Policy manuals and directives are replaced by commitments and covenants. As a result, members of the organization enjoy greater autonomy and creativity than their more rigidly supervised counterparts.

"How must we behave to create the school that will achieve our purpose?"

Leaders benefit from clearly defined commitments as well. When leaders in traditional hierarchical structures address an employee's inappropriate behavior and demand change, their rationale tends to be, "Because the rules say we have to do it," or "Because I am the boss, and I said so." If, however, the members of the organization have specified collective commitments, leaders operate with the full weight of the moral authority of the group behind them. Members perceive inappropriate behavior as a violation of collective commitments, and the leader moves from the role of "boss" to the promoter and protector of what the members have declared as important or sacred. Finally, achieving agreement about what we are prepared to start doing, and then *implementing* that agreement, is one of the most effective strategies for closing the knowing-doing gap. Those who "do" develop deeper knowledge, greater self-efficacy, and a stronger sense of ownership in results than those who only talk about what should be done.

We believe that attention to clarifying collective commitments is one of the most important and, regrettably, least utilized strategies in building a PLC. There is, once again, considerable evidence in organizational and educational research to support that belief (see page 34, Why Should We Articulate Collective Commitments?).

Goals

The final pillar of the foundation asks members to clarify the specific goals they hope to achieve as a result of their improvement initiative. The goals pillar identifies the targets and timelines that enable a staff to answer the question, "How will we know if all of this is making a difference?"

"How will we know if all of this is making a difference?"

Why Should We Articulate Collective Commitments?

"Culture and core values will be increasingly recognized as the vital social glue that infuses an organization with passion and purpose." (Bolman & Deal, 2000, p. 185)

With the democratization of organizations, especially schools, the leadership function becomes one of creating a "community of shared values" (Lezotte, 1991, p. 3).

To change culture, leaders must create a process to identify and articulate the shared values that people will commit to, examine structures to ensure they support the values, teach and model the values, and address behavior that is contrary to the values (Champy, 1995).

"Leaders of the best-performing organizations defined their jobs in terms of identifying and constantly communicating commonly held values, shaping such values to enhance performance, ensuring the capability of people around them, and living the commonly held values." (Heskett & Schlesinger, 1996, p. 112)

Both profit and nonprofit organizations should be grounded on "a timeless set of core values and an enduring purpose" (Collins & Porras, 1997, p. xxiv).

"Leaders must be able to build a community of shared values. Consensus about values creates commitment to where the organization is going and how it is going to get there." (Kouzes & Posner, 1996, p. 105)

"Values describe how we intend to operate, on a day-to-day basis, as we pursue our vision. . . . Values are best expressed in terms of behavior: If we act as we should, what would an observer see us doing? . . . If values are made a central part of the organization's shared vision effort, and put out in full view, they become like a figurehead on a ship: a guiding symbol of the behavior that will help move people toward the vision." (Senge et al., 1994, p. 302)

High-performing districts "tended to rely more on a common culture of values to shape collective action than on bureaucratic rules and controls. The shared values typically focused on improvement of student learning as the central goal" (Elmore, 2000, p. 26).

The three strands of strong school cultures are academic focus, shared beliefs and values, and productive professional relationships (Saphier, King, & D'Auria, 2006).

A professional community is characterized by "shared values and purpose" (Little, 2006, p. 14).

"Systems successful in improving student learning are characterized by articulated norms and values." (Garmston, 2007, p. 55)

"Values provide guidelines on how you should proceed as you pursue your purpose and picture of the future. They answer the question . . . 'How?' They need to be clearly described so that you know exactly what behaviors demonstrate that the value is being lived." (Blanchard, 2007, p. 30)

"When people gather together to . . . commit themselves to ideas, their relationships change—they have made promises to each other and are likely to feel morally obliged to keep their promises." (Sergiovanni, 2005, p. 32)

"Winning leaders are missionaries for their organization's values. They preach the values, embody them in their own actions, and encourage others to think about them and their application in everyday situations." (Tichy, 1997, p. 105)

"Clear shared values, collectively reinforced, increase the likelihood of teacher success." (Louis, Kruse, & Marks, 1996, p. 181)

"The core values of an institutional culture are the fundamental beliefs and commitments that drive what the organization does and how its members behave. Effective leaders begin the job of shaping a culture by leading the discussion about the institution's core values and beliefs." (Johnston, 1995, p. 12)

Goals provide staff members with a sense of their short-term priorities and the steps to achieve the benchmarks. Effective goals foster both the results orientation of a PLC and individual and collective accountability for achieving the results. They help close the gap between the current reality and where the staff hopes to take the school (the shared vision).

Furthermore, goals are absolutely essential to the collaborative team process. We define a team as a group of people working together *interdependently* to achieve a *common goal* for which members are held *mutually accountable*. In the absence of a common goal, there can be no true team. Effective goals generate joint effort and help collaborative teams clarify how their work can contribute to schoolwide or districtwide improvement initiatives.

When schools create short-term goals and routinely celebrate as those goals are achieved, they foster a sense of confidence and self-efficacy among the staff. Confidence is merely "the expectation of success" (Kanter, 2005), and when people expect to be successful they are more likely to put forth the effort to ensure it. Thus, goals play a key role in motivating people to honor their commitments so the school moves closer to fulfilling its fundamental purpose of learning for all students. Once again, educational researchers and organizational theorists consider measurable goals as a key element in improvement. We will examine that research in chapter 6.

The Importance of Effective Communication

Marcus Buckingham (2005) contends that the one thing leaders of any organization must know to be effective is the importance of clarity: communicating clearly and consistently the purpose of the organization, the primary clients it serves, the future it is creating, the indicators of progress it will track, and the specific actions members can take immediately to achieve its long-term purpose and short-term goals. Engaging staff in consideration of the mission, vision, collective commitments, and goals that constitute the foundation of a professional learning community is designed to address these very issues.

Leaders must realize that the most important element in communicating is congruency between their actions and their words.

Powerful communication is simple and succinct, driven by a few key ideas, and is repeated at every opportunity (Collins, 2001; Pfeffer & Sutton, 2000; Tichy, 1997). Leaders must realize, however, that the most important element in communicating is congruency between their actions and their words. It is not essential that leaders are eloquent or clever; it is imperative, however, that they demonstrate consistency between what they say and what they do (Collins & Porras, 1997; Covey, 2006; Drucker, 1992; Kouzes & Posner, 1987; Maxwell, 1995; Ulrich, 1996). When leaders' actions are inconsistent with what they contend are their priorities, those actions overwhelm all other forms of communication (Kotter, 1996).

One of the most effective ways leaders communicate priorities is by what they pay attention to (Kouzes & Posner, 1999; Peters & Austin, 1985).

Subsequent chapters provide specific examples of leaders communicating what is valued by creating systems and structures to promote priorities, monitoring what is essential, reallocating time, asking the right questions, and responding to conflict in strategic ways. In this chapter, we present a powerful tool for communication that is often overlooked and underutilized: celebration.

Celebration

Celebration is a particularly powerful tool for communicating what is valued and for building community (Deal & Key, 1998; Kouzes & Posner, 1999). When celebrations continually remind people of the purpose and priorities of their organizations, members are more likely to embrace the purpose and work toward agreed-upon priorities. Regular public recognition of specific collaborative efforts, accomplished tasks, achieved goals, team learning, continuous improvement, and support for student learning remind staff of the collective commitment to create a PLC. The word *recognize* comes from the Latin "to know again." Recognition provides opportunities to say, "Let us all be reminded, let us all know again, what is important, what we value, and what we are committed to do. Now let's all pay tribute to someone in the organization who is living that commitment."

Celebrations allow for expressions of both appreciation and admiration. Appreciation lets others know we have received something we value, something we are happy to have. Admiration conveys the message that we have been inspired or instructed by observing the work and commitments of others. When admiration and appreciation are repeatedly expressed, organizations create a culture of ongoing regard that sustains effort because such language is "like pumping oxygen into the system" (Kegan & Lahey, 2001, p. 102).

Celebrations also provide an opportunity to use one of the oldest ways in the world to convey the values and ideals of a community: telling stories. As Jim Kouzes and Barry Posner (1999) write: "The intention of stories is not just to entertain. . . . They are also intended to teach. Good stories move us. They touch us, they teach us, and they cause us to remember" (p. 25). Good stories appeal to both the head and the heart and are more compelling and convincing than data alone. They bring data and evidence to life and persuade people to act in new ways (Pfeffer & Sutton, 2006). The ability of an individual to weave vibrant stories that lead others to a shared understanding of a better future is the "ultimate hallmark of world-class champion leaders" (Tichy, 1997, p. 173). Good stories personify purpose and priorities. They put a human face on success by providing examples and role models that can clarify for others what is noted, appreciated, and valued. They represent one of the most powerful tools for shaping the thinking and feelings of others (Patterson, Grenny, Maxfield, McMillan, & Switzler, 2008).

Finally, a multiyear study of what motivates knowledge workers concluded that the best motivator was celebration of progress. The study advised leaders to set clear overall goals, sustain the commitment to the pursuit of those goals, proactively create both the reality and the perception of progress, and celebrate even incremental progress (Amabile & Kramer, 2010).

Most schools and districts, however, will face a significant challenge as they attempt to integrate meaningful celebration into their cultures. The excessively egalitarian culture of schools (Lortie, 1975) makes it difficult to publicly recognize either individuals or teams. In most schools and districts, generic praise ("You are the best darn faculty in the state!") or private praise ("I want to send you a personal note of commendation") are acceptable—public recognition is not. Generic and private praise are ineffective in communicating priorities because neither conveys to the members at large what specific actions and commitments are valued, and therefore neither is effective in shaping behavior or beliefs. As Peter Drucker (1992) advises, "Changing behavior requires changing recognition and rewards . . . [because] people in organizations tend to act in response to being recognized and rewarded" (p. 195). Tom Peters (1987) puts it this way: "Well-constructed recognition settings provide the single most important opportunity to parade and reinforce the specific kinds of new behaviors one hopes others will emulate" (p. 307).

An excellent predictor of the future behavior of any organization is to examine the people and events it elects to honor (Buckingham, 2005). This is true of schools in particular. In his study of school culture, sociologist Robert Evans (2001) concluded, "The single best low-cost, high-leverage way to improve performance, morale, and the climate for change is to dramatically increase the levels of meaningful recognition for—and among—educators" (p. 254).

We offer the following suggestions to those who face the challenge of incorporating celebration into the culture of their school or district.

1. **Explicitly state the purpose of celebration.** The rationale for public celebration should be carefully explained at the outset of every celebration. Staff members should be continually reminded that celebration represents:

    ■ An important strategy for reinforcing the shared purpose, vision, collective commitments, and goals of the school or district

    ■ The most powerful tool for sustaining the improvement initiative

2. **Make celebration everyone's responsibility.** Recognizing extraordinary commitment should be the responsibility of everyone in the organization, and each individual should be called upon to contribute to the effort. If the formal leader is the sole arbiter of who will be recognized, the rest of the staff can merely sit back and critique the choices. All staff members should have the opportunity to publicly report when they appreciate and admire the work of a colleague.

3. **Establish a clear link between the recognition and the behavior or commitment you are attempting to encourage and reinforce.** Recognition must be specifically linked to the purpose, vision, collective commitments, and goals of the organization if it is to play a role in shaping culture. As we wrote, "Recognition will have little impact if a staff believes the recognition is presented randomly, that each person deserves to be recognized regardless of his or her contribution to the improvement effort, or that rewards are given for factors unrelated to the goal of creating a learning community" (DuFour & Eaker, 1998, p. 145). It is imperative, therefore, that clear parameters are established for recognition and rewards. The answer to the question, "What behavior or commitment are we attempting to encourage with this recognition?" should be readily apparent. Recognition should always be accompanied with a story relating the efforts of the team or individual back to the core foundation of the school or district. It should not only express appreciation and admiration, but also provide others with an example they can emulate.

Recognition must be specifically linked to the purpose, vision, collective commitments, and goals of the organization if it is to play a role in shaping culture.

4. **Create opportunities to have many winners.** Celebration will not have a significant effect on the culture of a school if most people in the organization feel they have no opportunity to be recognized. In fact, celebration can be disruptive and detrimental if there is a perception that recognition and reward are reserved for an exclusive few. Establishing artificial limits on appreciation—such as, "We honor no more than five individuals per meeting," or, "Only those with five or more years of experience are eligible"—lessens the impact celebration can have on a school or district. Developing a PLC requires creating systems specifically designed not only to provide celebrations, but also to ensure that there are many winners.

Four Keys for Incorporating Celebration Into the Culture of Your School or District

1. Explicitly state the purpose of celebration.
2. Make celebration everyone's responsibility.
3. Establish a clear link between the recognition and the behavior or commitment you are attempting to encourage and reinforce.
4. Create opportunities for many winners.

Frequent public acknowledgments for a job well done and a wide distribution of small symbolic gestures of appreciation and admiration are far more powerful tools for communicating priorities than infrequent "grand prizes" that create a few winners and many losers. An effective celebration program will convince every member of the staff that he or she can be a winner and that his or her efforts can be noted and appreciated.

Adlai Stevenson High School in Lincolnshire, Illinois, is often cited as a school that has used celebration to communicate purpose and priorities and to shape culture (Deal & Peterson, 1999; DuFour & Eaker, 1998; Kanold, 2006; Schmoker, 2006). Stevenson does not offer a "Teacher of the Year" program, but over several decades it has distributed thousands of "Super Pat" awards (small tokens of appreciation that represent a "pat on the back" for a job well done) to hundreds of teachers. In fact, in the past twenty years, Stevenson has *never* had a faculty meeting without celebrating the effort and commitment of individuals and teams. Stevenson also surveys its seniors each year to ask, "Which member of the staff has had the most profound impact on your life, and why?" The heartfelt responses of the students are then published in an internal "Kudos Memorandum" and distributed to the entire staff each quarter. Staff members have read thousands of testimonials citing specific examples of how they and their colleagues are making a difference in the lives of students. Stevenson employees receive ongoing reminders of the priorities of their school and the commitments that are being honored in order to achieve those priorities, and every member of the staff feels like he or she has the opportunity to be recognized and celebrated as a winner.

Study after study of what workers want in their jobs offer the same conclusion: they want to feel appreciated (Kouzes & Posner, 1999). Yet Kegan and Lahey (2001) conclude that "nearly every organization or work team we've spent time with astonishingly undercommunicates the genuinely positive, appreciative, and admiring experiences of its members" (p. 92).

One of the most frequent concerns raised by educators who are wary of making celebration a part of their school or district is that if celebration is frequent, it will lose its impact to motivate. Yet research has drawn the opposite conclusion; it reaffirms that frequent celebration communicates priorities, connects people to the organization and to each other, and sustains improvement initiatives (Kegan & Lahey, 2001; Kouzes & Posner, 1999; Peters, 1987).

One challenge every organization will face in implementing a comprehensive improvement effort is sustaining the momentum of that effort over time. Experts on the process of organizational change offer very consistent advice regarding that question (see Why Should Celebration Be a Part of Our Culture?).

Can celebration be overdone? Absolutely. The criterion for assessing the appropriateness of recognition for a team or individual should be the sincerity with which the recognition is given. A commendation should represent genuine and heartfelt appreciation and admiration. If that sincerity is lacking, celebration can be counterproductive.

Why Should Celebration Be a Part of Our Culture?

"In successful change efforts, empowered people create short-term wins—victories that nourish faith in the change effort, emotionally reward the hard workers, keep the critics at bay, and build momentum. Without sufficient wins that are visible, timely, unambiguous, and meaningful to others, change efforts inevitably run into serious problems." (Kotter & Cohen, 2002, p. 125)

"Milestones that are identified, achieved, and celebrated represent an essential condition for building a learning organization." (Thompson, 1995, p. 96)

"Remembering to recognize, reward, and celebrate accomplishments is a critical leadership skill. And it is probably the most underutilized motivational tool in organizations." (Kanter, 1999)

"Win small. Win early. Win often." (Hamel, 2002, p. 202)

"Specific goals should be designed to allow teams to achieve small wins as they pursue their common purpose. Small wins are invaluable to building members' commitment and overcoming the obstacles that get in the way of achieving a meaningful, long-term purpose." (Katzenbach & Smith, 1993, p. 54)

"Reward small improvements in behavior along the way. Don't wait until people achieve phenomenal results." (Patterson et al., 2008, p. 205)

"Small successes stimulate individuals to make further commitments to change. Staffs need tangible results in order to continue the development of their commitment to the change program and small steps engender understanding as well." (Eastwood & Louis, 1992, p. 219)

"Visible measures of progress are critical for motivating and encouraging educators to persist in the challenging work of improvement. Even the most dedicated and optimistic among us will stop if there's no sign that what we're doing is making a difference, or might make a difference eventually." (Elmore & City, 2007)

Part Four

Assessing Your Place on the PLC Journey

The PLC Continuum

In each chapter of this handbook, you will be asked to reflect upon the current conditions in your school or district and assess the alignment of those conditions with the principles and practices of a PLC. The assessment will present a five-point continuum:

1. **Pre-Initiation Stage.** The school has not yet begun to address this principle or practice of a PLC.

2. **Initiation Stage.** The school has made an effort to address this principle or practice, but the effort has not yet begun to impact a critical mass of staff members.

3. **Implementation Stage.** A critical mass of staff members is participating in implementing the principle or practice, but many approach the task with a sense of compliance rather than commitment. There is some uncertainty regarding what needs to be done and why it should be done.

4. **Developing Stage.** Structures are being altered to support the changes, and resources are being devoted to moving them forward. Members are becoming more receptive to the principle, practice, or process because they have experienced some of its benefits. The focus has shifted from "Why are we doing this?" to "How can we do this more effectively?"

5. **Sustaining Stage.** The principle or practice is deeply embedded in the culture of the school. It is a driving force in the daily work of staff. It is deeply internalized, and staff would resist attempts to abandon the principle or practice.

This continuum can be administered across a district, school, or team. Many districts have converted it to an electronic format and used simple survey tools such as SurveyMonkey to gather information on staff perceptions. Whatever format is used, we recommend that the process begin by asking each individual to make anonymous, independent, candid assessments and to offer evidence and anecdotes to support his or her conclusions on each characteristic that is presented.

Once individual assessments are completed, the results should be compiled and shared with all participants. Members of the staff can then analyze the results and use them to begin dialogue to clarify the current reality of their team, school, or district. Participants should be particularly attentive to discrepancies in responses and explore reasons for the differences. Groups have a tendency to gloss over disagreements. One person contends the school is in the pre-initiation stage while another contends it is developing, and to avoid discussion, they merely compromise and settle for the initiation stage. Avoid that temptation. Delve into one another's thinking to see if you can clarify discrepancies and establish common ground.

Following this guidance, complete the first PLC continuum, called "Laying the Foundation," on pages 44–46.

Where Do We Go From Here?

You will complete this phase of the process by turning to the Where Do We Go From Here? planning worksheet that follows the continuum. Each worksheet presents a principle or practice of a PLC and calls upon participants to develop a specific plan for moving forward. *Beware of plans that call for study, training, discussions, or anything less than specific action to advance your school.* The plan should specify what needs to be done, by whom, a timeline for completion, and how both its implementation and impact will be monitored.

Consider each indicator of a professional learning community described in the left column of the Where Do We Go From Here? worksheet called "Laying the Foundation of a PLC" on page 47, and then answer the questions listed at the top of the remaining four columns.

Articulating the mission of the school or district, the vision of what it hopes to become, the collective commitments necessary to begin moving it in that direction, and the goals that will help monitor its progress are important steps on the PLC journey—but only if these elements of the foundation of a PLC are clearly communicated and widely understood. Assess the effectiveness of the communication in your school or district by completing the second PLC continuum (pages 48–49) and Where Do We Go From Here? worksheet (page 50).

The Professional Learning Communities at Work™ Continuum: Laying the Foundation

DIRECTIONS: Individually, silently, and *honestly* assess the current reality of your school's implementation of each indicator listed in the left column. Consider what evidence or anecdotes support your assessment. This form may also be used to assess district or team implementation.

We have a clear sense of our collective purpose, the school we are attempting to create to achieve that purpose, the commitments we must make and honor to become that school, and the specific goals that will help monitor our progress.

Indicator	Pre-Initiating	Initiating	Implementing	Developing	Sustaining
Shared Mission It is evident that learning for all is our core purpose.	The purpose of the school has not been articulated. Most staff members view the mission of the school as teaching. They operate from the assumption that although all students should have the opportunity to learn, responsibility for learning belongs to the individual student and will be determined by his or her ability and effort.	An attempt has been made to clarify the purpose of the school through the development of a formal mission statement. Few people were involved in its creation. It does little to impact professional practice or the assumptions behind those practices.	A process has been initiated to provide greater focus and clarity regarding the mission of learning for all. Steps are being taken to clarify what, specifically, students are to learn and to monitor their learning. Some teachers are concerned that these efforts will deprive them of academic freedom.	Teachers are beginning to see evidence of the benefits of clearly established expectations for student learning and systematic processes to monitor student learning. They are becoming more analytical in assessing the evidence of student learning and are looking for ways to become more effective in assessing student learning and providing instruction to enhance student learning.	Staff members are committed to helping all students learn. They demonstrate that commitment by working collaboratively to clarify what students are to learn in each unit, creating frequent common formative assessments to monitor each student's learning on an ongoing basis, and implementing a systematic plan of intervention when students experience difficulty. They are willing to examine all practices and procedures in light of their impact on learning.

Indicator	Pre-Initiating	Initiating	Implementing	Developing	Sustaining
Shared Vision We have a shared understanding of and commitment to the school we are attempting to create.	No effort has been made to engage staff in describing the preferred conditions for the school.	A formal vision statement has been created for the school, but most staff members are unaware of it.	Staff members have participated in a process to clarify the school they are trying to create, and leadership calls attention to the resulting vision statement on a regular basis. Many staff members question the relevance of the vision statement, and their behavior is generally unaffected by it.	Staff members have worked together to describe the school are trying to create. They have endorsed this general description and use it to guide their school improvement efforts and their professional development.	Staff members can and do routinely articulate the major principles of the school's shared vision and use those principles to guide their day-to-day efforts and decisions. They honestly assess the current reality in their school and continually seek more effective strategies for reducing the discrepancy between that reality and the school they are working to create.
Collective Commitments (Shared Values) We have made commitments to each other regarding how we must behave in order to achieve our shared vision.	Staff members have not yet articulated the attitudes, behaviors, or commitments they are prepared to demonstrate in order to advance the mission of learning for all and the vision of what the school might become.	Administrators or a committee of teachers have created statements of beliefs regarding the school's purpose and its direction. Staff members have reviewed and reacted to those statements. Initial drafts have been amended based on staff feedback. There is no attempt to translate the beliefs into the specific commitments or behaviors that staff will model.	A statement has been developed that articulates the specific commitments staff have been asked to embrace to help the school fulfill its purpose and move closer to its vision. The commitments are stated as behaviors rather than beliefs. Many staff object to specifying these commitments and prefer to focus on what other groups must do to improve the school.	Staff members have been engaged in the process to articulate the collective commitments that will advance the school toward its vision. They endorse the commitments and seek ways to bring them to life in the school.	The collective commitments are embraced by staff, embedded in the school's culture, and evident to observers of the school. They help define the school and what it stands for. Examples of the commitments are shared in stories and celebrations, and people are challenged when they behave in ways that are inconsistent with the collective commitments.

Indicator	Pre-Initiating	Initiating	Implementing	Developing	Sustaining
Common School Goals We have articulated our long-term priorities, short-term targets, and timelines for achieving those targets.	No effort has been made to engage the staff in establishing school improvement goals related to student learning.	Goals for the school have been established by the administration or school improvement team as part of the formal district process for school improvement. Most staff would be unable to articulate a goal that has been established for their school.	Staff members have been made aware of the long-term and short-term goals for the school. Tools and strategies have been developed and implemented to monitor the school's progress toward its goals. Little has been done to translate the school goal into meaningful targets for either collaborative teams or individual teachers.	The school goal has been translated into specific goals that directly impact student achievement for each collaborative team. If teams are successful in achieving their goals, the school will achieve its goal as well. Teams are exploring different strategies for achieving their goals.	All staff members pursue measurable goals that are directly linked to the school's goals as part of their routine responsibilities. Teams work interdependently to achieve common goals for which members are mutually accountable. The celebration of the achievement of goals is part of the school culture and an important element in sustaining the PLC process.

Where Do We Go From Here? Worksheet
Laying the Foundation of a PLC

Indicator of a PLC at Work	What steps or activities must be initiated to create this condition in your school?	Who will be responsible for initiating or sustaining these steps or activities?	What is a realistic timeline for each step or phase of the activity?	What will you use to assess the effectiveness of your initiative?
Shared Mission It is evident that learning for all is our core purpose.				
Shared Vision We have a shared understanding of and commitment to the school we are attempting to create.				
Collective Commitments (Shared Values) We have made commitments to each other regarding how we must behave in order to achieve our shared vision.				
Common School Goals We have articulated our long-term priorities, short-term targets, and timelines for achieving those targets.				

The Professional Learning Communities at Work™ Continuum: Effective Communication

DIRECTIONS: Individually, silently, and *honestly* assess the current reality of your school's implementation of each indicator listed in the left column. Consider what evidence or anecdotes support your assessment. This form may also be used to assess district or team implementation.

Indicator	Pre-Initiating	Initiating	Implementing	Developing	Sustaining
We understand the purpose and priorities of our school because they have been communicated consistently and effectively.					
The school has established a clear purpose and priorities that have been effectively communicated. Systems are in place to ensure action steps aligned with the purpose and priorities are implemented and monitored.	There is no sense of purpose or priorities. People throughout the school feel swamped by what they regard as a never-ending series of fragmented, disjointed, and short-lived improvement initiatives. Changes in leadership inevitably result in changes in direction.	Key leaders may have reached agreement on general purpose and priorities, but people throughout the organization remain unclear. Furthermore, if asked to explain the priorities of the school or the strategies to achieve those priorities, leaders would have difficulty articulating specifics. Staff members would offer very different answers if pressed to explain the priorities of the school.	There is general understanding of the purpose and priorities of the school, but many staff members have not embraced them. Specific steps are being taken to advance the priorities, but some staff members are participating only grudgingly. They view the initiative as interfering with their real work.	Structures and processes have been altered to align with the purpose and priorities. Staff members are beginning to see benefits from the initiative and are seeking ways to become more effective in implementing it.	There is almost universal understanding of the purpose and priorities of the school. All policies, procedures, and structures have been purposefully aligned with the effort to fulfill the purpose and accomplish the priorities. Systems have been created to gauge progress. The systems are carefully monitored, and the resulting information is used to make adjustments designed to build the collective capacity of the group to be successful.

Indicator	Pre-Initiating	Initiating	Implementing	Developing	Sustaining
The leaders in the school communicate purpose and priorities through modeling, allocation of resources, what they celebrate, and what they are willing to confront.	There is no sense of purpose and priorities. Different people in the school seem to have different pet projects, and there is considerable in-fighting to acquire the resources to support those different projects.	Leaders can articulate the purpose and priorities of the school with a consistent voice, but their behavior is not congruent with their words. The structures, resources, and rewards of the school have not been altered to align with the professed priorities.	The school has begun to alter the structures, resources, and rewards to better align with the stated priorities. Staff members who openly oppose the initiative may be confronted, but those confronting them are likely to explain they are doing someone else's bidding. For example, a principal may say, "The central office is concerned that you are overtly resisting the process we are attempting to implement."	People throughout the school are changing their behavior to align with the priorities. They are seeking new strategies for using resources more effectively to support the initiative, and are willing to reallocate time, money, materials, and people in order to move forward. Small improvements are recognized and celebrated. Leaders confront incongruent behavior.	The purpose and priorities of the school are evident by the everyday behavior of people throughout the school. Time, money, materials, people, and resources have been strategically allocated to reflect priorities. Processes are in place to recognize and celebrate commitment to the priorities. People throughout the school will confront those who disregard the priorities.

Where Do We Go From Here? Worksheet
Effective Communication

Indicator of a PLC at Work	What steps or activities must be initiated to create this condition in your school?	Who will be responsible for initiating or sustaining these steps or activities?	What is a realistic timeline for each step or phase of the activity?	What will you use to assess the effectiveness of your initiative?
The school has established a clear purpose and priorities that have been effectively communicated. Systems are in place to ensure action steps aligned with the purpose and priorities are implemented and monitored.				
The leaders in the school communicate purpose and priorities through modeling, allocation of resources, what they celebrate, and what they are willing to confront.				

Part Five

Tips for Moving Forward: Building the Foundation of a PLC

1 **Move quickly to action.** Remember that you will not progress on the PLC continuum or close the knowing-doing gap until people in the school or district begin to "do" differently. We have seen educators devote years to studying, debating, rewording, and revising different elements of the foundation, thereby giving the illusion of meaningful action. In most instances, a staff should be able to consider and resolve all of the questions of the foundation in a matter of weeks. They may need to return to the foundation in the future to make changes as the vision becomes clear, the need for additional commitments arises, or new goals emerge. Perfection is not the objective: action is. Once again, the school or district that actually does the work of a PLC will develop its capacity to help all students learn far more effectively than the school or district that spends years preparing to be a PLC.

2 **Build shared knowledge when asking people to make a decision.** Asking uninformed people to make decisions is bound to result in uninformed decisions. Members of a PLC resolve issues and answer important questions by asking, "What information do we need to examine together to make a good decision?" and then building shared knowledge regarding that information. Learning together is, by definition, the very essence of a *learning* community. Furthermore, giving people access to the same information increases the likelihood that they will arrive at the same conclusions. All staff should have direct access to user-friendly information on the current reality in their school or district as well as access to summaries of effective practices and best thinking regarding the issue under consideration. School and district leaders must take responsibility for gathering and disseminating this information, but all staff should be invited to present any information for distribution that they feel is relevant.

3 **Use the foundation to assist in day-to-day decisions.** Addressing the foundation of a PLC will impact the school only if it becomes a tool for making decisions. Posting mission statements in the building or inserting a vision statement or goals into a strategic plan does nothing to improve a school.

When proposals are considered, the first questions that should be asked are:

- Is this consistent with our purpose?

- Will it help us become the school we envision?

- Are we prepared to commit to do this?

- Will it enable us to achieve our goals?

An honest assessment of these questions can help shorten debate and lead the group to the right conclusion.

4 **Use the foundation to identify existing practices that should be eliminated.** Once your foundation has been established, use it to identify and eliminate any practices that are inconsistent with its principles. As Jim Collins (2001) writes:

> Most of us have an ever-expanding "to do" list, trying to build momentum by doing, doing, doing—and doing more. And it rarely works. Those who build good to great companies, however, made as much use of "stop doing" lists as "to do" lists. They had the discipline to stop doing all the extraneous junk. (p. 139)

5 **Translate the vision of your school into a teachable point of view.** Effective leaders create a "teachable point of view": a succinct explanation of the organization's purpose and direction that can be illustrated through stories that engage others emotionally and intellectually (Tichy, 1997). They have a knack for making the complex simple in ways that give direction to those in the organization (Collins, 2001). They use simple language, simple concepts, and the power of common sense (Pfeffer & Sutton, 2000). Develop a brief teachable point of view that captures the vision of your school in a message that is simple, direct, and jargon free. Practice presenting the vision until articulating it becomes second nature.

6 **Write value statements as behaviors rather than beliefs.** "We believe in the potential and worth of each of our students" is a morally impeccable statement; however, it offers little insight into what a staff is prepared to do to help each child realize that potential. Another difficulty with belief statements is their failure to assign specific, personal responsibility. A staff may agree with the statement, "We believe in a safe and orderly environment," but feel it is the job of the administration to create such an environment. Simple, direct statements of what we commit to do are preferable to the most eloquent statements of our beliefs. For example, "We will monitor each student's learning on a timely basis and provide additional time and support for learning until the student becomes proficient" helps to clarify expectations far more effectively than assertions about the potential of every child.

7 **Focus on yourself rather than others.** In our work with schools, we have found that educators rarely have difficulty in articulating steps that could be taken to improve their schools, but they call upon others to do it: parents need to be more supportive, students need to be more responsible, the district needs to reduce class size, the state needs to provide more funding, and so on. This external focus on what others must do fails to improve the situation and fosters a culture of dependency and resignation (Sparks, 2007). Furthermore, we cannot make commitments on behalf of others. We can only make them for ourselves. Members of a PLC have an internal focus that acknowledges there is much within their sphere of influence that could be done to improve their school. They create a culture of self-efficacy and optimism by concentrating on what is within their collective power to do (Goleman, Boyatzis, & McKee, 2002).

8 **Recognize that the process is nonlinear.** Although we present the four pillars sequentially, the process of clarifying purpose, vision, collective commitments, and goals is nonlinear, nonhierarchical, and nonsequential. Working on the foundation is cyclical and interactive. Writing purpose and vision statements can help shape commitments and goals, but it is not until those commitments are honored and goals are achieved that purpose and vision become more real, clearer, and more focused.

9 **It is what you do that matters, not what you call it.** Henry Mintzberg (1994) advises, "Never adopt a technique by its usual name . . . call it something different so that you have to think it through for yourself and work it out on your own terms" (p. 27). When concepts take on a label, they accumulate baggage. People get the impression that a proposal represents the latest fad, or they settle for a superficial understanding rather than really engaging in an assessment of the underlying ideas. There are schools and districts throughout North America that call themselves professional learning communities yet demonstrate none of the characteristics of a PLC. There are schools that could serve as model PLCs that are unfamiliar with the term. We are not advocating that faculties be asked to vote to become a PLC or take a PLC pledge. In fact, it may be more helpful to never use the term. What is important is that we first engage staff members in building shared knowledge of certain key assumptions and critical practices and then call upon them to act in accordance with that knowledge.

Part Six

Questions to Guide the Work of Your Professional Learning Community

For Clarifying the Mission of Your School or District, Ask:

1. What is our fundamental purpose?

2. Why was this school built? What have we been brought here to do together?

3. Does the concept of public education for all children mean that all students shall learn or merely that they will be required to attend school?

4. What happens in our school or district when a student experiences difficulty in learning?

For Clarifying the Vision for Your School or District, Ask:

1. Can you describe the school we are trying to create?

2. What would our school look like if it were a great place for students? What would it look like if it were a great place for teachers?

3. It is five years from now, and we have achieved our vision as a school. In what ways are we different? Describe what is going on in terms of practices, procedures, relationships, results, and climate.

4. Imagine we have been given sixty seconds on the nightly news to clarify the vision of our school or district to the community. What do we want to say?

For Clarifying the Collective Commitments (Values) of Your School or District, Ask:

1. What are the specific commitments we must honor to achieve our purpose and vision?

2. What are the specific behaviors we can exhibit to make a personal contribution to the success of our school?

3. What commitments are we prepared to make to each other?

4. What commitments or assurances are we prepared to make to every student in our school?

5. What are the "must dos" and the taboos for this staff?

6. What agreements are shared among all of us?

For Clarifying the Goals of Your School or District, Ask:

1. How will we know if we are making progress toward achieving our vision?

2. How will we know if we are more effective three years from now than we are today?

3. If we achieve our shared vision, what will student achievement look like in our school?

4. What are the most essential conditions and factors we must monitor on an ongoing basis?

For Clarifying How Effective You Are at Communicating Priorities, Ask:

1. What are the most important factors that drive the day-to-day decisions in our school or district?

2. What are the priorities in our school or district?

3. What systems have been put in place to monitor progress in our priority areas?

4. What gets paid the closest attention in this school or district?

Part Seven

Dangerous Detours and Seductive Shortcuts

Beware of mission statements that hedge on the collective commitment to promote high levels of learning for all students. References to "providing students with an opportunity to learn" or "helping each student learn according to the best of his or her ability" are subtle ways of distancing a school from a focus on the achievement of each student. Educators must do more than give students the chance to learn: they must align their practices to promote learning. They must reject the fixed mindset that attributes accomplishments to innate ability or dispositions that cannot be enhanced. They must instead embrace the *growth* mindset—the belief that students can cultivate their ability and talent through their own additional effort and the support of their educators (Dweck, 2006).

Educators must do more than give students the chance to learn: they must align their practices to promote learning.

Do not equate writing a mission statement with establishing shared purpose for your school. Shared purpose is ultimately revealed by what you do. The completion of a mission statement does not indicate that your work is over, but rather that it has just begun. The tenets of a mission statement must be translated into specific, actionable steps that bring the mission to life. Remember the advice of Jim Collins (1996), who wrote:

> Leaders spend too much time drafting, wordsmithing, and redrafting vision statements, mission statements, values statements, purpose statements, aspiration statements, and so on. They spend nowhere near enough time trying to align their organizations with the values and visions already in place. . . . When you have superb alignment, a visitor could drop into your organization from another planet and infer the vision without having to read it on paper. (pp. 19–20)

Final Thoughts

The consideration of these questions can help a staff lay the foundation for a professional learning community, but important work remains to be done. A staff that embraces the premise that the very purpose of the school is to help all students learn will face the very challenging questions, "Learn what?" and "How we will know if each student has learned?" We turn our attention to these critical questions in the next chapter.

Chapter 3

Creating a Focus on Learning

Part One

The Case Study: What Do We Want Our Students to Learn, and How Will We Know When They Have Learned It?

Principal Dan Matthews had worked successfully with a task force of committed teachers to build support for the professional learning community concept among the staff of Genghis Khan High School (nickname: the Fighting Horde). The task force drafted and the staff approved a new vision statement, endorsed their collective commitments, and established school improvement goals. The vision statement called for a school in which teachers would deliver a guaranteed and viable curriculum in each course that provided all students with access to the same knowledge, concepts, and skills regardless of the teacher to whom they were assigned. It also described a school in which the learning of each student would be monitored on a timely basis.

Principal Matthews and the task force hoped to use the vision statement as a catalyst for action. He asked department chairs to help teachers work together in their collaborative teams to clarify the most essential learning for students by asking, "What knowledge, skills, and dispositions should each student acquire as a result of this course and each unit of instruction within this course?" Matthews also asked the chairs to support the task force recommendation to help teams create a series of common formative assessments to monitor each student's acquisition of the essential outcomes.

After a few weeks, the department chairs proposed modifications to Principal Matthews' request. The math chair reported that teachers felt the state standards already clarified what students were to learn, and they saw no point in addressing a question that had already been answered. The English chair informed Principal Matthews that several teachers from her department had been members on the committee that wrote the district's language arts curriculum, and they felt their work was being dismissed as irrelevant or ineffective. The head of the social studies department complained that the teachers in her department were unable to agree on the most essential learning for students because so many were personally invested in particular units they refused to abandon. After considerable discussion, the principal accepted the following recommendations of the department chairs:

1. Every teacher would be provided with a copy of the state standards and the district curriculum guide for their curricular area.

2. Teachers would be asked to adhere to the state and district guidelines.

3. Teacher teams would no longer be required to clarify the essential learning of their courses.

The task force proposal to engage teachers in creating common assessments for their courses also met with resistance on the part of some teachers. Art teachers argued that there was no way to assess the most essential outcomes of their courses on paper-and-pencil tests; therefore, they believed they should be exempt from common assessments. Science teachers pointed out that their textbooks included test questions at the end of each chapter, and they could simply use these chapter tests as their common assessments. The English department noted that there were not enough copies of the required novels for all students to read the same novel simultaneously. They argued that since students were reading different novels at different times, common assessments were impossible. The social studies department insisted teachers lacked both the time and expertise to develop quality assessments. They took the position that if common assessments were to be created, the district office should develop them. The math department chair contended that he spent two years trying to get his teachers to embrace the only test that really mattered: the state test. He finally persuaded them to sit down as a department to analyze the results, assess strengths and weaknesses in student learning, and adjust their curriculum and instruction based on the results. To now ask them to create common, teacher-made assessments would send mixed messages and divert their attention from the state test.

After reviewing these concerns, Principal Matthews and the task force agreed to withdraw the proposal to require teams of teachers to develop common assessments.

Reflection

Consider Principal Matthews' efforts and the efforts of the task force to engage teachers in clarifying the essential outcomes of their courses and developing common assessments. If you were called upon to consult with the school, what advice would you offer?

Part Two

Here's How

The principal and task force in this case study confronted a common dilemma: there were certain important tasks in which they hoped to engage the staff in order to further their agreed-upon commitment to learning for all students; however, they wanted the staff to be a part of the process and to feel empowered as the school moved forward.

- Should they insist that the faculty develop common outcomes and common assessments for their courses, or should they abandon processes vital to a PLC because of the objections raised by the staff?

- Is the school better served by a culture of control that demands adherence to certain practices or a culture of freedom that encourages individual and/or departmental autonomy?

In their study of high-performing organizations, Collins and Porras (1997) discovered ineffective organizations succumbed to the "Tyranny of Or"—"the rational view that cannot easily accept paradox, that cannot live with two seemingly contradictory forces at the same time. We must be A or B, but not both" (p. 44). High-performing organizations, however, rejected this false dichotomy and embraced the "Genius of And" by demonstrating the ability to honor both extremes at the same time. Collins and Porras clarified that the Genius of And "is not just a question of 'balance' because balance implies going to the midpoint—fifty-fifty. A visionary company does not seek the gray of balance, but seeks to be distinctly both 'A' and 'B' at the same time" (p. 45).

If Principal Matthews and his task force were to apply these findings to their situation, they would embrace the concept of "directed empowerment" (Waterman, 1987) or "defined autonomy" (Marzano & Waters, 2009). In other words, they would create a school culture that was simultaneously loose and tight.

Create a school culture that is simultaneously loose and tight.

Schools and districts need not choose between demanding adherence to certain core principles and practices *or* empowering the staff. Certain critical issues must be addressed, and certain important tasks must be accomplished in a PLC. The school or district is tight in those areas, demanding faithfulness to specific principles and practices. At the same time, however, individuals and teams can benefit from considerable autonomy and freedom in terms of how things get done on a day-to-day basis because the school or district is loose about much of the implementation. Members of the school have the benefit of clear parameters that provide direction and coherence to the improvement process; however, they are also given the freedom and tools to make their own contribution to that process. This autonomy allows the school community to benefit from the insights and expertise of those who are called upon to do the actual work.

Principal Matthews has every right to expect faculty members to unite around and act in accordance with the common purpose, clear priorities, and systematic procedures of a PLC if the school is to become more effective in helping all students learn. At the same time, teachers have every right to enjoy considerable freedom and autonomy as they build their capacity to function as a PLC.

One "tight" expectation the school must establish is that every teacher will be called upon to work collaboratively with colleagues in clarifying the questions:

The questions "Learn what?" and "How will we know?" are two of the most significant questions a PLC will consider, the very basis of the collective inquiry that drives the work of collaborative teams.

- ■ What is it we want our students to learn?

- ■ How will we know when each student has learned it?

The pursuit of these questions cannot be assigned to others. The constant collective inquiry into these questions is a professional responsibility of *every* faculty member. The responsibility cannot be left to each teacher to address on his or her own in a school or district committed to providing all students with equal access to a common, challenging curriculum. The questions "Learn what?" and "How will we know?" are two of the most significant questions a PLC will consider, the very basis of the collective inquiry that drives the work of collaborative teams. Therefore, members of a PLC can neither ship the questions off to someone else to answer nor disregard their colleagues while exploring the questions.

By the same token, however, if Principal Matthews intends to hold collaborative teams accountable for addressing these questions, he has a responsibility to provide them with the clarity, parameters, resources, and support to help them succeed in what they are being asked to accomplish. This is the concept of reciprocal accountability we presented in the introduction. If Matthews intends to hold teams accountable for establishing a guaranteed curriculum and common assessments, he must be accountable to them. He must work with team leaders to provide clear answers to the important questions that accompany the charge he has presented to his teachers. We presented those questions on page 2 of the introduction. Let's consider how Principal Matthews might work with team leaders to address those questions.

What Questions

What do you mean by *guaranteed curriculum* and *common formative assessments*?

If the team is going to be asked to create a guaranteed curriculum and common formative assessments, members must be clear regarding what those terms represent and what they do not represent. Members of the collaborative teams should understand that a "guaranteed and viable curriculum" (1) gives students access to the same essential learning regardless of who is teaching the class *and* (2) can be taught in the time allotted (Marzano, 2003). It does not mean that teachers must adhere to lockstep pacing by which members are teaching from the same page on the same day. It does not mean that all teachers must use the same instructional strategies or same materials. It does mean that during a unit presented within a specific window of time established by the team (for example, three weeks), each member of the team will work to ensure every student acquires the knowledge and skills the team has agreed are most essential for that unit.

The term *common formative assessment* will certainly need clarification as well. *Common* assessment means student learning will be assessed using the same instrument or process and according to the same criteria. For example, a team will use the same test or assess a student's writing according to the same criteria.

A *formative* assessment is used to inform both the teacher and the student of the student's progress so that appropriate steps can be taken to advance the student's learning. It is not the content of the assessment or when it is administered that makes an assessment formative. It is how the results are used, or what happens *after* the assessment, that determines whether or not it is part of a formative process.

Three things must occur for the assessment to be formative: (1) the assessment is used to identify students who are experiencing difficulty, (2) those students are provided additional time and support to acquire the intended skill or concept, and (3) the students are given another opportunity to demonstrate that they have learned.

In the context of PLCs, collaborative teams of teachers create multiple common formative assessments and use the results to identify (1) individual students who need additional time and support for learning, (2) the teaching strategies that proved effective in helping students acquire the intended knowledge and skills, (3) program concerns—areas in which students generally are having difficulty achieving the intended standard—and (4) improvement goals for individual teachers and the team.

Staff members should also understand that common formative assessments are only one element of an effective and balanced assessment *process* for monitoring student learning. That process will continue to rely on individual teachers' assessments within the classroom on a day-by-day basis, assessments created by individual teachers for their own students, occasional district benchmark assessments, summative assessments created by the team or the district, or the state or provincial assessments.

What resources can you provide to assist us?

Of course, one of the most important resources school leaders must provide teachers who are engaged in this process is time. We will devote a portion of chapter 5 to how schools and districts are meeting the challenge of time for collaboration; however, teams will need other resources as well.

As part of his reciprocal accountability to his staff, Principal Matthews should provide all staff member with the parameters in which they should operate and the pertinent resources to help them address the question of "learn what." For example, Matthews might specifically stipulate that:

1. The essential learning established by teams must align with state or provincial standards and district curriculum guides.

2. The identified essential learning must ensure students are well prepared to demonstrate proficiency on high-stakes assessments.

Some of the resources Principal Matthews should provide to the teacher teams to assist in creating a guaranteed curriculum include:

- State or provincial standards

- Recommended standards from professional organizations (for example, from the National Council of Teachers of Mathematics)

- District curriculum guides

- A list of prerequisite skills that colleagues at the next course or grade level have established as essential for success at that level

- Assessment frameworks (how students will be assessed on state, provincial, national, and district assessments)

- Data on student performance on past assessments

- Examples of student work and of specific criteria that could be used in judging the quality of student work

- Recommendations and standards for workplace skills

- Recommendations on standards and curriculum design from authors such as Doug Reeves, Heidi Hayes Jacobs, Robert Marzano, Grant Wiggins, and Jay McTighe

What process can we use to engage in this work?

The process to establish a guaranteed and *viable* curriculum should be specifically designed to eliminate content from the curriculum. It is impossible for American teachers, for example, to address adequately all the state and national standards they have been urged to teach (Consortium on Productivity in Schools, 1995; Kendall & Marzano, 2000; Popham, 2004). Ultimately, the problem of too much content and too little time forces teachers to either rush through content or to exercise judgment regarding which standards are the most significant and essential. In a PLC, this issue is neither left to each teacher to resolve individually nor allowed to deteriorate into a debate regarding teachers' opinions on what students must learn. Instead, collaborative teams of teachers work together to *build shared knowledge* regarding essential curriculum. They do what people do in learning communities: they learn together.

The insights of Doug Reeves (2002) are particularly helpful in guiding this work. He offers a three-part test for teams to consider as they assess the significance of a particular standard:

1. **Does it have endurance?** Do we really expect our students to retain the knowledge and skills over time as opposed to merely learning it for a test?

2. **Does it have leverage?** Will proficiency in this standard help the student in other areas of the curriculum and other academic disciplines?

3. **Does it develop student readiness for the next level of learning?** Is it essential for success in the next unit, course, or grade level?

The teams would also benefit from the discussion of a fourth question as they determine the most essential learning for their students: "What content do we currently teach that we can eliminate from the curriculum because it is not essential?" Principal Matthews could help foster a new mindset in the school if he asked each team to identify content it was removing from the curriculum each time the team planned a unit of instruction.

"What content do we currently teach that we can eliminate from the curriculum because it is not essential?"

Keep, Drop, and Create

When Tom Many works with schools, he uses a simple process called "Keep, Drop, Create" to engage teachers in dialogue regarding essential learning. At least once a quarter, teachers devote a grade level or departmental meeting to analysis of the intended versus the implemented curriculum. Each member of the team brings his or her lesson plan books and a copy of the essential curriculum. Three pieces of butcher paper are posted on the wall of the meeting room and labeled with one of the three categories: Keep, Drop, or Create. Each member of the team is then given sticky notes in three colors—yellow for Keep, pink for Drop, and green for Create—and is asked to reflect honestly on his or her teaching.

Teams begin their analysis using their lesson plan books as the record of what was actually taught (the implemented curriculum) and copies of state or district curriculum guides to review the intended curriculum. Topics identified in the essential curriculum documents and included in each teacher's lesson plan book are recorded on the Keep page. Topics identified as essential but not addressed in a teacher's lesson plan book (either because the topics have not yet been taught or because they have been omitted) are listed on the Create page. Finally, topics included in a teacher's lesson plan book but not reflected in the essential curriculum documents are put on the Drop page.

"What must our students know and be able to do as a result of this unit we are about to teach?"

This process not only assists in discovering curriculum gaps and topics that must be addressed in upcoming units, but it also helps teams create a "stop doing" list of topics that are not essential. As teachers engage in this activity over time, they become more clear, more consistent, and more confident in their response to the question, "What must our students know and be able to do as a result of this unit we are about to teach?"

What will proficiency look like?

"What would this standard, if mastered, look like in terms of student work?"

The White River School District in Buckley, Washington, engages teachers in a process to clarify essential standard by asking them to address the question, "What would this standard, if mastered, look like in terms of student work?" This strategy of clarifying standards through the lens of student work leads teams through a natural progression of questions: What is it we want our students to learn? What is the evidence we expect students to generate in order to demonstrate proficiency? What will the student work look like? What will our assessments look like in order to gather the appropriate evidence?

Tracy Nelson, a third-grade teacher, explained the process:

When our team was focusing on standards related to developing and organizing expository and narrative writing, we viewed these standards through the lens of our learners. Our student editing and revising checklists are generated as a team and are specific to the power standard being taught—in kid language! Learners self-assess along the way, study and assess samples from others, and conference with a teacher to explain their perception of the quality of the work they have done. We want our learners to have a clear understanding of what they know and what they still need to work on—not because the teacher told them, but because they really understand the expectations for the standard and why the standard has importance in their lives. This is only possible if the team has a clear understanding of what the standard looks like in day-to-day student work. (personal communication to Robert Eaker, January 8, 2010)

Cody Mothershead, an Advanced Placement (AP) statistics teacher, described how his team has benefitted from the process:

> Even though our team had previously decided how many points would be given for the main parts of each question in order to meet a particular standard, when we looked at student work, we realized we still had lots of differences in our expectations. For instance, I had my classes make t-proofs for each problem, while others accepted one or two word answers and drawings that included the main parts. After discussing this range in perception regarding what student work should look like if the standard were met, we realized that, as a team, we needed to engage in more specific discussions about what student work should look like prior to teaching each standard. (personal communication to Robert Eaker, January 8, 2010)

White River teachers have discovered that the richest team dialogue occurs when the team places actual student work alongside the standard. The standard now comes alive visually! The team examines different approaches students used to meet the standard, looks for differences in the quality of the work from student to student and classroom to classroom, discusses different instructional strategies, and checks to make sure team members are consistent in their assessment of student work.

What are effective strategies for monitoring student learning?

Principal Matthews must also resist any effort to exempt teachers from working together to create the frequent common formative assessments that enable a team to verify the proficiency of each student in each skill. Frequent monitoring of each student's learning is an essential element of effective teaching, and no teacher should be absolved from that task or allowed to assign responsibility for it to state test makers, central office coordinators, or textbook publishers.

Frequent monitoring of each student's learning is an essential element of effective teaching, and no teacher should be absolved from that task.

Teachers should again be guided by clear expectations and parameters as they develop their common formative assessments. Such guidelines might call upon teams to:

- Create a specific minimum number of common assessments to be used in their course or grade level during the semester to ensure student learning is monitored on a timely basis.

- Demonstrate how each item on the assessment is aligned to an essential outcome of the course or grade level.

- Specify the proficiency standard for each skill or concept so that teachers and students alike are able to identify, with precision, where the student needs help.

- Clarify the conditions for administering the test consistently.

- Ensure that demonstration of proficiency on the team assessment will be highly correlated to success on high-stakes testing at the district, state, provincial, or national level.

- Assess a few key concepts frequently rather than many concepts infrequently.

Once again, if Principal Matthews calls upon teachers to create common assessments, reciprocal accountability demands he must support their efforts—by providing them with time to address the task and resources to help them build quality assessments. Such resources might include:

- State or provincial assessment frameworks to make sure staff are familiar with the format and rigor of the state or provincial test

- Released items from state, provincial, and national assessments (for example, see the National Assessment of Educational Progress website for released items of different disciplines at different grade levels: http://nces.ed.gov/nationsreportcard/)

- Data on student performance on past indicators of achievement

- Examples of rubrics for performance-based assessments

- Recommendations from assessment experts such as Rick Stiggins, W. James Popham, Dylan Wiliam, and Larry Ainsworth

- Websites on quality assessments such as the National Center for Research on Evaluation, Standards, and Student Testing (CRESST, www.cse.ucla.edu) and the Assessment Training Institute (www.assessmentinst.com)

- Tests developed by individual members of the team

Teams should have the autonomy to develop the kind of assessments they believe will result in valid and authentic measures of the learning of their students. They should have autonomy in designating the proficiency targets for each skill; however, they should also be called upon to demonstrate that student success on their assessments is strongly correlated to success on other indicators of achievement the school is monitoring.

When Alisa Papas, an assessment coach for the Fairfax County Public Schools in Virginia, works with teams to create common assessments, she guides them through a series of questions prior to teaching a new unit. The questions include:

- What is the purpose of the assessment? What are you attempting to discover, and whom will the assessment inform?

- What essential standard or standards are you addressing with this assessment? What specific knowledge and skills lead to proficiency in this standard?

■ How can you plan to gather the information that is most important to you?

In this step, teams decide how many and what kind of items to include on the assessment. Options include (1) selected response, such as multiple choice, (2) constructed response, such as short answer or essay, (3) performance assessment, which requires a rubric, or (4) personal communication, such as an interview or individual reading inventory. Once these first three questions have been addressed, the team turns its attention to creating the assessment.

■ How will you choose items and questions? Who will be responsible for pulling it together?

Any item to be included on the test must be reviewed and endorsed by the team.

■ What must students score to be deemed proficient in each essential standard?

The processes being used in White River and Fairfax County are helping educators clarify how students will demonstrate that they have acquired the intended knowledge, skills, and dispositions. This clarity on the part of educators puts them in a better position to help students understand what they are to learn and how they will be called upon to provide evidence of their learning.

Part Three

Here's Why

Reciprocal accountability requires leaders not only to help educators understand how to address a task, but also to make the case for why the task is essential. Organizations are most effective when the people throughout the organization are clear regarding its fundamental purpose. Employees can play a role in the success of their organizations when they know not only how to perform their specific tasks, but also understand why they do them—how their work contributes to a larger purpose (Covey, 1996; Handy, 1996; Kouzes & Posner, 1987). This clarity of purpose directs their day-to-day actions and decisions. As Jim Collins (2001) noted, "Great organizations simplify a complex world into a single organizing idea, a basic principle or concept that unifies and guides everything" (p. 91).

Organizations are most effective when the people throughout the organization are clear regarding its fundamental purpose.

In chapter 2 we argued that the fundamental purpose—the single organizing idea—that unifies and guides the work of a PLC is ensuring high levels of learning for all students. No school or district can accomplish that purpose unless it can answer the questions:

- Exactly what is it each student is expected to learn?

- How will students be called upon to demonstrate their learning?

School districts are most effective when these questions are addressed in a systematic way by the professionals most responsible for ensuring learning: classroom teachers.

The premise that every teacher must know what he or she must teach and what students must learn is found in virtually every credible school improvement model (see Why Should We Ensure Students Have Access to a Guaranteed and Viable Curriculum?).

To ensure all students have an opportunity to master the same essential learning, school and district leaders must . . . engage every teacher in a collaborative process to study, to clarify, and most importantly, to commit to teaching the curriculum.

Research points to the same conclusion: teachers are most effective in helping all students learn when they are clear regarding exactly what their students must know and be able to do as a result of the course, grade level, or unit of instruction.

This finding presents schools and districts with an important question: "What is the best way to ensure each teacher knows what students must learn?" One approach is to provide each teacher with a copy of the standards that have been established for their subject area or grade level as well as a district curriculum guide for addressing those standards. The assumption behind this practice is that if the right documents are distributed to individual teachers, each will teach the same curriculum as his or her colleagues. This assumption lingers despite decades of evidence that it is erroneous. Almost every veteran educator would agree with the research that there is a huge discrepancy between the intended curriculum and the implemented curriculum (Marzano, 2003). The former specifies what teachers are called upon to teach; the latter reflects what is actually taught. The idea that all students within the same school have access to the same curriculum has been described as a "gravely misleading myth" (Hirsch, 1996, p. 26), and district curriculum guides have been characterized as "well intended, but fundamentally fictional accounts" of what students are actually learning (Jacobs, 2001, p. 20).

To ensure all students have an opportunity to master the same essential learning, school and district leaders must do more than deliver curriculum documents to teachers. They must engage every teacher in a collaborative process to study, to clarify, and most importantly, to commit to teaching the curriculum. All teachers should be expected to clarify essential learning with their colleagues—even in states or provinces with delineated standards

Why Should We Ensure Students Have Access to a Guaranteed and Viable Curriculum?

One of the most significant factors that impacts student achievement is that teachers commit to implementing a guaranteed and viable curriculum *to ensure no matter who teaches a given class, the curriculum will address certain essential content* (Marzano, 2003).

To improve student achievement, educators must determine the power standards—*learning standards that are most essential because they possess the qualities of endurance, leverage, and readiness for success at the next level; "the first and most important practical implication of power standards is that leaders must make time for teachers to collaborate within and among grade levels to identify the power standards"* (Reeves, 2002, p. 54).

One of the keys to improving schools is to ensure teachers "know the learning intentions *and success criteria of their lessons, know* how well they are attaining *these criteria for all their students, and know where to go next in light of the gap between students' current knowledge and understanding and the success criteria"; this can be maximized in a safe and collaborative environment where teachers talk to each other about teaching* (Hattie, 2009, p. 239).

"The staff in the effective school accepts responsibility for the students' learning of the essential curricular goals." (Lezotte, 2002, p. 4, emphasis added)

Professional learning communities are characterized by an academic focus that begins with a set of practices that bring clarity, coherence, and precision to every teacher's classroom work. Teachers work collaboratively to provide a rigorous curriculum that is crystal clear and includes a compact list of learning expectations *for each grade or course and tangible exemplars of student proficiency for each learning expectation* (Saphier, 2005).

"[Effective teachers] clarify . . . goals and assessment criteria *in ways that will help students understand what they need to learn and what strategies are likely to be most useful in enabling them to do so."* (Brophy, 2004, p. 79, emphasis added)

"Implementing a strategy of common, rigorous standards *with differentiated resources and instruction can create excellence and equity for all students."* (Childress, Doyle, & Thomas, 2009, p. 133, emphasis added)

and in districts with highly developed curriculum guides. They should do so because:

1. **Collaborative study of essential learning promotes clarity.** Even if individual teachers take the time to review state and district curriculum standards, it is unlikely they will interpret those standards consistently. Dialogue clarifying what standards mean and what they look like in the classroom helps promote a more consistent curriculum.

2. **Collaborative study of essential learning promotes consistent priorities.** Just because teachers interpret a learning standard consistently does not guarantee that they will assign the same priority to the standard. One teacher may conclude a particular standard is very significant and devote weeks to teaching it, while another teacher may choose to spend only a day on the same standard.

3. **Collaborative study of essential learning is crucial to the common pacing required for common formative assessments.** If teachers have not agreed on the meaning and significance of what they are being asked to teach, they will not be able to establish common pacing in their courses and grade levels. Common pacing is a prerequisite for common formative assessments, which we have concluded are some of the most powerful tools for improvement available to a school.

4. **Collaborative study of essential learning can help establish a curriculum that is viable.** One of the most significant barriers to clarity regarding essential learning for students is curriculum overload (Consortium on Productivity in Schools, 1995; Reeves, 2004). One analysis concluded it would take up to twenty-three years to cover adequately all the standards that have been established at the state and national levels (Marzano, 2003). As a result, individual teachers are constantly making decisions regarding what content to omit in their classrooms, making it difficult for subsequent teachers to know what has been taught and what has not (Stevenson & Stigler, 1992). If teachers work together to make these decisions, they can establish a curriculum that can be taught in the allotted time, and they can clarify the scope and sequence of the curriculum with colleagues who teach in the preceding and subsequent courses or grade levels.

5. **Collaborative study of essential learning creates ownership of the curriculum among those who are called upon to teach it.** Attempts to create a guaranteed curriculum for every child throughout a state, province, or district often create a uniform *intended* curriculum but do little to address the *implemented* curriculum. Teachers throughout North America often

feel neither ownership of nor accountability for the content they are being asked to teach. They were not meaningfully involved in the process of creating that content, and they often critique the decisions of those who were: state or provincial departments of education, district committees, central office curriculum coordinators, and so on. Others do not debate the merits of the curriculum; they simply ignore it. A guaranteed curriculum exists in theory but not in fact.

Certainly teacher ownership of and commitment to the curriculum their students will be expected to master play an important role in the quality of student learning. Successful implementation of any course of study requires people who care about intended outcomes and have a determination to achieve them. One strategy to promote stronger ownership would simply allow each teacher to determine what he or she will teach; however, that strategy eliminates any hope students will have an equal opportunity to learn the same essential content.

Teacher ownership of and commitment to the curriculum their students will be expected to master play an important role in the quality of student learning.

> **Collaborative Study of Essential Learning . . .**
>
> - Promotes clarity
> - Promotes consistent priorities
> - Is crucial to the common pacing required for formative assessments
> - Can help establish a curriculum that is viable
> - Creates ownership of the curriculum among those who are asked to teach it

So should districts opt for the uniformity that accompanies a curriculum prescribed by a state, province, or district, or should they promote individual teacher autonomy in an effort to generate greater enthusiasm and ownership? The attentive reader will recognize that the wisest course is to reject this Tyranny of Or and seek the Genius of And by creating processes that promote both equity and allegiance.

Ownership and commitment are directly linked to the extent to which people are engaged in the decision-making process (Axelrod, 2002). Stephen Covey (1989) was emphatic on this point, writing, "Without involvement there is no commitment. Mark it down, asterisk it, circle it, underline it. *No involvement, no commitment*" (p. 143). As a result, there is a direct correlation between participation and improved results (Wheatley, 1999). An attempt to bring about significant change in a school without first engaging those who will be called upon to do the work in meaningful dialogue creates a context for failure. Seymour Sarason (1996), who studied the culture of schools for over a quarter of a century, described the typical change process:

"Someone" decides that something will be changed and "others" are then *required* appropriately to implement that change. If others have had no say in the decision, if there was no forum or allotted time for others to express their ideas or feelings, if others come to feel they are not respected, if they feel their professionalism has been demeaned, the stage is set for the change to fail. *The problem of change is the problem of power, and the problem of power is how to wield it in ways that allow others to identify with, to gain a sense of ownership of the process and the goals of the change.* (p. 335, emphasis in the original)

So what is the best way to engage staff in an improvement process? The greatest ownership and strongest levels of commitment flow to the smallest part of the organization because that is where people's *engagement* levels are highest. Teachers are de facto members of their state or provincial systems of education, but they feel greater allegiance to their local district than they do to the state or province. Most teachers, however, feel greater loyalty to their individual schools than to their districts. Teachers are likely to feel even greater allegiance to their departments than to their schools. If their departments have been organized into teams, they probably feel greater loyalty to their teammates than to the department as a whole. It is at the team level that teachers have the greatest opportunity for engagement, dialogue, and decision making. When teachers have collaboratively studied the question, "What must our students learn?," when they have created common formative assessments as a team to monitor student learning on a timely basis, and when they have promised each other to teach essential content and prepare students for the assessments, they have exponentially increased the likelihood that the agreed-upon curriculum will actually be taught.

We are not advocating that a team of teachers should be free to disregard state, provincial, or district guidelines and pursue their own interests. We are instead contending that one of the most powerful ways to bring the guidelines to life is to create processes to ensure every teacher becomes a true student of them.

When school leaders establish clear expectations and parameters like those we list earlier in this chapter, they create a process that promotes consistency *and* engages teachers in ways that encourage ownership and commitment. Those guidelines also demand accountability because a team must be able to demonstrate that its decisions have led to more students achieving at higher levels as measured by multiple indicators. Furthermore, the team format itself promotes accountability. Teachers recognize that failure to address agreed-upon content will have an adverse impact on their students when they take common assessments and will prevent the team from achieving its goals. Few teachers will be cavalier about letting down their students and their teammates, particularly when evidence of their failure to honor commitments is readily available with each common assessment.

For too long, administrators have settled for the illusion of uniformity across the entire district: they dictated curriculum to schools while teachers provided students in the same course or grade level with vastly different experiences. Effective leaders will view engagement with the question, "What do we want our students to know and be able to do?" as a professional obligation incumbent upon every teacher, and they will create the processes and parameters to promote far greater consistency in the *implemented* curriculum.

The Power of Common Formative Assessments

One of the most powerful, high-leverage strategies for improving student learning available to schools is the creation of frequent, high-quality, common formative assessments by teachers who are working collaboratively to help a group of students acquire agreed-upon knowledge and skills. Such assessments serve a distinctly different purpose than the state and provincial tests that have become the norm in North America. State and provincial tests typically serve as summative assessments: attempts to determine if students have met intended standards by a specified deadline. They are assessments *of* learning, typically measuring many things infrequently. They can provide helpful information regarding the strengths and weaknesses of curricula and programs in a district, school, or department, and they often serve as a means of promoting institutional accountability. The infrequency of these end-of-process measurements, however, limits their effectiveness in providing the timely feedback that guides teacher practice and student learning (Stiggins & DuFour, 2009).

Summative assessments determine if students have met intended standards by a specified deadline.

Formative assessments, or assessments *for* learning, are part of an ongoing process to monitor each student's learning on a continuous basis. Formative assessments typically measure a few things frequently and are intended to inform teachers regarding the effectiveness of their practice and students of their next steps on the scaffolding of learning. When done well, formative assessment advances and motivates, rather than merely reports on student learning. The clearly defined goals and descriptive feedback to students provide them with specific insights regarding how to improve, and the growth they experience helps build their confidence as learners (Stiggins & DuFour, 2009).

Formative assessments typically measure a few things frequently and are intended to inform teachers regarding the effectiveness of their practice and students of their next steps on the scaffolding of learning.

Doug Reeves (2000) uses an analogy to draw a sharp distinction between summative and formative assessments, comparing the former to an autopsy and the latter to a physical examination. A summative test, like an autopsy, can provide useful information that explains why the patient has failed, but the information comes too late, at least from the patient's perspective. A formative assessment, like a physical examination, can provide both the physician and the patient with timely information regarding the patient's well-being and can help in prescribing antidotes to help an ailing person or to assist a healthy patient in becoming even stronger.

The case for formative assessment is compelling (see page 77, Why Should We Use Formative Assessments?). Of course, the most effective teachers are constantly assessing student learning. Multiple times each day, they check for student understanding, use precise assessments, and engage students in reviewing their own comprehension and progress. Most of the research on formative assessment focuses on this ongoing, daily assessment. It is crucial to good teaching and can serve as a powerful motivator for students. We endorse it wholeheartedly. There will be times, however, that assessments become more formal, and there are compelling reasons that at least some of those formal assessments be developed by the team rather than by the individual teacher. The case for team-developed common formative assessments as a powerful tool for school improvement is also compelling (see page 78, Why Should We Use Common Assessments?).

We argue that the benefits of team-developed common assessments used for formative purposes are so powerful that no team of teachers should be allowed to opt out of creating them. We are not suggesting that they take the place of the ongoing checks for understanding that should occur in individual teacher's classroom each day. Furthermore, schools should certainly use a variety of assessments: those developed by individual teachers, a state or provincial test, district tests, national tests, tests that accompany textbooks, and so on. But school leaders should *never* allow the presence of these other assessments to be an excuse for ignoring the need for common, team-made formative assessments for the following reasons:

1. **Common assessments promote efficiency for teachers.** If all students are expected to demonstrate the same knowledge and skills regardless of the teacher to whom they are assigned, it only makes sense that teachers would work together to assess student learning. For example, suppose four third-grade teachers will assess their students on four reading skills during a unit. It would be more efficient for each teacher to develop activities or questions for one skill and present them to teammates for review for inclusion on the common assessment than for each teacher to work separately on all four skills, thereby duplicating and replicating the effort of his or her colleagues. It is ineffective and inefficient for teachers to operate as independent subcontractors who are stationed in proximity to others, yet work in isolation. Those who are called upon to complete the same task benefit by pooling their efforts.

2. **Common assessments promote equity for students.** When schools utilize common assessments, they are more likely to:

   - Ensure that students have access to the same essential curriculum

   - Use common pacing

   - Assess the quality of student work according to the same standards

Why Should We Use Formative Assessments?

Effective use of formative assessment, developed through teacher learning communities, promises not only the largest potential gains in student achievement but also a process for affordable teacher professional development (Wiliam & Thompson, 2007).

"There is strong and rigorous evidence that improving formative assessment can raise standards of pupils' performance. There have been few initiatives in education with such a strong body of evidence to support a claim to raise standards." (Black & Wiliam, 1998, p. 20)

"Assessment for learning . . . when done well, this is one of the most powerful, high-leverage strategies for improving student learning that we know of. Educators collectively *at the district and school levels become more skilled and focused at assessing, disaggregating, and using student achievement as a tool for ongoing improvement."* (Fullan, 2005, p. 71)

"Studies have demonstrated assessment for learning rivals one-on-one tutoring in its effectiveness and that the use of assessment particularly benefits low-achieving students." (Stiggins, 2004, p. 27)

"Formative assessments are one of the most powerful weapons in a teacher's arsenal. An effective standards-based, formative assessment program can help to dramatically enhance student achievement throughout the K–12 system." (Marzano, 2006, back cover)

"Formative assessment is a potentially transformative instructional tool that, if clearly understood and adroitly employed, can benefit both educators and their students . . . formative assessment constitutes the key cornerstone of clearheaded instructional thinking. Formative assessment represents evidence-based *instructional decision-making. If you want to become more instructionally effective, and if you want your students to achieve more, then formative assessments should be for you."* (Popham, 2008, p. 3, 15)

Why Should We Use Common Assessments?

Reviews of accountability data from hundreds of schools reveal the schools with the greatest gains in achievement consistently employ common assessments, nonfiction writing, and collaborative scoring by faculty (Reeves, 2004).

Powerful, proven structures for improved results are at hand. "It starts when a group of teachers meet regularly as a team to identify essential and valued student learning, develop common formative assessments, analyze current levels of achievement, set achievement goals, and then share and create lessons and strategies to improve upon those levels." (Schmoker, 2004b, p. 48).

"[Common formative assessments provide] regular and timely feedback regarding student attainment of the most critical standards . . . [and] also foster consistent expectations and priorities within a grade level, course, and department regarding standards, instruction, and assessment. . . . Most importantly, common formative assessment results enable educators to diagnose student learning needs accurately in time to make instructional modifications." (Ainsworth, 2007, pp. 95–96)

The schools and districts that doubled student achievement added another layer of testing—common formative or benchmark assessments. These assessments were designed to provide detailed and concrete information on what students know and do not know with respect to specific learning targets (Odden & Archibald, 2009).

The key to improved student achievement was moving beyond an individual teacher looking at his or her classroom data. Instead, it took getting same-grade teacher teams to meet, analyze the results of each interim assessment to understand what concepts in the curriculum were posing difficulty for students, share ideas, figure out the best interventions, and actually follow up in their classrooms (Christman et al., 2009).

In schools that help students burdened by poverty achieve remarkable success, teachers work in collaborative teams to build common formative assessments and use the data to identify which students need help and which need greater challenges. But they also use data to inform teachers' practice, to discuss why one teacher is having success in teaching a concept and others are not, and what the more successful teacher can teach his or her colleagues (Chenoweth, 2009).

It is ironic that schools and districts often pride themselves in the fair and consistent application of rules and policies while at the same time ignoring the tremendous inequities in the opportunities students are given to learn and the criteria by which their learning is assessed. Schools will continue to have difficulty helping all students achieve high standards if the teachers within them cannot develop the capacity to define a standard with specificity and assess it with consistency.

3. **Common assessments represent a powerful strategy for determining whether the guaranteed curriculum is being taught and, more importantly, learned.** Doug Reeves (2004) refers to common, teacher-made formative assessments as the "best practice in assessment" (p. 71) and the "gold standard in educational accountability" (p. 114) because they promote consistency in expectations and provide timely, accurate, and specific feedback to both students and teachers. Furthermore, as teachers work together to study the elements of effective assessment and critique one another's ideas for assessment, they improve their assessment literacy. Perhaps most importantly, teachers' active engagement in the development of the assessment leads them to accept greater responsibility for the results.

4. **Common assessments inform the practice of individual teachers.** Tests constructed by an individual teacher generate plenty of data (mean, mode, median, percentage of failing students, and so on), but they do little to inform the teacher's practice by identifying strengths and weaknesses in his or her teaching. Common assessments provide teachers with a basis of comparison as they learn, skill by skill, how the performance of their students is similar to and different from the other students who took the assessment. With this information, a teacher can seek assistance from teammates on areas of concern and can share strategies and ideas on skills in which his or her students excelled. For generations, teachers have been told that effective teaching is preceded by planning and followed by reflection. But the single greatest determinant of how a teacher will teach is not reflection, but rather how he or she has taught in the past (Elmore, 2010). One of the most comprehensive studies ever conducted of factors that impact student achievement concluded that reflection enhances student learning only when it is collective—a team of teachers reflecting rather than an individual—and based on actual evidence of student learning rather than an appraisal of particular teaching strategies (Hattie, 2009). Team-developed common assessments are ideally suited to this *collective reflection based on evidence.*

5. **Common assessments build a team's capacity to improve its program.** When collaborative teams of teachers have the opportunity to examine indicators of the achievement of all students in their course or grade level and track those indicators over time, they are able to identify and address problem areas in their program. Their collective analysis can lead to new curriculum, pacing, materials, and instructional strategies designed to strengthen the academic program they offer. A longitudinal study of schools engaged in reform efforts found that for two years those schools could show no gains despite the fact that teachers were meeting in teams. It wasn't until the collaborative teams of teachers looked at evidence of student learning from common assessments, identified the consistent problems students were experiencing, and then developed specific action plans to resolve those problems that students experienced dramatic gains in their learning (Gallimore, Ermeling, Saunders, & Goldenberg, 2009).

6. **Common assessments facilitate a systematic, collective response to students who are experiencing difficulty.** Common assessments help identify a group of students who need additional time and support to ensure their learning. Because the students are identified at the same time and because they need help with the same specific skills that have been addressed on the common assessment, the team and school are in a position to create a timely, systematic program of intervention. We will address this topic in detail in the next chapter.

7. **Common formative assessments are one of the most powerful tools for changing the professional practice of educators.** We explore this assertion in detail in chapter 7.

Common Formative Assessments . . .

- Promote efficiency for teachers
- Promote equity for students
- Provide an effective strategy for determining whether the guaranteed curriculum is being taught and, more importantly, learned
- Inform the practice of individual teachers
- Build a team's capacity to improve its program
- Facilitate a systematic, collective response to students who are experiencing difficulty
- Offer the most powerful tool for changing adult behavior and practice

One of the most important factors in student learning is the quality of the teaching they receive (Hattie, 2009; Haycock, 1998; Marzano, 2003; Wright, Horn, & Sanders, 1997). And the "most immediate and direct influence on teaching expertise is the workplace of the school itself" (Saphier, 2005, p. 220). As Jonathan Saphier (2005) goes on to say:

> The reason Professional Learning Communities increase student learning is that they produce more good teaching by more teachers more of the time. Put simply, PLC improves teaching, which improves student results, especially for the least advantaged of students. (p. 23)

The reason that PLCs improve teaching is, paradoxically, because they focus on learning. Educators in a PLC work together collaboratively in constant, deep collective inquiry into the questions, "What is it our students must learn?" and "How will we know when they have learned it?" The dialogue generated from these questions results in the academic focus, collective commitments, and productive professional relationships that enhance learning for teachers and students alike. School leaders cannot waffle on this issue. Working with colleagues on these questions is an ongoing professional responsibility from which no teacher should be exempt.

Part Four

Assessing Your Place on the PLC Journey

Complete the PLC continuum and Where Do We Go From Here? worksheets as outlined in chapter 2.

The Professional Learning Communities at Work™ Continuum: Learning as Our Fundamental Purpose (Part I)

DIRECTIONS: Individually, silently, and *honestly* assess the current reality of your school's implementation of each indicator listed in the left column. Consider what evidence or anecdotes support your assessment. This form may also be used to assess district or team implementation.

We acknowledge that the fundamental purpose of our school is to help all students achieve high levels of learning, and therefore, we work collaboratively to clarify what students must learn and how we will monitor each student's learning.

Indicator	Pre-Initiating	Initiating	Implementing	Developing	Sustaining
We work with colleagues on our team to build shared knowledge regarding state, provincial, and/ or national standards; district curriculum guides; trends in student achievement; and expectations for the next course or grade level. This collective inquiry has enabled each member of our team to clarify what all students must know and be able to do as a result of every unit of instruction.	Teachers have been provided with a copy of state, provincial, and/or national standards and a district curriculum guide. There is no process for them to discuss curriculum with colleagues and no expectation they will do so.	Teacher representatives have helped to create a district curriculum guide. Those involved in the development feel it is a useful resource for teachers. Those not involved in the development may or may not use the guide.	Teachers are working in collaborative teams to clarify the essential learning for each unit and to establish a common pacing guide. Some staff members question the benefit of the work. They argue that developing curriculum is the responsibility of the central office or textbook publishers rather than teachers. Some are reluctant to give up favorite units that seem to have no bearing on essential standards.	Teachers have clarified the essential learning for each unit by building shared knowledge regarding state, provincial, and/or national standards; by studying high-stakes assessments; and by seeking input regarding the prerequisites for success as students enter the next grade level. They are beginning to adjust curriculum, pacing, and instruction based on evidence of student learning.	Teachers on every collaborative team are confident they have established a guaranteed and viable curriculum for their students. Their clarity regarding the knowledge and skills students must acquire as a result of each unit of instruction, and their commitment to providing students with the instruction and support to achieve the intended outcomes, give every student access to essential learning.

Page 1 of 2

Indicator	Pre-Initiating	Initiating	Implementing	Developing	Sustaining
We work with colleagues on our team to clarify the criteria by which we will judge the quality of student work, and we practice applying those criteria until we can do so consistently.	Each teacher establishes his or her own criteria for assessing the quality of student work.	Teachers have been provided with sample rubrics for assessing the quality of student work.	Teachers working in collaborative teams are attempting to assess student work according to common criteria. They are practicing applying the criteria to examples of student work, but they are not yet consistent. The discrepancy is causing some tension on the team.	Teachers working in collaborative teams are clear on the criteria they will use in assessing the quality of student work and can apply the criteria consistently.	Collaborative teams of teachers frequently use performance-based assessments to gather evidence of student learning. Members have established strong inter-rater reliability and use the results from these assessments to inform and improve their individual and collective practice. The team's clarity also helps members teach the criteria to students, who can then assess the quality of their own work and become more actively engaged in their learning.
We monitor the learning of each student's attainment of all essential outcomes on a timely basis through a series of frequent, team-developed common formative assessments that are aligned with high-stakes assessments students will be required to take.	Each teacher creates his or her own assessments to monitor student learning. Assessments are typically summative rather than formative. A teacher can teach an entire career and not know if he or she teaches a particular skill or concept better or worse than the colleague in the next room.	The district has established benchmark assessments that are administered several times throughout the year. Teachers pay little attention to the results and would have a difficult time explaining the purpose of the benchmark assessments.	Teachers working in collaborative teams have begun to create common assessments. Some attempt to circumvent the collaborative process by proposing the team merely use the quizzes and tests that are available in the textbook as their common assessments. Some administrators question the ability of teachers to create good assessments and argue that the district should purchase commercially developed tests.	Teachers working in collaborative teams have created a series of common assessments and agreed on the specific standard students must achieve to be deemed proficient. The user-friendly results of common assessments are providing each member of the team with timely evidence of student learning. Members are using that evidence to improve their assessments and to develop more effective instructional strategies.	Collaborative teams of teachers gather evidence of student learning on a regular basis through frequent common formative assessments. The team analysis of results drives the continuous improvement process of the school. Members determine the effectiveness of instructional strategies based on evidence of student learning rather than teacher preference or precedent. Members who struggle to teach a skill are learning from those who are getting the best results. The frequent common formative assessments provide the vital information that fuels the school's system of intervention and enrichment. The assessments are formative because (1) they are used to identify students who need additional time and support for learning, (2) the students receive the additional time and support for learning, and (3) students are given another opportunity to demonstrate that they have learned.

Where Do We Go From Here? Worksheet
Clearly Defined Outcomes

Indicator of a PLC at Work	What steps or activities must be initiated to create this condition in your school?	Who will be responsible for initiating or sustaining these steps or activities?	What is a realistic timeline for each step or phase of the activity?	What will you use to assess the effectiveness of your initiative?
We work with colleagues on our team to build shared knowledge regarding state, provincial, and/or national standards; district curriculum guides; trends in student achievement; and expectations for the next course or grade level. This collective inquiry has enabled each member of our team to clarify what all students must know and be able to do as a result of every unit of instruction.				

Where Do We Go From Here? Worksheet
Monitoring Each Student's Learning

Indicator of a PLC at Work	What steps or activities must be initiated to create this condition in your school?	Who will be responsible for initiating or sustaining these steps or activities?	What is a realistic timeline for each step or phase of the activity?	What will you use to assess the effectiveness of your initiative?
We work with colleagues on our team to clarify the criteria by which we will judge the quality of student work, and we practice applying those criteria until we can do so consistently.				
We monitor the learning of each student's attainment of all essential outcomes on a timely basis through a series of frequent, team-developed common formative assessments that are aligned with high-stakes assessments students will be required to take.				

Part Five

Tips for Moving Forward: Clarifying and Monitoring Essential Learning

1 **Less is more.** Remember that the main problem with curricula in North America is not that we do not do enough, but rather that we attempt to do too much. As Doug Reeves (2005) writes, "While academic standards vary widely in their specificity and clarity, they almost all have one thing in common: there are too many of them" (p. 48). We recommend that teams start by identifying the eight to ten most essential outcomes students will be expected to achieve in their course or subject area for that semester. There is nothing sacred about that total; it is merely meant to serve as a guideline for team dialogue.

2 **Focus on proficiency in key skills—not coverage.** Teachers throughout North America are confronted with a multitude of standards, and they fear that any one of them may be addressed on state and provincial tests. Therefore, they focus on covering the content rather than ensuring students become proficient in the most essential skills. But not all standards are of equal importance. Some are vital to a student's success, and others are simply nice to know. By focusing on essential skills, teachers prepare students for 80 to 90 percent of the content that will be addressed on state and provincial tests and provide them with the reading, writing, and reasoning skills to address any question that could appear (Reeves, 2002).

A common core curriculum can allow for some variation within courses and grade levels. A frequent but often unstated objection to common curriculum is that teachers may be forced to forgo their favorite unit, the one they most enjoy and are most passionate about. But a common core curriculum does not mean a uniform curriculum. A team could develop a curriculum and pacing guide that members feel will enable them to address all of the essential skills in fifteen weeks of an eighteen-week semester. This provides each member of the team with three weeks to teach his or her favorite unit. The team's common assessment will cover the common curriculum, while individual teachers can create their own assessments for content unique to their students.

3 **Recognize that common assessments might create teacher anxiety.** Common assessments are likely to create anxiety among teachers who recognize that the results from these assessments could be used to expose weaknesses in their instruction. The inner voice of teachers may very well say,

> But what if I am the weakest teacher on my team? My teammates will lose respect for me. The principal may use the results in my evaluation. If the results become public, parents may demand that their children be removed from my class. I don't want to participate in a process that can be used to humiliate or punish me. I would rather work in blissful ignorance than become aware that I may be ineffective.

These very real and understandable human emotions should be acknowledged, but should not be allowed to derail the effort to create a common curriculum and common assessments. There are certain things leaders can do in an attempt to address these initial concerns, such as assuring teachers that their individual results from the assessments will not be distributed to their teammates. Each teacher would be able to see how his or her students performed on each skill compared to the total group of students who took the test, but not compared to other individual teachers on the team. Principals can promise teachers that the results will not leave the building, appear in board of education reports, or show up in district newsletters. They can assure staff that student performance on common assessments will not be used as a factor in teacher evaluation. The process to assess student learning should be distinct from the process to evaluate teachers. Certainly a teacher's failure to contribute to the team process or unwillingness to change practices to improve results when students are not being successful can be addressed in the teacher's evaluation; however, scores from common assessments should not be. We will address this topic in more detail in chapter 7.

 Districts can play a role. Districts make a mistake when they create common assessments as a substitute for teacher-developed assessments at the team level. Districts can create their own assessments to monitor student learning throughout the entire district, but these assessments should supplement rather than replace team-level assessments. Districts can also create test-item banks as a resource for teachers, but teams should be expected to engage in the process of developing their own tools to answer the question, "How do we know our students are learning?"

 Create shared understanding of the term *common assessment*. Once again, we have discovered that people who use the same terms do not necessarily assign them the same meaning.

For example, a team of teachers that agrees to use the quiz provided at the end of each chapter of the textbook could claim they are using common assessments, but they would not experience the benefits we have outlined. Common assessments in the PLC context "are developed *collaboratively* in grade-level and departmental teams and incorporate each team's collective wisdom (professional knowledge and experience) in determining the selection, design, and administration of those assessments" (Ainsworth & Viegut, 2006, p. 13).

District and school leaders in Countryside Kildeer School District 96 in suburban Chicago worked with staff to create a shared understanding of the term. Teachers there recognized that their common assessments were to be:

- Connected to the guaranteed and viable curriculum

- Given on a regular and frequent basis to all students enrolled in the same course or grade level

- Administered at about the same time

- Created by a collaborative team of teachers

- Analyzed by that collaborative team of teachers

- Considered highly formative (to identify weaknesses in student learning in order to provide students with additional opportunities to learn)

- Used to help students see their progress toward a well-defined standard

 Use assessments as a means rather than an end. In too many schools in North America, staff have become preoccupied with the pursuit of higher test scores. Test scores should be an indicator of our effectiveness in helping all students learn rather than the primary focus of the institution. They should be viewed as a means rather than an end. Doug Reeves (2004) does a wonderful job of providing schools with fail-safe strategies to improve test scores: increase the dropout rate, assign higher percentages of students to special education, warehouse low-performing students in one school, create magnet programs to attract enough high-performing students to a low-performing school to raise its average, eliminate electives to devote more time to areas of the curriculum that are tested, and so on. Sadly, these strategies are routinely being used in schools that are attempting to increase scores without improving learning.

Educators will not be driven to extraordinary effort and relentless commitment to achieve the goal of increasing student performance on the state test by five points. Most entered the profession because they felt they could make a significant difference in the lives of their students, and school leaders are more effective in marshalling and motivating faculty efforts when they appeal to that moral purpose.

Test scores will take care of themselves when schools and the people within them are passionately committed to helping each student develop the knowledge, skills, and dispositions essential to his or her success.

Part Six

Questions to Guide the Work of Your Professional Learning Community

To Clarify Essential Learning, Ask:

1. What is it we want all students to know and be able to do as a result of this course, grade level, or unit of instruction?

2. How can we be sure each student has access to the same knowledge and skills regardless of who is teaching the course?

3. What knowledge and which skills in our curriculum pass the three-part test: endurance, leverage, and necessity for success at the next level?

4. What material can we eliminate from our curriculum?

5. Is our curriculum preparing students for success on high-stakes tests?

6. Is our curriculum preparing students for success at the next level?

7. How should we pace the curriculum to ensure that all students have the opportunity to master the essential learning?

To Monitor Student Learning, Ask:

1. How will we monitor the learning of each student, on each essential skill, on a timely basis?

2. What are the criteria we will use in judging the quality of student work?

3. What evidence do we have that we apply the criteria consistently?

4. What evidence do we have that we are using the results of common assessments to identify students who require additional time and support for learning?

5. What evidence do we have that we are using the results from common assessments to identify strengths and weaknesses in our individual teaching?

6. What evidence do we have that we are using the results of common assessments as part of a continuous improvement process that is helping our team get better results?

7. Does student performance on our team assessments correlate with their achievement on other assessments at the district, state, provincial, or national level?

   ■ Does student performance on our assessments correlate with the grades they are earning in my course or grade level?

   ■ Do our assessment practices encourage or discourage learning on the part of our students?

Part Seven

Dangerous Detours and Seductive Shortcuts

Beware of any action that removes teachers from the process or minimizes their role because in every instance the impact of the process will be diminished.

It is the *process* of team members collaboratively building shared knowledge and collectively making decisions about curriculum and assessment that results in adult learning and improved professional practice. Beware of any action that removes teachers from the process or minimizes their role because in every instance the impact of the process will be diminished. Examples of shortcuts that are frequently used to circumvent this critical collaborative team dialogue include:

- Distributing state and district guidelines to individual teachers as a substitute for team dialogue

- Assigning a committee of teachers to establish the curriculum and present it to their colleagues

- Purchasing the curriculum

- Allowing the textbook to determine the curriculum

- Substituting district benchmark assessments, textbook assessments, or commercially prepared assessments for team-developed common assessments

- Failing to include team dialogue based on evidence of student learning as part of the curriculum and assessment process

Teachers and administrators both may argue that teachers are too busy to clarify curriculum and/or create assessments. They may assert that having someone else do the work provides teachers with an important service. Some may argue that teachers lack the knowledge and skills to do the work well. It is certainly true that school leaders will need to provide collaborative teams of teachers with time, resources, and training to assist them in this important work. Once again, however, the critical questions, "What must our students learn?" and "How will we know if they have learned it?" must be addressed in a systematic way by the professionals most responsible for ensuring learning—classroom teachers. It is by engaging the process that teachers learn, so do not remove them from the process.

Final Thoughts

When teachers work together to establish clarity regarding the knowledge, skills, and dispositions all students are to acquire as a result of each course, grade level, and unit of instruction, schools take a significant step forward on their PLC journey. When those same teachers establish frequent common formative assessments that provide timely feedback on each student's proficiency, their schools advance even further, because these assessments help identify students who are experiencing difficulty in their learning. If, however, the school does nothing to assist those students, little has been accomplished. The next chapter explores the critical question, "What happens in your school when kids don't learn?"

Chapter 4

How Will We Respond When Some Students Don't Learn?

Part One

The Case Study: Systematic Interventions Versus an Educational Lottery

Marty Mathers, principal of the Puff Daddy Middle School (nickname: the Rappers), knew that his eighth-grade algebra teachers were his most challenging team on the faculty. The team was comprised of four people with very strong personalities who had difficulty finding common ground.

Peter Pilate was the most problematic teacher on the team from Principal Mather's perspective. The failure rate in his classes was three times higher than the other members of the team, and parents routinely demanded that their students be assigned to a different teacher. Ironically, many of the students who failed Mr. Pilate's class demonstrated proficiency on the state math test. Principal Mathers had raised these issues with Peter, but found Peter to be unreceptive to the possibility of changing any of his practices. Peter insisted that the primary reason students failed was because they did not complete their daily homework assignments in a timely manner. He refused to accept late work, and he explained that the accumulation of zeros on missed assignments led to the high failure rate. He felt strongly that the school had to teach students to be responsible, and he made it clear that he expected the principal to support him in his effort to teach responsibility for getting work done on time.

The students knew Alan Sandler as the "cool" teacher. He had excellent rapport with his students and a great sense of humor that made his classroom an entertaining environment. Most of his students earned As and Bs in his course; however, each spring, almost half of them would fail to meet the proficiency standard on the state exam.

Principal Mathers was aware of yet another trend in Charlotte Darwin's math classes. He knew that although her algebra sections might start out with a large number of students, by early October she would recommend transferring many of them to the pre-algebra program. She felt it was unfair to keep students in a program where they lacked the skills for success. The students who remained in her algebra class usually scored slightly above the state average on their proficiency examination.

Henrietta Higgins was a true joy to have on the faculty. She was relentless in holding students accountable but perfectly willing to sacrifice her personal time to help students be successful. She monitored their achievement constantly, and if a student began to fall behind, she required the student to meet with her before or after school for intensive tutoring. Her students always met or exceeded the proficiency standard on the state assessment.

Principal Mathers was increasingly uncomfortable knowing that students' experiences in the eighth-grade math program varied so greatly depending on which teacher they had, but he was uncertain of how to address the situation. Two parent phone calls in late September convinced him he could no longer ignore the disparities in the program.

The first phone call came from a parent who objected to Charlotte Darwin's recommendation to move her student to pre-algebra. The parent was familiar with the math program at the high school and recognized that if her son did not complete algebra in the eighth grade, he would never have access to the honors math program there. She was certain her son could be successful if he received some extra time and support to master content in which he was experiencing some initial difficulty. She had asked Ms. Darwin to help her son before or after school, and Ms. Darwin had flatly refused to do so. The parent was aware that Ms. Higgins routinely tutored students after school, and she demanded that Principal Mathers either direct Ms. Darwin to provide the same service for her son or transfer her son to Ms. Higgins' class.

Principal Mathers knew he could not demand that Ms. Darwin extend her contractual day to work with students after school. He also realized that she was a single parent who constantly struggled to find quality daycare for her preschool-aged child. He felt the only solution was to transfer the student to Ms. Higgins' class.

Before he could make the transfer, however, he received a second parent complaint. This time Ms. Higgins was the target. The parent objected to the fact that Ms. Higgins was demanding her son stay after school to get extra help in math. She needed her son to come home immediately after school because he was responsible for caring for his younger sister until his mother came home from work. She did not want her daughter left unsupervised. Her son could not come in before school either because he walked his sister to school. She argued that none of the other math teachers required students to stay after school, and she felt it was unfair for Ms. Higgins to do so.

Principal Mathers certainly did not want to undermine Ms. Higgins. His initial thought was to pursue the easy solution: transfer the two students into the other teacher's class. He recognized, however, that this strategy offered only a temporary solution and left the real problem unresolved. He was uneasy about a program that he perceived as inherently unfair to students. It was as if the school was playing an educational lottery with the lives of children—rolling the dice to see which students would receive an excellent opportunity to learn algebra and which would not. He was determined to address this inequity, but he was not sure how.

Reflection

Consider the dilemma presented in this case study; it is played out in schools throughout North America each day. Assuming that Principal Mathers has no additional resources to hire after-school tutors, how can he best address this problem?

Part Two

Here's How

Principal Mathers and his school are confronting the question, "How will we respond when our students don't learn?" Each individual teacher has been left to resolve this question on his or her own. The result is that students who experience difficulty in learning are subject to very different experiences. The solution requires a *systematic* process of intervention to ensure students receive additional time and support for learning according to a schoolwide plan:

- The process should ensure students receive the intervention in a timely fashion—at the first indication they are experiencing difficulty.

- The process should direct rather than invite students to devote the extra time and take advantage of the additional support until they are experiencing success.

- Most importantly, students should be guaranteed they will receive this time and support regardless of who their teacher might be.

Principal Mathers should present the current reality to the staff and ask them to assess that reality in terms of its effectiveness, efficiency, and most importantly, its equity. An honest evaluation of the facts could only lead to certain conclusions. The current practice is ineffective as demonstrated by both local and state indicators: a high failure rate in some classes and a high percentage of students failing to meet the state proficiency standard in others. It is inefficient: some teachers give up personal time, the school staff has to make schedule changes, and students sacrifice time in the summer to repeat failed courses. Finally, it is patently unfair.

Once the staff has confronted the "brutal facts" of their current situation, Principal Mathers could lead them through an analysis of best practices in responding to students who are not learning. The research in this area is clear: in order to help all students learn at high levels, schools must provide students who are experiencing difficulty in learning with additional time and support for learning.

The next step in this process requires the principal and staff to brainstorm ideas to create a multitiered intervention system that is timely, directive, systematic, and within the school day. Then staff members would identify the collective commitments essential to the success of their new intervention system. They would set specific, results-oriented student achievement goals to help monitor the effectiveness of the system. Finally, they would implement that system, monitor its impact, and make adjustments and improvements based on their results.

In our video program *Through New Eyes: Examining the Culture of Your School* (DuFour, 2003), we ask audiences to view a scene of a student who experiences difficulty in making the transition from middle school to high school and, very importantly, to view the scenario through the eyes of the student. Three different teachers respond to the student in three very different ways, but in each case, the burden for addressing the student's problems in the course falls to the respective teacher. In fact, the individual teacher is the only person who even realizes the student is having difficulty for the first nine weeks of the school year.

After viewing and discussing the scene with us, teachers acknowledge that the *school* never responded to the student; there was no *collective* response. When the student struggled, he was abandoned to the idiosyncrasies and beliefs of each of the school's overburdened teachers. We then ask, "Is what you saw in the scene a fairly accurate account of what typically happens in school?" Every audience has answered in the affirmative.

We then show a second scene with the same student experiencing the same difficulty in school; however, this school makes a collective response to the student. He is provided with a study hall to ensure he has extra time during the school day to receive additional support. He also meets daily with a faculty advisor and an upperclassman mentor. His counselor visits with him each week. His grades are monitored every three weeks. When he continues to experience difficulty, he is assigned to a tutoring center in place of his study hall, and his grades are monitored on a weekly basis. When his struggles persist, he is moved from the tutoring center to a guided study hall where his homework is monitored each day and all materials are provided to ensure he will complete his work. He is required to join a cocurricular activity, and his coach advises him he must be passing all of his classes if he wants to remain on the team. His progress is monitored on a weekly basis by a student support team led by his counselor. In short, he is *surrounded* by caring adults, all of whom attempt to help him be successful in his classes and consistently express their confidence in his ability to be successful through additional effort.

Audiences invariably acknowledge that the caring environment created through this timely, directive, and systematic intervention plan benefits the student far more than what traditional schools typically offer. *But it is not just the student who benefits from this systematic support.* In the first scene (and in most schools), the only professional who knows the student is struggling in algebra is the algebra teacher. The only person responsible for resolving the student's algebra problem is the algebra teacher. In the second scene, an army of adults is there to support the algebra teacher in helping the student. The teacher is not alone.

The good news is that the second scenario is not merely a dream, but something that is happening in schools throughout North America. In *Raising the Bar and Closing the Gap: Whatever it Takes* (DuFour, DuFour, Eaker, & Karhanek, 2010), we describe nine very different schools and three very different districts that have created systematic interventions to ensure their students receive additional time and support for learning. In each case, the schools and districts created their systems using their existing resources. In each case, however, it was imperative that the staff agreed to modify the schedule and assume new roles and responsibilities.

We know of schools at all levels and very diverse districts that have built systems of time and support within the constraints of union contracts and state mandates. The website www.allthingsplc.info provides information on more than 150 of those schools and districts. Although it is impossible to anticipate all the nuances of all the schedules of all schools and districts, and then offer specific solutions to scheduling questions, we can offer this generalization: faculties determined to work together to create a schedule that ensures students will receive extra time and support for learning in a timely, directive, and systematic way will be able to do so. The key question the staff of any school must consider in assessing the appropriateness and effectiveness of their daily schedule is whether the schedule provides access to students who need additional time and support during the school day in a way that does not require them to miss new direct instruction.

The caring environment created through this timely, directive, and systematic intervention plan benefits the student far more than what traditional schools typically offer. But it is not just the student who benefits from this systematic support.

Faculties determined to work together to create a schedule that ensures students will receive extra time and support for learning in a timely, directive, and systematic way will be able to do so.

What Questions

What do you mean by *system of intervention*?

Staff members must understand that a multitiered system of intervention is a schoolwide plan that ensures every student in every course or grade level will receive additional time and support for learning as soon as they experience difficulty in acquiring essential knowledge and skills. The intervention occurs during the school day and students are required rather than invited to devote the extra time and secure the extra support for learning. A system of intervention means that providing this support for students is a collective, schoolwide responsibility rather than the sole responsibility of the individual teacher.

When the leaders of Kildeer Countryside School District 96 in suburban Chicago asked each of its schools to create a "system of intervention" to provide students with additional time and support for learning, district leaders discovered schools were interpreting the term in very different ways. Therefore, district leaders worked with representatives of the schools to create the SPEED Intervention Criteria to guide the process. According to the criteria, interventions must be:

- Systematic

- Practical

- Effective

- Essential

- Directive

SPEED Intervention Goals

Systematic: The intervention plan is schoolwide, independent of the individual teacher, and communicated in writing (who, why, how, where, and when) to everyone: staff, parents, and students.

Practical: The intervention plan is affordable with the school's available resources (time, space, staff, and materials). The plan must be sustainable and replicable so that its programs and strategies can be used in other schools.

Effective: The intervention plan must be effective and available and operational early enough in the school year to make a difference for the student. It should have flexible entrance and exit criteria designed to respond to the ever-changing needs of students.

Essential: The intervention plan should focus on agreed-upon standards and the essential learning outcomes of the district's curriculum and be targeted to a student's specific learning needs as determined by formative and summative assessments.

Directive: The intervention plan should be directive. It should be mandatory—not invitational—and a part of the student's regular school day. Students should not be able to opt out, and parents and teachers cannot waive the student's participation in the intervention program.

What resources can you provide to assist us?

Intervention systems do not require additional resources, but they do require schools to use their existing resources—time, personnel, and materials—differently. The schools with exemplary intervention systems that we featured in *Raising the Bar and Closing the Gap* were not flush with resources. For example, Lakeridge Junior High School is in Orem, Utah, and Utah ranks last among the fifty states in per-pupil expenditure. Yet this school was recognized as the best school in Utah for two consecutive years because, principal Garrick Peterson advises, "We realized we were in control of time in our school" (personal communication to Rick DuFour, May 1, 2008).

Intervention systems do not require additional resources, but they do require schools to use their existing resources— time, personnel, and materials— differently.

Schools must come to regard time as a tool rather than a limitation. For too long, learning has been a prisoner of time, with clock and calendar holding students and teachers captive (Goldberg & Cross, 2005). Of course, schools could lengthen the school day or the school year to create more time, but faculties typically are not in a position to do so unilaterally and are understandably unwilling to do so unless they are compensated accordingly. Faculties can, however, examine the way they are using the existing time available to them to create more opportunities for students to learn. The answer to the scheduling challenge lies within the school. For examples of schools at all levels and all sizes that have built systems of intervention into their school day, go to www.allthingsplc.info and click on "Evidence of Effectiveness."

Part Three

Here's Why

We have known for more than thirty years that effective schools create a climate of high expectations for student learning; that is, such schools are driven by the assumption that all students are able to achieve the essential learning of their course or grade level (Cotton, 2000; Georgiades, Fuentes, & Snyder, 1983; Good & Brophy, 2002; Lezotte, 1991; Newmann & Wehlage, 1996; Purkey & Smith, 1983). One of the most authentic ways to assess the degree to which a school is characterized by "high expectations" is to examine "how the organization responds when some students do not learn" (Lezotte, 1991).

Key to an effective response for students who struggle is the provision of additional time and support for learning. Benjamin Bloom's research on mastery learning in the 1960s established that if all students were to learn, some students would need additional time and support for learning. Bob Marzano's (2003) meta-analysis of research on school-level factors that impact student learning revealed that the schools that have a profound impact on student achievement "provide interventions that are designed to overcome student background characteristics." Doug Reeves (2006, p. 87), in his studies of high-poverty, high-minority, high-achieving schools, found that those schools implement a plan for "immediate and decisive intervention" when students don't learn. In their study of school districts that were able to double student achievement, Allan Odden and Sarah Archibald (2009) found that those districts extended learning time for struggling students. A decade of research by the Southern Regional Education Board (2000) into "things that matter most in student achievement" concluded that "extra help and time are important if they are designed to help students meet the standards of higher-level academic courses" (p. 8). Schools that improved most required students to get extra help when they performed poorly on tests. The message is clear: some students will require a greater opportunity to learn—they will need more time and support than others—and the most effective schools ensure that they receive it. (See Why Should We Implement Systematic Interventions?, for expert commentary on this issue.)

Some students will require a greater opportunity to learn—they will need more time and support than others—and the most effective schools ensure that they receive it.

Another reason to create a timely, multitiered system of intervention for any student who experiences difficulty is because that is exactly what the Individuals with Disabilities Education Improvement Act of 2004 calls upon schools to do. That law called for an end to the artificial division between special and regular education, an end to the discrepancy model that required students to fail for an extended period of time before becoming eligible for additional support, and an end to a focus on compliance with special education regulations rather than a focus on results. Schools are now asked to implement a systematic response to intervention (RTI)—"to integrate assessment and intervention within a multi-level prevention system to maximize student achievement and reduce behavior problems" (National Center on Response to Intervention, 2008). In short, RTI aligns perfectly with the timely, directive, systematic process to provide students with additional time and support for learning that constitutes such a vital element of a PLC (Buffum, Mattos, & Weber, 2008).

There is nothing that is counterintuitive in what we are proposing regarding systematic intervention. Whenever a school makes time and support for learning constant (that is, fixed), the variable will always be student learning. Some students, probably most students, will learn the intended skill or concept in the given time and with the given support. Some students will not. What happens to them is left to the discretion of the individual teachers to whom they are assigned.

Professional learning communities make a conscious and sustained effort to reverse this equation: they advise students that learning is the constant—"All of you will learn this essential skill"—and then recognize that if they are to keep that commitment, they must create processes to ensure that students who need additional time and support for learning will receive it.

Why Should We Implement Systematic Interventions?

"High-performing schools and school systems set high expectations for what each and every child should achieve, and then monitor performance against the expectations, intervening whenever they are not met. . . . The very best systems intervene at the level of the individual student, developing processes and structures within schools that are able to identify whenever a student is starting to fall behind, and then intervening to improve that child's performance." (Barber & Mourshed, 2007, p. 34)

In order to raise student achievement, schools must use diagnostic assessments to measure students' knowledge and skills at the beginning of each curriculum unit, on-the-spot assessments to check for understanding during instruction, and end-of-unit assessments and interim assessments to see how well students learned. "All of these enable teachers to make mid-course corrections and to get students into intervention earlier" (Odden, 2009, p. 23).

"A criterion for schools that have made great strides in achievement and equity is immediate and decisive intervention. . . . Successful schools do not give a second thought to providing preventive assistance for students in need." (Reeves, 2006, p. 87)

"The most significant factor in providing appropriate interventions for students was the development of layers of support. Systems of support specifically addressed the needs of students who were 'stretching' to take more rigorous coursework." (Dolejs, 2006, p. 3)

"Reforms must move the system toward early identification and swift intervention, using scientifically based instruction and teaching methods." (President's Commission on Excellence in Special Education, 2002, p. 8)

Characteristics of high performing schools include setting high expectations for all students . . . using assessment data to support student success . . . and employing systems for identifying intervention (Council of Chief School Officers, 2002).

"Opportunity to learn" has been recognized as a powerful variable in student achievement for more than thirty years (Lezotte, 2005). In fact, Marzano (2003) concluded that "opportunity to learn has the strongest relationship with student achievement of all school level factors" (p. 22). Research on the topic has typically focused on whether or not the intended curriculum was actually implemented in the classroom; that is, were the essential skills actually taught? We are arguing that opportunity to learn must move beyond the question, "Was it taught?" to the far more important question: "Was it learned?" If the answer is no for some students, then the school must be prepared to provide additional opportunities to learn during the regular school day in ways that students perceive as helpful rather than punitive.

In the previous chapter, we made the case for the use of common, formative, teacher-developed assessments as a powerful tool for school improvement. These assessments help collaborative teams of teachers answer the question, "How do we know if our students are learning?" It is pointless to raise this question, however, if the school is not prepared to intervene when it discovers that some students are not learning. The lack of a systematic response to ensure that students receive additional opportunities for learning reduces the assessment to yet another summative test administered solely to assign a grade. The response that occurs *after* the test has been given will truly determine whether or not it is being used as a formative assessment. If it is used to ensure students who experience difficulty are given additional time and support as well as additional opportunities to demonstrate their learning, it is formative; if additional support is not forthcoming, it is summative.

Many teachers have come to the conclusion that their job is not just difficult—it is *impossible*. If schools continue to operate according to traditional assumptions and practices, we would concur with that conclusion. Individual teachers working in isolation as they attempt to help all of their students achieve at high levels will eventually be overwhelmed by the tension between covering the content and responding to the diverse needs of their students in a fixed amount of time with virtually no external support.

It is disingenuous for any school to claim its purpose is to help all students learn at high levels and then fail to create a system of intervention to give struggling learners additional time and support for learning.

We cannot make this point emphatically enough: it is disingenuous for any school to claim its purpose is to help all students learn at high levels and then fail to create a system of intervention to give struggling learners additional time and support for learning. If time and support remain constant in schools, learning will always be the variable.

Furthermore, we cannot meet the needs of our students unless we assume collective responsibility for their well-being. Seymour Sarason (1996) described schools as a "culture of individuals, not a group . . . [with] each concerned about himself or herself" (p. 367), a place in which "each teacher dealt alone with his or her problems" (p. 321), an environment in which teachers "are only interested in what they do and are confronted within their encapsulated classrooms" (p. 329). The idea so frequently heard in schools— "These are *my* kids, *my* room, and *my* materials"—must give way to a new paradigm of "These are *our* kids, and we cannot help all of them learn what they must learn without a collective effort." As the president of the National Commission on Teaching and America's Future wrote, "The idea that a single teacher, working alone, can know and do everything to meet the diverse learning needs of 30 students every day throughout the school year has rarely worked, and it certainly won't meet the needs of learners in years to come" (Carroll, 2009, p. 13). Jonathan Saphier (2005) was exactly correct when he wrote, "The success of our students is our joint responsibility, and when they succeed, it is to our joint credit and cumulative accomplishment" (p. 28).

Part Four

Assessing Your Place on the PLC Journey

Complete the PLC continuum and Where Do We Go From Here? worksheets as outlined in chapter 2.

The Professional Learning Communities at Work™ Continuum: Learning as Our Fundamental Purpose (Part II)

DIRECTIONS: Individually, silently, and *honestly* assess the current reality of your school's implementation of each indicator listed in the left column. Consider what evidence or anecdotes support your assessment. This form may also be used to assess district or team implementation.

We acknowledge that the fundamental purpose of our school is to help all students achieve high levels of learning, and therefore, we provide students with systematic interventions when they struggle and enrichment when they are proficient.

Indicator	Pre-Initiating	Initiating	Implementing	Developing	Sustaining
We provide a system of interventions that guarantees each student will receive additional time and support for learning if he or she experiences initial difficulty. Students who are proficient have access to enriched and extended learning opportunities.	What happens when a student does not learn will depend almost exclusively on the teacher to whom the student is assigned. There is no coordinated school response to students who experience difficulty. Some teachers allow students to turn in late work; some do not. Some teachers allow students to retake a test; some do not. The tension that occurs at the conclusion of each unit when some students are proficient and ready to move forward and others are failing to demonstrate proficiency is left to each teacher to resolve.	The school has attempted to establish specific policies and procedures regarding homework, grading, parent notification of student progress, and referral of students to child study teams to assess their eligibility for special education services. If the school provides any additional support for students, it is either a "pull-out" program that removes students from new direct instruction or an optional after-school program. Policies are established for identifying students who are eligible for more advanced learning.	The school has taken steps to provide students with additional time and support when they experience difficulty. The staff is grappling with structural issues such as how to provide time for intervention during the school day in ways that do not remove the student from new direct instruction. The school schedule is regarded as a major impediment to intervention and enrichment, and staff members are unwilling to change it. Some are concerned that providing students with additional time and support is not holding them responsible for their own learning.	The school has developed a schoolwide plan to provide students who experience difficulty with additional time and support for learning in a way that is timely, directive, and systematic. It has made structural changes such as modifications in the daily schedule to support this system of interventions. Staff members have been assigned new roles and responsibilities to assist with the interventions. The faculty is looking for ways to make the system of interventions more effective.	The school has a highly coordinated system of intervention and enrichment in place. The system is very proactive. Coordination with sender schools enables the staff to identify students who will benefit from additional time and support for learning even before they arrive at the school. The system is very fluid. Students move into intervention and enrichment easily and remain only as long as they benefit from it. The achievement of each student is monitored on a timely basis. Students who experience difficulty are required, rather than invited, to utilize the system of support. The plan is multilayered. If the current level of time and support is not sufficient to help a student become proficient, he or she is moved to the next level and receives increased time and support. All students are guaranteed access to this system of intervention regardless of the teacher to whom they are assigned. The *school* responds to students and views those who are failing to learn as "undersupported" rather than "at risk."

Where Do We Go From Here? Worksheet

Systematic Intervention

Indicator of a PLC at Work	What steps or activities must be initiated to create this condition in your school?	Who will be responsible for initiating or sustaining these steps or activities?	What is a realistic timeline for each step or phase of the activity?	What will you use to assess the effectiveness of your initiative?
We provide a system of interventions that guarantees each student will receive additional time and support for learning if he or she experiences initial difficulty. Students who are proficient have access to enriched and extended learning opportunities.				

Part Five

Tips for Moving Forward: Creating Systematic Interventions to Ensure Students Receive Additional Time and Support for Learning

Beware of appeals to mindless precedent. Appeals to mindless precedent include the phrases, "But we have always done it this way," "We have never done it that way," and the ever-popular, "The schedule won't let us." These appeals pose a formidable barrier to the creation of a PLC.

We have carefully perused both the Old and New Testaments and can find no evidence that any school schedule was carved into stone tablets and brought down from Mount Sinai. Yet in schools throughout North America, the schedule is regarded an unalterable, sacrosanct part of the school not to be tampered with in any way. The reverence afforded the schedule is puzzling. Mere mortals created it, and educators should regard it as a tool to further priorities rather than as an impediment to change.

One way to address mindless precedent is to invite those who resort to it to reflect upon and articulate the assumptions that led them to their position. In effect, they are invited to bring their perhaps unexamined assumptions to the surface for dialogue. Advocates for change can inquire about and probe those assumptions, articulate their own assumptions, and invite others to inquire about them as well. The likelihood of well-intentioned people learning from one another and arriving at similar conclusions increases when individual thinking is in clear view and accessible for examination and dialogue (Senge et al., 1994).

An advocate for a schedule that provides additional time and support for student learning might present the following argument:

- We contend that our fundamental purpose and most vital priority is to ensure all students learn at high levels.

- Research, as well as our own experience and intuition, make it clear that it is impossible for all students to learn at high levels if some do not receive additional time and support for learning. Even the most ardent advocates of the premise that all students can learn acknowledge that they will not learn at the same rate and with the same support.

- If the only time we offer this service is before or after school, some of our students cannot or will not utilize the services. It will be difficult for us to require those students to do what is necessary to be successful if our only access to them is beyond the school day.

- Therefore, the priority in designing our schedule should be ensuring we have access to students for intervention during the school day in ways that do not deprive them of new direct instruction in their classroom.

- Help me clarify my thinking. Where do you see errors in my logic? What priorities have you identified that are more significant and should take precedence over interventions for students as we build our schedule?

2 **The system of intervention should be fluid.** The system of intervention should not be designed as a permanent support for individual students. When students are experiencing difficulty, they should be directed to the appropriate level of intervention, but only until they have acquired the intended knowledge and skill. Once they have become proficient in the problem area, they should be weaned from the system until they experience difficulty in the future. There should be an easy flow of students into and out of the various levels of the program of support.

3 **Systems of intervention work most effectively when they are supporting teams rather than individual teachers.** We know of a school that convinced the board of education to provide additional funding to create a support system for students during the day. Three certified teachers were hired to provide tutoring throughout the school day, and each created a sign-up sheet that stipulated designated blocks of time they were available to work with students. The sign-up sheets were posted in the faculty workroom, and teachers assigned individual students into a designated block on the schedule to utilize the service. This process often proved problematic because the only time available to tutor a student in reading might occur when the classroom teacher was teaching math. Providing the student with extra time in one area meant a loss of instructional time in another. Furthermore, the teachers had not created common essential learning, pacing guides, or assessments. As a result, tutors were often uncertain regarding the specific skills with which a student required assistance. Therefore, teachers were asked to provide materials when they assigned a student to tutoring to ensure the tutor was focused on the right skills and concepts. As time went on, teachers began to regard the tutoring program as a burden that was creating more work for them rather than a helpful service. At the end of the year, the program was abandoned.

This example stands in stark contrast to one of the schools featured in *Raising the Bar and Closing the Gap* (DuFour et al., 2010). This rural school had access to very limited resources, and there were no additional dollars available for funding an intervention program; however, the staff chose to reallocate discretionary funds in their site-based budget and to shift dollars from their state remediation funds in order to create a system of intervention. Two part-time "floating" tutors were hired to support that system, but neither was a certified teacher.

The teachers in this school were organized into six grade-level teams of four or five members, and each team had clarified the essential learning, adhered to a common pacing guide, and administered common assessments throughout the year. Furthermore, each team had designated a specific thirty-minute block of time during the school day when no new direct instruction would take place so that students could be provided either additional time and support or enrichment, depending upon their demonstrated proficiency.

Following each assessment, the teams identified the students who had been unable to meet the proficiency standard on a particular skill. The tutors would report to the team at the designated period of the day and would typically release the two teachers who had been most effective in teaching that skill to work with struggling students. Thus, the students who experienced the greatest difficulty in mastering a concept were given small-group instruction and individual tutoring by the strongest teachers in that particular concept. During this same thirty-minute tutorial block, the tutors and remaining teachers of the grade level provided a variety of enrichment and extension activities to students who had mastered the skill. Each team created its own activities, such as learning centers, silent sustained reading, teacher read-alouds, junior great books groups, computer-based learning activities, and so on. The one rule observed by each team during this tutorial time was that no new direct instruction would take place.

The floating tutors and teaching teams were assisted by a cadre of volunteers recruited by the school: college students, high school students, employees from area businesses, parents, and grandparents. Volunteers were assigned to a specific grade level during the tutoring period and supported both students in the tutorial program and students in the enrichment activities. Most importantly, the volunteers were assured they would able to work directly with students while they were in the school.

Thus, a school with significantly fewer resources but coordinated collaborative teams was able to be successful in creating a system of intervention for students, while a school with extraordinary resources failed because it could not break free from its traditional structure of twenty-eight classrooms that functioned as twenty-eight independent kingdoms. We have witnessed the same lesson repeated over and over again in our work with schools: schools can dabble in the PLC process or any other school improvement model of their choice, but they will never experience significant gains in student achievement if they value individual teacher autonomy more than helping all students learn.

 An intervention plan should recognize the unique context of the school. Faculties should create their own plans rather than merely adopting the program of another school. In *Raising the Bar and Closing the Gap* (DuFour et al., 2010), we offer specific and detailed explanations and examples of how intervention plans operate in elementary, middle, and high schools. It is important that faculties realize, however, that eventually they are called upon to create their own systems of intervention within the context of their own schools. Once again, engaging staff in the process of exploring and resolving the question, "What will we do when students do not learn in our school?" creates far more ownership in and commitment to the resulting plan than the adoption of someone else's plan.

 More of the same is not effective intervention. Effective intervention will be characterized by differentiation and precision. Intervention will offer a setting and strategies that are different from those that have already proven to be ineffective for the student. A student who failed to grasp a concept that was taught in a large-group setting by a teacher using a particular strategy is not likely to learn the concept if the intervention takes place in another large-group setting and replicates the same instructional strategy. Effective intervention will require diverse formats for delivery and truly differentiated instruction. Furthermore, an intervention system that merely reports a student is failing math will not be as effective as a system that can identify the precise skill or skills that are causing the students difficulty.

 Realize that no support system will compensate for bad teaching. A school characterized by weak and ineffective teaching will not solve its problems by creating a system of timely intervention for students. Eventually, that system will be crushed by the weight of the mass of students it is attempting to support. At the same time the school is creating its system of intervention, it must also take steps to build the capacity of every teacher in the school to become more effective in meeting the needs of students. The battle to help all students learn must be fought on both fronts: support for students and support for the professional staff. To focus on one and exclude the other will never result in victory. Principals and teachers must engage in a process of continuous improvement, constantly examining their practices and expanding their repertoire of skills. But no matter how skillful the professional, at the end of each unit of instruction, it is likely some students will not master the intended learning. At that point the system of intervention comes to the aid of both students and teachers. Schools need both skillful teachers and effective, schoolwide interventions.

Part Six

Questions to Guide the Work of Your Professional Learning Community

To Develop Systematic Interventions That Ensure Students Receive Additional Time and Support for Learning on a Timely and Directive Basis, Ask:

1. How do we respond in our school when students don't learn?

2. How timely is our response? How quickly can we identify a student who is experiencing difficulty?

3. How proactive are we? What steps do we take to identify the students who will need us most before they come to our school?

4. How directive is our response? Do we require students to put in extra time and utilize the extra support, or do we merely encourage them to do so?

5. How systematic is our response? Is there a plan in place that ensures students will receive additional time and support for learning independent of the classroom teacher?

6. Who oversees the system of response? Who makes the determination to move a student from one level of intervention to another?

7. How extensive is our response? How much time do we have each day and each week to support student learning through our interventions? Do we have multiple layers in our intervention plan?

8. How might we adjust our schedule to give us greater access to students who are not successful within the traditional school schedule?

9. How fluid is our response? Can we easily move students in and out of interventions based on their demonstrated proficiency?

Part Seven

Dangerous Detours and Seductive Shortcuts

Beware of pseudo plans of intervention. For example, an after-school tutoring program for students who elect to seek help is not systematic intervention. The students who need help most are typically the least likely to seek it. Furthermore, it is difficult for educators to insist that students remain after school given busing, family requirements, jobs, and so on that make it impossible for some students to remain after school. An intervention plan that is directive will occur during the school day when educators serve in loco parentis.

If the time scheduled for intervention is so infrequent that the school must attempt to support every student who needs assistance during that narrow window of opportunity, the effectiveness of intervention is diminished. A high school of two thousand students that attempts to support all students who are struggling during the same single thirty-minute period will not be as effective as a school that builds time for intervention for small groups of students throughout the entire day.

Finally, beware of attempts to use intervention to further exonerate educators from responsibility for student learning. In the wrong school culture, a system of intervention could be viewed as yet another reason the teacher is not responsible for student learning—"I taught it, they didn't get it, so let the intervention people deal with it." To be effective, it must be just one part of an explicit schoolwide commitment to help all students learn by providing those who struggle with additional time and support at the same time that the school establishes a process to inform and improve the professional practice of every teacher and every team.

An after-school tutoring program for students who elect to seek help is not systematic intervention. The students who need help most are typically the least likely to seek it.

Final Thoughts

A schoolwide system of intervention requires a collaborative culture: a school culture in which staff members work together to provide each student with access to the same essential learning and a culture in which the proficiency of each student is assessed in a way that is timely, authentic, and consistent. In many schools and districts, however, educators squander precious time that has been provided for collaboration on topics that have no impact on student achievement. Chapter 5 delves into this problem and offers strategies for creating high-performing collaborative teams.

Building the Collaborative Culture of a Professional Learning Community

Part One

The Case Study: Are We Engaged in Collaboration or "Coblaboration"?

Principal Joe McDonald was puzzled. He knew that building a collaborative culture was the key to improving student achievement. He could cite any number of research studies to support his position. He had worked tirelessly to promote collaboration and had taken a number of steps to support teachers working together. He organized each grade level in Nemo Middle School (nickname: the Fish) into an interdisciplinary team composed of individual math, science, social studies, and language arts teachers. He created a schedule that gave teams time to meet together each day. He trained staff in collaborative skills, consensus building, and conflict resolution. He emphasized the importance of collaboration at almost every faculty meeting. He felt he had done all the right things, and for three years he had waited patiently to reap the reward of higher levels of student learning. But to his dismay and bewilderment, every academic indicator of student achievement monitored by the school had remained essentially the same.

Principal McDonald decided to survey the faculty to see if he could discover why all the collaboration had yielded no gains in student achievement. The satisfaction survey he developed revealed that, with very few exceptions, teachers felt their collaborative time had strengthened the bond between teachers. Specialist teachers—those in art, music, physical education, technical education, and special education—were less enthusiastic and expressed some resentment about being lumped together in one collaborative team. In general, however, teachers seemed to enjoy working together.

Principal McDonald then decided to make a concerted effort to observe personally the workings of the teams. At the first meeting he attended, a seventh-grade team focused on the behavior of a student who had become increasingly disruptive. The team agreed to schedule a parent conference so they could present their concerns to the parent as a group. An eighth-grade team brainstormed strategies for achieving their team goal of reducing disciplinary referrals for tardiness to class. At a meeting of a second seventh-grade team, he observed a lively debate about whether or not members should accept late work from students, and if so, how many points they should deduct for each day the work was late. The fourth team he observed assigned roles and responsibilities to each member to ensure all the tasks associated with an upcoming field trip were addressed.

By the end of the fourth meeting, Principal McDonald had a revelation: there had been no gains in student achievement because the collaborative teams addressed topics that were only remotely related to student learning! Armed with this insight, he convened a meeting of the faculty and shared his conclusion that teams needed to shift the focus of their dialogues to curriculum, assessment, and instruction.

His proposal met with less than wild enthusiasm. Teachers pointed out that each member of their interdisciplinary teams taught different content. How could a seventh-grade science teacher engage in meaningful work on curriculum, assessment, and instruction with a seventh-grade social studies teacher? The team of specialist teachers was even more emphatic that it was impossible for them to have meaningful conversations on those topics because of the different courses they taught. Teachers argued that since they did not share content with the colleagues on their team, it made sense that they would use their team time to focus on the one thing they did have in common: their students.

Other teachers accused Principal McDonald of abandoning the middle school concept and its commitment to the "whole child." One highly emotional teacher charged Principal McDonald with selling out—of disregarding the emotional well-being of the children in the pursuit of higher test scores.

Principal McDonald was genuinely stunned by the reaction of the staff. He had always believed they enjoyed working together in their teams, and he assumed that merely shifting the focus of their collaboration would be a relatively simple matter. It now appeared, however, that although the staff was happy to collaborate regarding some aspects of the school's program, they were either disinterested or adamantly opposed to addressing others. Dispirited, he retreated to his office to ponder next steps.

Reflection

Why did Principal McDonald's efforts to build a collaborative culture in his school go awry? What steps might he take to improve upon the situation?

Part Two

Here's How

The situation in this school reflects one of the most pervasive problems in building PLCs. Many educators have gradually, sometimes grudgingly, come to acknowledge that collaborating with one's colleagues is preferable to working in isolation. Slowly, structures have been put in place to support collaboration. Staff members are increasingly assigned to teams, given time for collaboration during their contractual day, and provided with training to assist them as they begin the challenge of working together. Administrators and teachers alike take pride that the goal has been accomplished: professionals in the building are collaborating with each other on a regular basis. The anticipated gains in student achievement, however, often fail to materialize.

We cannot stress this next point too emphatically: *the fact that teachers collaborate will do nothing to improve a school.* The pertinent question is not, "Are they collaborating?" but rather, "What are they collaborating about?" Collaboration is not a virtue in itself, and building a collaborative culture is simply a means to an end, not the end itself. The purpose of collaboration—to help more students achieve at higher levels—can only be accomplished if the professionals engaged in collaboration are focused on the right work.

The purpose of collaboration—to help more students achieve at higher levels—can only be accomplished if the professionals engaged in collaboration are focused on the right work.

What is the "right work" that would occupy the collaborative efforts of a team committed to higher levels of learning for all students? Once again, we return to the four questions that drive the work of a PLC:

1. What is it we want our students to learn?

2. How will we know if each student has learned it?

3. How will we respond when some students do not learn it?

4. How can we extend and enrich the learning for students who have demonstrated proficiency?

Principal McDonald must first form an alliance with key members of the staff to help build a deeper understanding of the real purpose of their collaboration and then create supports and parameters to guide staff dialogue to the right topics. He must do more than assign people to teams and hope for the best. If Principal McDonald is to build the capacity of the staff to function as members of high-performing teams, he must demonstrate reciprocal accountability by providing those teams with the focus, support, and resources to be successful.

What Questions

What do you mean by *team* and *collaboration*?

Educators who are asked to work in collaborative teams will continue to struggle unless they come to a shared understanding of these terms. Principal McDonald must clarify that in asking educators to work in teams, he is asking them to work interdependently to achieve a common goal for which members are mutually accountable. Furthermore, since the purpose of the school is to ensure high levels of learning, the goals of the team must be explicitly and directly tied to that purpose. A collection of teachers does not truly become a team until they must rely upon one another to accomplish a goal that none could achieve individually. We will have more to say about the importance of goals in the next chapter.

In asking teachers to collaborate, Principal McDonald is asking them to engage in a *systematic* process in which they work together, interdependently, to analyze and *impact* their professional practice in order to improve individual and collective results. A *systematic process* is a combination of related parts, organized into a whole in a methodical, deliberate, and orderly way, toward a particular aim. It is not intended to be invitational or indiscriminate. Those who develop systematic practices do not hope things happen a certain way; they create specific structures to ensure certain steps are taken.

A deeper understanding of the meaning and purpose of teams and collaboration could help the educators in this school recognize that they have not been focusing on the right work in the right way.

What resources can you provide to assist us?

One of the ways Principal McDonald can support teachers in the effort to create high-performing collaborative teams is to ensure that each member of the staff is assigned to a meaningful team. It is important for principals to recognize that the task of building a collaborative culture requires more than bringing random adults together in the hope they will discover a topic of conversation. *The fundamental question in organizing teams is, "Do the members of this team have a shared responsibility for responding to the four critical questions in ways that enhance the learning of their students?"*

Much work will remain in terms of helping teams develop their capacity to improve student learning, but that outcome is far more difficult to achieve without organizing teams appropriately.

Possible Team Structures

Let's examine some possible team structures that support meaningful collaboration.

Same Course or Grade Level

The best team structure is simple: a team of teachers who teach the same course or grade level. These teachers have a natural common interest in exploring the critical questions of learning. Furthermore, there is considerable research that indicates that this structure is best suited for the ongoing professional learning that leads to improved student achievement (Darling-Hammond, Wei, Andree, Richardson, & Orphanos, 2009; Gallimore et al., 2009; Little, 2006; Saphier et al., 2006; Stigler & Hiebert, 2009). In some instances, however, a single person may be the only teacher of a grade level or content area (such as in very small schools or courses outside of the core curriculum). How does the only first-grade teacher or the only art teacher in a school become a member of a meaningful collaborative team?

The best team structure is simple: a team of teachers who teach the same course or grade level.

Vertical Teams

Vertical teams link teachers with those who teach content above and/or below their students. For example, the sole first-grade teacher could join the kindergarten and second-grade teacher to create school's primary team. The members of that team would work together to:

- Clarify the essential outcomes for students in kindergarten, first grade, and second grade

- Develop assessments for the students in each grade level

- Analyze the results of each assessment

- Offer suggestions for improving results

In this structure, each teacher has the benefit of two "critical friends" who can offer suggestions for improvement as the team examines indicators of student achievement. Furthermore, when teachers examine evidence indicating students are having difficulty in a particular skill in the grade level beyond the one they are teaching, they can make adjustments to their own instruction, pacing, and curriculum to better prepare students for that content.

Vertical teams can also cut across schools. A middle school band director, for example, could join the high school band director to create a vertical team responsible for creating a strong band program. An elementary school art teacher could work with the middle school teacher to clarify the prerequisite skills students should have acquired as they enter the middle school art program. The K–12 vertical team format can be a powerful tool for strengthening the program of an entire district.

Electronic Teams

Proximity is not a prerequisite for an effective collaborative team.

Proximity is not a prerequisite for an effective collaborative team. Teachers can use technology to create powerful partnerships with colleagues across the district, the state, or the world. As Ken Blanchard (2007) concluded in his study of effective organizations, "There is no reason that time and distance should keep people from interacting as a team. With proper management and the help of technology, virtual teams can be every bit as productive and rewarding as face-to-face teams" (p. 173). Any teacher with access to a computer can create an electronic team of colleagues who teach the same course or grade level by using Skype to engage in real-time dialogue with a colleague, Google docs to share files, and Mikogo to see each other's desktops. Using technology, the members of the team can clarify what students should learn, develop common pacing guides, create common assessments, and share information regarding the learning of their students. Principals of schools in the same district can facilitate the process by coordinating with their colleagues to provide a common planning period for singleton teachers in different schools. For example, all of the elementary physical education teachers in the district could become a team to answer the critical questions of learning related to their content area of expertise.

Furthermore, most professional organizations will assist teachers in finding colleagues to form a collaborative team. The College Board has created electronic discussion groups for each area of the AP program along with sample syllabi, course descriptions, free-response questions, and tips for teaching the AP content. A French teacher in Madison, Wisconsin, can no longer complain he has no opportunity to be a member of a collaborative team when he can meet electronically each week with a French teacher in Green Bay. The fact that there is no teammate across the hall does not eliminate the possibility of powerful collaboration, and it is time to quit pretending that it does.

Interdisciplinary Teams

The interdisciplinary team model used in the case-study school can be an effective structure for collaboration, but only if certain steps are taken to change the nature of the conversation. If teachers share no common content or objectives, they will inevitably turn their attention to the one thing they do have in common: their students. A seventh-grade team's discussions regarding Johnny's behavior and Mary's attitude can be appropriate and beneficial, but at some point the team must clarify the knowledge, skills, and dispositions Johnny and Mary are to acquire as a result of their seventh-grade experience.

In an interdisciplinary structure, each team in the school should be asked to create an overarching curricular goal that members will work together interdependently to achieve.

Therefore, in an interdisciplinary structure, each team in the school should be asked to create an overarching curricular goal that members will work together interdependently to achieve. For example, Principal McDonald could make staff aware of the power of nonfiction writing to improve student achievement in mathematics, science, social studies, and reading (Reeves, 2006). He could then ask each grade-level team to develop a goal to increase student achievement by becoming more effective in the instruction of nonfiction writing. The seventh-grade team would confront a series of questions as they worked together to achieve this goal, questions such as:

- How can we integrate nonfiction writing into each of our different subject areas?

- What criteria will we use to assess the quality of student writing?

- How will we know if we are applying the criteria consistently?

- What are the most effective ways to teach nonfiction writing?

- Is there a member of the team with expertise in this area who can help the rest of us become more effective?

- How will we know if our students are becoming better writers?

- How will we know if the focus on writing is impacting achievement in our respective courses?

- What strategies will we put in place for students who struggle with nonfiction writing?

- How can we enrich the learning experience for students who are already capable writers?

- Are there elements of the seventh-grade curriculum we can eliminate or curtail to provide the necessary time for greater emphasis on nonfiction writing?

Principal McDonald could also foster a greater focus on learning if he created a schedule that allowed teachers to meet in content-area teams as well as in grade-level teams. Once again, research has found this structure the most conducive to meaningful dialogue and the continuing professional learning of a team. Middle schools make a mistake when they put all their eggs in the interdisciplinary basket. A seventh-grade math teacher can certainly benefit from conversations with colleagues who teach language arts, social studies, or science, but just as certainly, that math teacher can also benefit from conversations with other math teachers. The best middle schools embrace the Genius of And to utilize both team structures to focus on and improve the academic achievement of their students.

Logical Links

Specialist teachers can become members of grade-level or course-specific teams that are pursuing outcomes linked to their areas of expertise. A physical education teacher can join a sixth-grade team in an effort to help students learn percentages. Each day he or she could help students learn to calculate the percentage of free throws they made in basketball or their batting averages. A music teacher we know joined the fourth-grade team and wrote a musical based on key historical figures students were required to learn that year. A special education teacher joined a biology team because of the difficulties her students were experiencing in that course. She disaggregated the scores of special education students on each test and became a consultant to the team on supplementary materials, instructional strategies, and alternative assessments to help special education students achieve the intended outcomes of the course. She then worked as a member of the special education team to help her colleagues recognize the specific biology skills and concepts that were causing difficulty for students in special education and to provide them with resources and ideas for supporting students in those areas during their resource period with their special education teacher.

Team Structures

- **Same course or grade-level teams** are those in which, for example, all the geometry teachers or all the second-grade teachers in a school form a collaborative team.

- **Vertical teams** link teachers with those who teach content above or below their students.

- **Electronic teams** use technology to create powerful partnerships with colleagues across the district, the state, or the world.

- **Interdisciplinary teams** found in middle schools and small high schools can be an effective structure if members work interdependently to achieve an overarching curricular goal that will result in higher levels of student learning.

- **Logical links** put teachers together in teams that are pursuing outcomes linked to their areas of expertise.

Teachers should be organized into structures that allow them to engage in meaningful collaboration that is beneficial to them and their students.

In short, teachers should be organized into structures that allow them to engage in meaningful collaboration that is beneficial to them and their students. Once again, the fundamental question in organizing teams is this: "Do the people on this team have a shared responsibility for responding to the critical questions in ways that enhance the learning of their students?" The effectiveness of any particular team structure will depend on the extent to which it supports teacher dialogue and action aligned with those questions.

Making Time for Collaboration

Reciprocal accountability demands that leaders who ask educators to work in collaborative teams provide those educators with time to meet during their contractual day. We believe it is insincere for any district or school leader to stress the importance of collaboration and then fail to provide time for it. One of the ways in which organizations demonstrate their priorities is allocation of resources, and in schools, one of the most precious resources is time. Thus, school and district leaders must provide teachers with time to do the things they are being asked to do.

School and district leaders must provide teachers with time to do the things they are being asked to do.

We also recognize that many districts face real-world constraints in providing time for collaboration. Releasing students from school so that teachers can collaborate may create childcare hardships for some families. In fact, we have seen several instances where community pressure has put an end to collaborative time for teachers. In almost every instance, it was not the fact that teachers were collaborating that sparked the opposition, but that the strategy for providing time for collaboration created problems for families. Other districts have paid teachers to extend their school day to provide time for collaboration, but often that time is axed when money gets tight. Furthermore, this strategy conveys the message that collaboration is an "add-on" to the teacher workday rather than an integral part of teaching. Hiring substitute teachers to give teams of teachers time to work together is a possible strategy but may be cost prohibitive in some districts—and gives teachers the added burden of creating plans for the substitute. Furthermore, teachers and administrators alike are often reluctant to lose precious instructional time so that teachers can meet in teams. Nonetheless, we have worked with school districts throughout North America that have been able to create regularly scheduled weekly time for collaboration within real-world parameters: they bring teachers together during their contractual day while students are on campus, in ways that do not cost money and that result in little or no loss of instructional time.

The issue of finding time for collaboration has been addressed effectively—and often—in the professional literature and is readily available for those who are sincerely interested in exploring alternatives. The National Staff Development Council alone has addressed the issue hundreds of times in its publications, and the www.allthingsplc.info website lists over 150 schools that have created time for teachers to collaborate in ways that don't require the school to be shut down, don't cost money, and don't result in significant loss of instructional time. The following strategies do not form a comprehensive list; rather, they illustrate some of the steps schools and districts have taken to create the prerequisite time for collaboration.

Common Preparation

Build the master schedule to provide daily common preparation periods for teachers of the same course or department. Each team should then designate one day each week to engage in collaborative, rather than individual, planning.

Parallel Scheduling

Schedule common preparation time by assigning the specialists (physical education teachers, librarians, music teachers, art teachers, instructional technologists, guidance counselors, foreign language teachers, and so on) to provide lessons to students across an entire grade level at the same time each day. The team should designate one day each week for collaborative planning. Some schools build back-to-back specials classes into the master schedule on each team's designated collaborative day, thus creating an extended block of time for the team to meet. Specials teachers must also be given time to collaborate.

Adjusted Start and End Time

Gain collaborative time by starting the workday early or extending the workday one day each week. In exchange for adding time to one end of the workday, teachers get the time back on the other end of that day. For example, on Tuesdays, the entire staff of Adlai Stevenson High School in Lincolnshire, Illinois, begins their workday at 7:30 am rather than the normal 7:45 a.m. start time. From 7:30 to 8:30 a.m., the entire faculty engages in collaborative team meetings. Classes, which usually begin at 8:05 a.m., are delayed until 8:30 a.m. Students who can arrange for their own transportation arrive to school then. Buses run their regular routes so that no parent is inconvenienced and deliver students to the school at 7:40 a.m. Upon their arrival they are supervised by administrative and noninstructional staff in a variety of optional activities (such as breakfast, library and computer research, open gym, study halls, and tutorials) until classes begin. To make up for the twenty-five minutes of lost instructional time, five minutes is trimmed from five of the eight fifty-minute class periods. The school day ends at the usual time (3:25 in the afternoon), and again buses run on their regular schedules. Because they began work fifteen minutes early (7:30 rather than 7:45), Stevenson teachers are free to leave fifteen minutes earlier than the normal conclusion of their workday (3:30 rather than 3:45). By making these minor adjustments to the schedule one day each week, the entire faculty is guaranteed an hour of collaborative planning without extending their workday or workweek by a single minute.

Shared Classes

Combine students across two different grade levels or courses into one class for instruction. While one teacher or team instructs the students, the other team engages in collaborative work. The teams alternate instructing and collaborating to provide equity in learning time for students and teams. Some schools coordinate shared classes so older students adopt younger students and serve as literacy buddies, tutors, and mentors during shared classes.

Group Activities, Events, and Testing

Teams of teachers coordinate activities that require supervision of students rather than instructional expertise, such as watching an instructional DVD or video, conducting resource lessons, reading aloud, attending assemblies, or testing. Nonteaching staff members supervise students while teachers engage in team collaboration.

Banked Time

Over a designated period of days, extend the instructional minutes beyond the required school day. After you have banked the desired number of minutes, end the instructional day early to allow for faculty collaboration and student enrichment. For example, in a middle school, the traditional instructional day ends at 3:00 p.m., students board buses at 3:20, and the teachers' contractual day ends at 3:30. The faculty may decide to extend the instructional day until 3:10. By teaching an extra ten minutes for nine days in a row, they "bank" ninety minutes. On the tenth day, instruction stops at 1:30, and the entire faculty has collaborative team time for two hours. The students remain on campus and are engaged in clubs, enrichment activities, assemblies, and so on, sponsored by a variety of parent and community partners and cosupervised by the school's nonteaching staff.

In-Service and Faculty Meeting Time

Schedule extended time for teams to work together on staff development days and during faculty meeting time. Rather than requiring staff to attend a traditional whole-staff in-service session or sit in a faculty meeting while directives and calendar items are read aloud, shift the focus and use of these days and meetings so members of teams have extended time to learn with and from each other.

> ## Making Time for Collaboration
>
> - Provide common preparation time.
> - Use parallel scheduling.
> - Adjust start and end times.
> - Share classes.
> - Schedule group activities, events, and testing.
> - Bank time.
> - Use in-service and faculty meeting time wisely.

Clarifying the Right Work

Another way in which Principal McDonald could support his teams and increase the likelihood of their success is to ensure they are clear on the nature of the work to be done. Once again, merely assigning teachers to groups will not improve a school, and much of what passes for collaboration among educators is more aptly described as *coblaboration*, a term coined by David Perkins (2003). Ineffective or unproductive team meetings create cynicism and only serve to sour teachers' attitudes towards teaming while simultaneously reinforcing the norms of isolation so prevalent in our schools. Those who hope to improve student achievement by developing the capacity of staff to function as a professional learning community must create and foster the conditions that move educators from mere work groups to high-performing collaborative teams.

In a PLC, the process of collaboration is specifically designed to *impact* educator practice in ways that lead to better results. Over and over again, we have seen schools in which staff members are willing to collaborate about any number of things—dress codes, tardy policies, the appropriateness of Halloween parties—provided they can return to their classrooms and continue to do what they have always done. Yet in a PLC, the reason teachers are organized into teams, the reason they are provided with time to work together, the reason they are asked to focus on certain topics and complete specific tasks, is so that when they return to their classrooms they will possess and *utilize* an expanded repertoire of skills, strategies, materials, assessments, and ideas in order to impact student achievement in a positive way.

One of the most important elements of reciprocal accountability that district and school leaders must address is establishing clear parameters and priorities that guide the work of the teams toward the goal of improved student learning.

Therefore, *one of the most important elements of reciprocal accountability that district and school leaders must address is establishing clear parameters and priorities that guide the work of the teams toward the goal of improved student learning.* The Critical Issues for Team Consideration worksheet (pages 130–131) is a useful tool toward that end. First, it directs the team's attention to issues that impact practice and, thus, student achievement. Second, it calls upon the team to generate products that flow directly from the dialogue and decisions regarding those issues. One of the most effective ways to enhance and monitor the productivity of a team is to insist that it *produce*. In this case, it must produce artifacts related to the team's collective inquiry into the critical questions that reflect the right work.

Principal McDonald might have avoided some of the initial confusion regarding how teams were expected to use their time had he presented them with the Critical Issues for Team Consideration worksheet and then worked with the team leaders to help them establish a timeline for the completion of team products. Imagine if the principal and staff had created the following timeline to guide the dialogue of teams:

By the end of . . .

- *The second week of school we will present our team norms.*

- *The fourth week of school we will present our team SMART goal.*

- *The sixth week of school we will present our list of the essential knowledge, skills, and dispositions our students will acquire during this semester.*

- *The eighth week of school we will present our first common assessment.*

- *The tenth week of school we will present our analysis of the results from the common assessments, including areas of strength and strategies for addressing areas of concern.*

Clearly established expectations and timelines are a tremendous benefit to teams. Members lose no time debating "Why are we here?" or focusing on the trivial because they have been guided toward conversations specific to teaching and learning. Furthermore, this process of gathering and reviewing team products on a regular basis is one of the most effective strategies for monitoring the progress of teams. A principal who creates a process to review the products on an ongoing basis and who meets with teams each quarter to discuss their products will know when a team is struggling and can provide support on a timely basis. We highly recommend that school leadership teams use the Critical Issues for Team Consideration or a similar tool to help clarify exactly what collaborative teams are expected to do and to monitor the progress they are making.

Critical Issues for Team Consideration

Team Name:

Team Members:

Use the following rating scale to indicate the extent to which each statement is true of your team.

1	2	3	4	5	6	7	8	9	10

Not True of Our Team   **Our Team Is Addressing This**   **True of Our Team**

1. _____ We have identified team norms and protocols to guide us in working together.

2. _____ We have analyzed student achievement data and established SMART goals to improve upon this level of achievement we are working interdependently to attain. (SMART Goals are Strategic, Measurable, Attainable, Results oriented, and Time bound. SMART Goals are discussed at length in chapter 6.)

3. _____ Each member of our team is clear on the knowledge, skills, and dispositions (that is, the essential learning) that students will acquire as a result of (1) our course or grade level and (2) each unit within the course or grade level.

4. _____ We have aligned the essential learning with state and district standards and the high-stakes assessments required of our students.

5. _____ We have identified course content and topics we can eliminate to devote more time to the essential curriculum.

6. _____ We have agreed on how to best sequence the content of the course and have established pacing guides to help students achieve the intended essential learning.

7. _____ We have identified the prerequisite knowledge and skills students need in order to master the essential learning of each unit of instruction.

8. _____ We have identified strategies and created instruments to assess whether students have the prerequisite knowledge and skills.

9. _____ We have developed strategies and systems to assist students in acquiring prerequisite knowledge and skills when they are lacking in those areas.

10. _____ We have developed frequent common formative assessments that help us determine each student's mastery of essential learning.

11. _____ We have established the proficiency standard we want each student to achieve on each skill and concept examined with our common assessments.

12. _____ We use the results of our common assessments to assist each other in building on strengths and addressing weaknesses as part of an ongoing process of continuous improvement designed to help students achieve at higher levels.

13. _____ We use the results of our common assessments to identify students who need additional time and support to master essential learning, and we work within the systems and processes of the school to ensure they receive that support.

14. _____ We have agreed on the criteria we will use in judging the quality of student work related to the essential learning of our course, and we continually practice applying those criteria to ensure we are consistent.

15. _____ We have taught students the criteria we will use in judging the quality of their work and provided them with examples.

16. _____ We have developed or utilized common summative assessments that help us assess the strengths and weaknesses of our program.

17. _____ We have established the proficiency standard we want each student to achieve on each skill and concept examined with our summative assessments.

18. _____ We formally evaluate our adherence to team norms and the effectiveness of our team at least twice each year.

Establishing Collective Commitments to Enhance the Effectiveness of Teams

A reluctance to change their traditional classroom practices is not the only reason educators tend to drift away from substantive conversations about teaching and learning if parameters are not in place to guide their work. Conversations about the trivial are safer. If teachers are to work collaboratively to clarify the essential learning for their courses and grade levels, write common assessments, and jointly analyze the results, they must overcome the fear that they may be exposed to their colleagues and principals as ineffective. After all, you were hired for your professional expertise, but what if the results from a common assessment demonstrate that while students taught by your colleagues are successful, your students are not? We have seen evidence that some teachers would prefer not to know their strengths and weaknesses in relation to their colleagues' because it is not worth the risk of being exposed and vulnerable.

In his review of the dysfunctions of a team, Patrick Lencioni (2003) contends that the first and most important step in building a cohesive and high-performing team is the establishment of vulnerability-based trust. Individuals on effective teams learn to acknowledge mistakes, weaknesses, failures, and the need for help. They also learn to recognize and value the strengths of other members of the team and are willing to learn from one another.

The fear of vulnerability leads to the second dysfunction of a team: avoidance of productive conflict. Dysfunctional teams prefer artificial harmony to insightful inquiry and advocacy. As a result, they avoid topics that require them to work interdependently. Even decisions that would appear to require joint effort fail to generate genuine commitment from individuals on the team. Members settle for the appearance of agreement rather than pushing each other to pledge to honor the agreement through their actions. The avoidance of conflict and lack of commitment lead to yet another dysfunction of a team: avoidance of accountability. Team members are unwilling to confront peers who fail to work toward team goals or to honor team decisions. Finally, since members are unwilling to commit to purpose, priorities, and decisions, and are unwilling to hold each other accountable, they inevitably are inattentive to results. When groups demonstrate the five dysfunctions of a team—the inability to (1) establish trust, (2) engage in honest dialogue regarding disagreements, (3) make commitments to one another, (4) hold each other accountable, and (5) focus on results—the team process begins to unravel (Lencioni, 2003).

Leaders can help teams avoid these dysfunctions in several ways. First, and very importantly, they can model vulnerability, enthusiasm for meaningful exploration of disagreements, articulation of public commitments, willingness to confront those who fail to honor decisions, and an unrelenting focus on and accountability for results. For example, Principal

McDonald could acknowledge that he made a mistake in his initial approach to creating high-performing teams and admit that he needs the help of the faculty in altering the team process so that it benefits students. He could invite open dialogue about specific proposals to refocus teams on matters impacting learning and help build shared knowledge regarding the advantages and disadvantages of each proposal. He could make commitments to the staff regarding what he is prepared to do to support their efforts and address their concerns. He could demonstrate his commitment to the decisions they reach by confronting those who violate them. Finally, he could clarify the indicators they would monitor as a school to maintain their focus on results.

Furthermore, Principal McDonald could help staff members engage in professional dialogue designed to address the dangers of a dysfunctional team. Teams benefit not only from clarity regarding the purpose of their collaboration, but also from clarity regarding how they will work together and what is expected of each member. Once again, simply putting people in groups does not ensure a productive, positive experience for participants. Most educators can remember a time when they worked in a group that was painfully inefficient and excruciatingly ineffective. But teams increase their likelihood of performing at high levels when they clarify their expectations of one another regarding procedures, responsibilities, and relationships.

Teams increase their likelihood of performing at high levels when they clarify their expectations of one another regarding procedures, responsibilities, and relationships.

All groups establish norms—"ground rules or habits that govern the group" (Goleman et al., 2002, p. 173)—regardless of whether or not they take the time to reflect upon and articulate the norms they prefer for their team. But when individuals work through a process to create explicitly stated norms, and then commit to honor those norms, they increase the likelihood they will begin to function as a collaborative team rather than as a loose collection of people working together.

Team norms are not intended to serve as rules, but rather as collective commitments: public agreements shared among the members (Kegan & Lahey, 2001). Effective teams do not settle for "sorta" agreements; they identify the very specific commitments members have made to each other.

Here again, members of a learning community will begin the challenging task of articulating collective commitments for each team by *building shared knowledge* regarding best practices and strategies for implementing those practices. For example, one study of high-performing teams (Druskat & Wolf, 2001) found that members consistently demonstrated high emotional intelligence as evidenced by the following characteristics:

- **Perspective taking.** Members are willing to consider matters from the other person's point of view.

- **Interpersonal understanding.** Members demonstrate accurate understanding of the spoken and unspoken feelings, interests, and concerns of other group members.

- **Willingness to confront.** Members speak up when an individual violates commitments, but they confront in a caring way aimed at building consensus and shared interpretations of commitments.

- **Caring orientation.** Members communicate positive regard, appreciation, and respect. A close personal relationship is not a prerequisite of an effective team, but mutual respect and validation are critical.

- **Team self-evaluation.** The team is willing and able to evaluate its effectiveness.

- **Feedback solicitation.** The team solicits feedback and searches for evidence of its effectiveness from external sources as part of a process of continuous improvement.

- **Positive environment.** The team focuses on staying positive: positive affect, positive behavior, and the pursuit of positive outcomes. Members cultivate positive images of the group's past, present, and future.

- **Proactive problem solving.** Members actively take the initiative to resolve issues that stand in the way of accomplishing team goals.

- **Organizational awareness.** Members understand their connection to and contribution to the larger organization.

- **Building external relationships.** The team establishes relationships with others who can support their efforts to achieve their goals.

Garmston and Wellman (1999, p. 37) identified seven norms of collaboration for teams. They contend that when team members practice the following norms, they promote the productive dialogue essential to effective teams:

1. Pausing

2. Paraphrasing

3. Probing for specificity

4. Putting ideas on the table

5. Paying attention to self and others

6. Presuming positive intentions

7. Pursuing a balance between advocacy and inquiry

In their Protocols for Effective Advocacy and Protocols for Effective Inquiry, Senge and his colleagues (1994) offer detailed suggestions to assist teams in moving from polite acquiescence to meaningful dialogue that helps clarify the thinking of each member of the group. The National Staff Development Council (1999) devoted an entire issue of their publication *Tools for Schools* to the topic of team norms. The issue includes a rationale for norms, a format for creating norms, sample team norms, and sources for exploring the topic more fully. All of this information should be made available to teams who are called upon to articulate collective commitments (see pages 137–138).

Protocols for Effective Advocacy

1.	State your assumptions.	*Here is what I think.*
2.	Describe your reasoning.	*Here are some reasons why I arrived at this conclusion.*
3.	Give concrete examples.	*Let me explain how I saw this work in another school.*
4.	Reveal your perspective	*I acknowledge that I am looking at this from the perspective of a veteran teacher.*
5.	Anticipate other perspectives.	*Some teachers are likely to question . . .*
6.	Acknowledge areas of uncertainty.	*Here is one issue you could help me think through.*
7.	Invite others to question your assumptions and conclusions.	*What is your reaction to what I said? In what ways do you see things differently?*

Protocols for Effective Inquiry

1.	Gently probe underlying logic.	*What led you to that conclusion?*
2.	Use nonaggressive language.	*Can you help me understand your thinking here?*
3.	Draw out their thinking.	*Which aspects of what you have proposed do you feel are most significant or essential?*
4.	Check for understanding.	*I'm hearing that your primary goal is . . .*
5.	Explain your reason for inquiring.	*I'm asking about your assumption because I feel . . .*

We also recommend that members of a team have an honest and open dialogue about the expectations they bring to the process by asking each member to reflect upon and discuss his or her past experience with groups.

Ask each participant to describe a time when he or she was a member of a group, committee, task force, or so on that proved to be a negative experience. Then ask each participant to explain the specific behaviors or conditions that made it so negative. Next, invite each participant to describe a personal experience in which he or she felt the power and synergy of an effective team. Record the answers and turn the group's attention to identifying commitments that would avoid the negative and promote the positive aspects of membership on a team if all participants pledged to honor those norms.

We offer the following additional tips for creating norms.

1. **Each team should create its own norms.** Asking a committee to create norms all teams will honor is ineffective. Norms are collective commitments that members make to each other, and committees cannot make commitments for us. Furthermore, norms should reflect the experiences, hopes, and expectations of the members of a specific team.

2. **Norms should be stated as commitments to act or behave in certain ways rather than as beliefs.** The statement, "We will arrive to meetings on time and stay fully engaged throughout the meeting," is more powerful than, "We believe in punctuality."

3. **Norms should be reviewed at the beginning and end of each meeting for at least six months.** Norms only impact the work of a team if they are put into practice over and over again until they become internalized. Teams should not confuse writing norms with living norms.

4. **Teams should formally evaluate their effectiveness at least twice a year.** This assessment should include exploration of the questions:

    ■ Are we adhering to our norms?

    ■ Do we need to establish a new norm to address a problem occurring on our team?

    ■ Are all members of the team contributing to its work?

    ■ Are we working interdependently to achieve our team goal?

5. **Teams should focus on a few essential norms rather than creating an extensive laundry list.** Less is more when it comes to norms. People do not need a lot of rules to remember, just a few commitments to honor.

6. **Violations of team norms must be addressed.** Failure to confront clear violations of the commitments members have made to each other will undermine the entire team process. We will address the issue of how to confront violations in chapter eight.

Developing Norms

Comments to the Facilitator: This activity will enable a group to develop a set of operating norms or ground rules. In existing groups, anonymity will help ensure that everyone is able to express their ideas freely. For this reason, it is essential to provide pens or pencils or to ask that everyone use the same type of writing implement.

Supplies: Index cards, pens or pencils, poster paper, display board, tape, tacks

Time: Two hours

Directions

1. Explain to the group that effective groups generally have a set of norms that govern individual behavior, facilitate the work of the group, and enable the group to accomplish its task.

2. Provide examples of norms.

3. Recommend to the group that it establish a set of norms:

   - To ensure that all individuals have the opportunity to contribute in the meeting;

   - To increase productivity and effectiveness; and

   - To facilitate the achievement of its goals.

4. Give five index cards and the same kind of writing tool to each person in the group.

5. Ask each person to reflect on and record behaviors they consider ideal behaviors for a group. Ask them to write one idea on each of their cards. Time: 10 minutes.

6. Shuffle all the cards together. Every effort should be made to provide anonymity for individuals, especially if the group has worked together before.

7. Turn cards face up and read each card aloud. Allow time for the group members to discuss each idea. Tape or tack each card to a display board so that all group members can see it. As each card is read aloud, ask the group to determine if it is similar to another idea that already has been expressed. Cards with similar ideas should be grouped together.

8. When all of the cards have been sorted, ask the group to write the norm suggested by each group of cards. Have one group member record these new norms on a large sheet of paper.

9. Review the proposed norms with the group. Determine whether the group can support the norms before the group adopts them.

Used with permission of the National Staff Development Council, www.nsdc.org, 2006. All rights reserved. Adapted from *Tools for Change Workshops* by Robby Champion. Oxford, OH: National Staff Development Council, 1993.

When Establishing Norms, Consider:	Proposed Norm
Time ■ When do we meet? ■ Will we set a beginning and ending time? ■ Will we start and end on time?	
Listening ■ How will we encourage listening? ■ How will we discourage interrupting?	
Confidentiality ■ Will the meetings be open? ■ Will what we say in the meeting be held in confidence? ■ What can be said after the meeting?	
Decision Making ■ How will we make decisions? ■ Are we an advisory or a decision-making body? ■ Will we reach decisions by consensus? ■ How will we deal with conflicts?	
Participation ■ How will we encourage everyone's participation? ■ Will we have an attendance policy?	
Expectations ■ What do we expect from members? ■ Are there requirements for participation?	

Used with permission of the National Staff Development Council, www.nsdc.org, 2006. All rights reserved. From *Keys to Successful Meetings* by Stephanie Hirsh, Ann Delehant, and Sherry Sparks. Oxford, OH: National Staff Development Council, 1994.

When done well, norms can help establish the trust, openness, commitment, and accountability that move teams from the trivial to the substantive. No team should work without the benefit of these clearly defined collective commitments.

Leaders can and should take each of the purposeful steps presented in this chapter: creating teams on the basis of a common responsibility for pursuing the critical questions of learning, providing them with time to collaborate, guiding them to the most powerful questions that impact learning, asking teams to create specific products that should flow naturally from the dialogue of a team focused on the right work, and helping them create collective commitments that facilitate the trust, openness, and clarity of expectations essential to effective teams. Those steps can help create the structure for meaningful team dialogue; however, two more critical steps must be taken to help turn the focus of the team to improved student learning:

1. Collaborative teams must develop and pursue SMART goals.

2. Individual teachers and teams must have access to relevant and timely information.

These steps will be considered in the following chapters.

Part Three

Here's Why

Why is it so important to organize a staff into collaborative teams in which people work together interdependently to achieve common goals rather than continuing the longstanding tradition of teacher isolation? The very reason any organization is established is to bring people together in an organized way to achieve a collective purpose that cannot be accomplished by working alone. As Jeffrey Pfeffer and Robert Sutton (2000) wrote, "Interdependence is what organizations are all about. Productivity, performance, and innovation result from *joint* action, not just individual efforts and behavior" (p. 197). The degree to which people are working together in a coordinated, focused effort is a major determinant of the effectiveness of any organization, and the inability to work interdependently has been described as the "biggest opponent" and the "mortal enemy" of those who confront complex tasks in their daily work (Patterson et al., 2008, p. 192). Certainly there are few tasks more complex than accomplishing something that has never been done—helping all students learn at high levels.

The very reason any organization is established is to bring people together in an organized way to achieve a collective purpose that cannot be accomplished by working alone.

Furthermore, the collaborative team has been cited repeatedly in organizational literature as the most powerful structure for promoting the essential interdependence of an effective enterprise. Experts on effective teams offer very consistent advice regarding the benefits of teams (see Why Should We Use Teams as Our Basic Structure?).

As we mentioned earlier in the chapter, simply organizing people into teams does not improve a school. Steps must be taken to ensure that those team members engage in *collaboration* on the issues that most impact student learning. Educational research has repeatedly linked collaborative cultures with school improvement. In fact, the case for teachers working together collaboratively is so compelling that we are not aware of any credible research explicitly opposed to the concept (see pages 142–143, Why Should We Collaborate?).

We have, however, heard individuals oppose providing educators with time to collaborate. They typically frame their objection by arguing the time a teacher spends collaborating with colleagues is time that could have been spent teaching students, and thus represents unproductive time. Once again, research from both organizational development and education refute that position. Effective organizations and effective schools build time for reflection and dialogue into every process. The goal is not merely to do more of what we have always done (regardless of its effectiveness), but to create a culture of continuous improvement, to discover ways to become better at achieving our purpose, forever (Black, Harrison, Lee, Marsh, & William, 2004; Champy, 1995; Collins & Porras, 1997; Darling-Hammond, 1996; Dolan, 1994; Goldsmith, 1996; Kouzes & Posner, 1987; Schein, 1996).

Common sense advises, however, that collaborative time can be squandered if educators do not use that time to focus on issues most directly related to teaching and learning. Michael Fullan's (2001) caution should be self-evident: "Collaborative cultures, which by definition have close relationships, are indeed powerful, but unless they are focusing on the right things they may end up being powerfully wrong" (p. 67).

Effective leaders will direct the work of teams to the critical questions, because those are the conversations that have the biggest impact on student achievement. Clarifying what students must learn, monitoring the learning of each student, responding to students who need additional time and support for learning, and challenging students who have already mastered the intended outcomes are the most critical tasks in a school. It is imperative, therefore, that educators work together interdependently to become more skillful in these critical areas, and that these questions become the priority within and among collaborative teams. The extensive research base to support the focus on these questions was presented in chapter 3.

School and district leaders should also be prepared to provide the research rationale regarding why collaborative teams should establish the norms or collective commitments to clarify their expectations of one another and guide their collective efforts (see page 144, Why Should We Create Norms?).

Why Should We Use Teams as Our Basic Structure?

"Empowered teams are such a powerful force of integration and productivity that they form the basic building block of any intelligent organization." (Pinchot & Pinchot, 1993, p. 66)

"We are at a point in time where teams are recognized as a critical component of every enterprise—the predominant unit for decision making and getting things done. . . . Working in teams is the norm in a learning organization." (Senge et al. 1994, pp. 354–355)

"Leaders of the future will have to master the art of forming teams. . . . Future leaders will have to master teamwork . . . and work with and through others because no one person can possibly master all the divergent sources of information necessary to make good decisions." (Ulrich, 1996, p. 213)

Teams *"bring together complementary skills and experience that . . . exceed those of any individual on the team."* Teams are more effective in problem solving, *"provide a unique social dimension that enhances . . . work,"* motivate, and foster peer pressure and internal accountability (Katzenbach & Smith, 1993, p. 18).

The best way to achieve challenging goals is through teamwork: *"Teams nurture, support and inspire each other"* (Tichy, 1997, p. 180).

"We have known for nearly a quarter of a century that self-managed teams are far more productive than any other form of organizing. . . . by joining with others we can accomplish something important that we could not accomplish alone." (Wheatley, 1999, pp. 152–153)

"A team can make better decisions, solve more complex problems, and do more to enhance creativity and build skills than individuals working alone . . . They have become the vehicle for moving organizations into the future. . . . Teams are not just nice to have. They are hard-core units of the production." (Blanchard, 2007, p. 17)

"Influencers increase the capacity of others by asking them to work in teams with interdependent relationships. . . . We increase capacity when we work together rather than in isolation." (Patterson et al., 2008, p. 183)

Why Should We Collaborate?

When teachers work in collaborative teams schools are more likely to see gains in student achievement, find higher quality solutions to problems, promote increased confidence among staff, create an environment in which teachers support one another's strengths and accommodate weaknesses, provide support for new teachers, and provide all staff with access to an expanded pool of ideas, materials, and methods (Little, 1990).

"The single most important factor for successful school restructuring and the first order of business for those interested in increasing the capacity of their schools is building a collaborative internal environment." (Eastwood & Seashore Louis, 1992, p. 215)

Improving schools requires a collaborative culture: "without collaborative skills and relationships it is not possible to learn and to continue to learn" (Fullan, 1993, p. 18).

When groups, rather than individuals, are seen as the main units for implementing curriculum, instruction, and assessment, they facilitate development of shared purpose for student learning and collective responsibility to achieve it (Newmann & Wehlage, 1995).

High-performing schools promote collaborative problem solving and support professional communities and exchanges among all staff. Teachers and staff collaborate to remove barriers to student learning and communicate regularly with each other about effective teaching and learning strategies. They have regularly scheduled time to learn from one another (National Education Association, 2003).

"[High-achieving schools] build a highly collaborative school environment where working together to solve problems and to learn from each other become cultural norms." (WestEd, 2000, p. 12)

"It is imperative that professional learning be directed at improving the quality of collaborative work." (National Staff Development Council, 2006)

"The key to ensuring that every child has a quality teacher is finding a way for school systems to organize the work of qualified teachers so they can collaborate with their colleagues in developing strong learning communities that will sustain them as they become more accomplished teachers." (National Commission on Teaching and America's Future, 2003, p. 7)

"Collaboration and the ability to engage in collaborative action are becoming increasingly important to the survival of the public schools. Indeed, without the ability to collaborate with others, the prospect of truly improving schools is not likely." (Schlechty, 2005, p. 22)

"It is time to end the practice of solo teaching in isolated classrooms." (Fulton, Yoon, & Lee, 2005)

"[Today's teachers must] transform their personal knowledge into a collectively built, widely shared and cohesive professional knowledge base." (Chokshi & Fernandez, 2004, cited in Fulton, Yoon, & Lee, 2005)

Teacher collaboration in strong professional learning communities improves the quality and equity of student learning, promotes discussions that are grounded in evidence and analysis rather than opinion, and fosters collective responsibility for student success (McLaughlin & Talbert, 2006).

"Quality teaching is not an individual accomplishment, it is the result of a collaborative culture that empowers teachers to team up to improve student learning beyond what any one of them can achieve alone." (Carroll, 2009, p. 13)

High-performing, high-poverty schools build deep teacher collaboration that focuses on student learning into the culture of the school. Structures and systems are set up to ensure teachers work together rather than in isolation, and "the point of their collaboration is to improve instruction and ensure all students learn" (Chenoweth, 2009, p. 17).

Why Should We Create Norms?

Teams improve their ability to grapple with the critical questions when they clarify the norms that will guide their work. These collective commitments represent the "promises we make to ourselves and others, promises that underpin two critical aspects of teams—commitment and trust" (Katzenbach & Smith, 1993, p. 60).

Norms can help clarify expectations, promote open dialogue, and serve as a powerful tool for holding members accountable (Lencioni, 2005).

"When self-management norms are explicit and practiced over time, team effectiveness improves dramatically, as does the experience of team members themselves. Being on the team becomes rewarding in itself—and those positive emotions provide energy and motivation for accomplishing the team's goals." (Goleman et al., p. 182)

Explicit team norms help to increase the emotional intelligence of the group by cultivating trust, a sense of group identity, and belief in group efficacy (Druskat & Wolf, 2001).

Referring back to the norms can help "the members of a group to 're-member,' to once again take out membership in what the group values and stands for; to 'remember,' to bring the group back into one cooperating whole" (Kegan & Lahey, 2001, p. 194).

Inattention to establishing specific team norms is one of the major reasons teams fail (Blanchard, 2007).

Part Four

Assessing Your Place on the PLC Journey

Complete the PLC continuum and Where Do We Go From Here? worksheets as outlined in chapter 2.

The Professional Learning Communities at Work™ Continuum: Building a Collaborative Culture Through High-Performing Teams

DIRECTIONS: Individually, silently, and *honestly* assess the current reality of your school's implementation of each indicator listed in the left column. Consider what evidence or anecdotes support your assessment. This form may also be used to assess district or team implementation.

We are committed to working together to achieve our collective purpose of learning for all students. We cultivate a collaborative culture through the development of high-performing teams.

Indicator	Pre-Initiating	Initiating	Implementing	Developing	Sustaining
We are organized into collaborative teams in which members work interdependently to achieve common goals that directly impact student achievement. Structures have been put in place to ensure:	Teachers work in isolation with little awareness of the strategies, methods, or materials that colleagues use in teaching the same course or grade level. There is no plan in place to assign staff members into teams or to provide them with time to collaborate.	Teachers are encouraged but not required to work together collaboratively. Some staff may elect to work with colleagues on topics of mutual interest. Staff members are congenial but are not co-laboring in an effort to improve student achievement.	Teachers have been assigned to collaborative teams and have been provided time for collaboration during the regular contractual day. Teams may be unclear regarding how they should use the collaborative times. Topics often focus on matters unrelated to teaching and learning. Some teachers believe the team meeting is not a productive use of their time.	Teachers have been assigned to collaborative teams and have been provided time for collaboration on a weekly basis during the regular contractual day. Guidelines, protocols, and processes have been established in an effort to help teams use collaborative time to focus on topics that will have a positive impact on student achievement. Team leaders are helping lead the collaborative process, and the work of teams is monitored closely so assistance can be provided when a team struggles. Teams are working interdependently to achieve goals specifically related to higher levels of student achievement and are focusing their efforts on discovering better ways to achieve those goals.	The collaborative team process is deeply engrained in the school culture. Staff members view it as the engine that drives school improvement. Teams are self-directed and very skillful in advocacy and inquiry. They consistently focus on issues that are most significant in improving student achievement and set specific, measurable goals to monitor improvement. The collaborative team process serves as a powerful form of job-embedded professional development because members are willing and eager to learn from one another, identify common problems, engage in action research, make evidence of student learning transparent among members of the team, and make judgments about the effectiveness of different practices on the basis of that evidence. The team process directly impacts teacher practice in the classroom, helping each teacher clarify what to teach, how to assess, and how to improve instruction.
1. Collaboration is embedded in our routine work practice.					
2. We are provided with time to collaborate.					
3. We are clear on the critical questions that should drive our collaboration.					
4. Our collaborative work is monitored and supported.					

Indicator	Pre-Initiating	Initiating	Implementing	Developing	Sustaining
We have identified and honor the commitments we have made to the members of our collaborative teams in order to enhance the effectiveness of our team. These articulated collective commitments or norms have clarified expectations of how our team will operate, and we use them to address problems that may occur on the team.	No attention has been paid to establishing clearly articulated commitments that clarify the expectations of how the team will function and how each member will contribute to its success. Norms do emerge from each group based on the habits that come to characterize the group, but they are neither explicit nor the result of a thoughtful process. Several of the norms have an adverse effect on the effectiveness of the team.	Teams have been encouraged by school or district leadership to create norms that clarify expectations and commitments. Recommended norms for teams may have been created and distributed. Norms are often stated as beliefs rather than commitments to act in certain ways.	Each team has been required to develop written norms that clarify expectations and commitments. Many teams have viewed this as a task to be accomplished. They have written the norms and submitted them, but do not use them as part of the collaborative team process.	Teams have established the collective commitments that will guide their work, and members have agreed to honor the commitments. The commitments are stated in terms of specific behaviors that members will demonstrate. The team begins and ends each meeting with a review of the commitments to remind each other of the agreements they have made about how they will work together. They assess the effectiveness of the commitments periodically and make revisions when they feel that will help the team become more effective.	Team members honor the collective commitments they have made to one another regarding how the team will operate and the responsibility of each member to the team. The commitments have been instrumental in creating an atmosphere of trust and mutual respect. They have helped members work interdependently to achieve common goals because members believe they can rely upon one another. The commitments facilitate the team's collective inquiry and help people explore their assumptions and practices. Members recognize that their collective commitments have not only helped the team become more effective, but have also made the collaborative experience more personally rewarding. Violations of the commitments are addressed. Members use them as the basis for crucial conversations and honest dialogue when there is concern that one or more members are not fulfilling commitments.

Where Do We Go From Here? Worksheet

Collaborative Culture

Indicator of a PLC at Work	What steps or activities must be initiated to create this condition in your school?	Who will be responsible for initiating or sustaining these steps or activities?	What is a realistic timeline for each step or phase of the activity?	What will you use to assess the effectiveness of your initiative?
We are organized into collaborative teams in which members work interdependently to achieve common goals that directly impact student achievement. Structures have been put in place to ensure: 1. Collaboration is embedded in our routine work practice. 2. We are provided with time to collaborate. 3. We are clear on the critical questions that should drive our collaboration. 4. Our collaborative work is monitored and supported.				
We have identified and honor the commitments we have made to the members of our collaborative teams in order to enhance the effectiveness of our team. These articulated collective commitments or norms have clarified expectations of how our team will operate, and we use them to address problems that may occur on the team.				

Part Five

Tips for Moving Forward: Building a Collaborative Culture Through High-Performing Teams

1   **Create meaningful teams.** Ensure that teams are created on the basis of shared responsibility for pursuing the critical questions of teaching and learning with a particular group of students: for example, by course or by grade level.

2   **Make time for collaboration.** Work with staff to find creative ways to provide more time for team collaboration, including ways of using existing time more effectively.

3   **Develop widespread leadership.** Disperse leadership more widely by identifying team leaders for any team with more than three people. Meet with team leaders on a regular basis to identify problematic areas of the process, and develop strategies for resolving those problems.

4   **Make decisions on the basis of evidence.** Ask teams to build shared knowledge—to learn together—as they approach each new task in the collaborative process.

5   **Build the capacity of teams to succeed in the PLC process by providing them with essential tools.** Make supporting research, templates, exemplars, worksheets, and timelines available to teams to assist them in each step of the process.

6   **Continually assess the progress of teams.** Monitor the work of each team through ongoing assessment of their products, regular meetings with team leaders, and formal self-evaluations. Respond immediately to a team that is having difficulty.

7   **Lead by example.** Building-level leadership teams should model everything being asked of the collaborative teams, including meeting on a regular basis, staying focused on issues with the greatest impact on student achievement, establishing and honoring collective commitments, and working toward SMART goals.

8 **Provide for cross-team collaboration.** Create procedures to ensure teams are able to learn from one another.

9 **Expand the knowledge base available to teams.** Look for ways to link teams with relevant resources inside and outside of your building.

10 **Celebrate teams.** Make teams the focus of recognition and celebration (see chapter 2). Take every opportunity to acknowledge the efforts and accomplishments of teams.

Part Six

Questions to Guide the Work of Your Professional Learning Community

To Promote a Collaborative Culture in Your School or District, Ask:

1. Have we organized our staff into collaborative teams?

2. Have teams been organized on the basis of common courses and common grade levels whenever possible?

3. If we have used the interdisciplinary team structure, have members of the team identified specific, overarching student-achievement goals, and do they use those goals to guide their work?

4. Have specialist teachers and singleton teachers found meaningful collaborative teams?

5. Have we avoided assigning people to teams whose disparate assignments make it difficult if not impossible to focus on the critical questions of learning?

6. Have we provided time for teachers to meet in their collaborative teams on a regular basis?

7. Do teams focus on the critical questions of learning identified in *Learning By Doing*?

8. Are teams asked to submit specific products according to a designated timeline? Do these products reflect their focus on the critical questions?

9. What systems are in place to monitor the work and the effectiveness of the teams on a timely basis?

10. Has every team developed explicit norms that clarify the commitments members have made to one another regarding how they will work together as a team?

11. Do teams honor the norms they have established? What happens when faculty members do not honor their commitments?

12. Have we given teams the knowledge base, time, and support essential for their effectiveness?

Part Seven

Dangerous Detours and Seductive Shortcuts

Many schools and districts are organizing educators into what are simply groups rather than teams. Unless educators are working interdependently to achieve a common goal for which members are mutually accountable, they are not a team.

Beware of artificial teams. We have seen schools create "the leftover team" that combines unrelated singleton teachers under the pretext that they will function as a collaborative team. The likelihood that this disparate group will actually function as a collaborative team is extremely remote. Work with singletons to make them members of meaningful teams, even if the team is vertical or electronic and includes members outside of the building.

Most importantly, remember that a collaborative team will have no impact on student achievement unless its members are co-laboring on the right work. Systems must be in place to clarify what teams are to accomplish, monitor their progress, and provide assistance when they struggle.

Unless educators are working interdependently to achieve a common goal for which members are mutually accountable, they are not a team.

Final Thoughts

A collaborative culture does not simply emerge in a school or district: leaders *cultivate* collaborative cultures when they develop the capacity of their staffs to work as members of high-performing teams. People throughout the organization, however, must always remember that collaboration is a means to an end—to higher levels of learning—rather than the end itself. Chapter 6 addresses the challenge of creating a results orientation that impacts the work of teams, the school, and the district.

Creating a Results Orientation in a Professional Learning Community

Part One

The Case Study: Creating a Results Orientation at the School, Team, and Teacher Levels

When Aretha Ross was hired as a new superintendent of the Supreme School District, the board of education made it clear that its strategic plan for school improvement was the pride of the district. Every five years, the board engaged the community and staff in a comprehensive planning process intended to provide a sense of direction for the district and all of its schools and programs. A committee of key stakeholders oversaw the creation of the plan during a six-month development process. Each member was responsible for reporting back periodically to the group he or she represented to ensure accurate representation and ongoing communication. The committee held a series of community focus groups to solicit feedback from hundreds of parents, analyzed quantitative data, and generated qualitative data through a series of surveys to community, staff, and parents. The district mission statement provided the foundation of the document:

> It is the mission of our schools to provide a rigorous academic curriculum in a safe, caring, and enjoyable learning environment that enables each and every child to realize his or her potential and become a responsible and productive citizen and lifelong learner fully equipped to meet the challenges of the twenty-first century.

The plan provided the vision for the district and its schools, as well as core beliefs, strategic goals, key objectives, operational principles, and performance outcomes. With its adoption by the board of education, it became the blueprint for school improvement in the district. Each school was then called upon to create an extensive annual school improvement plan (SIP) aligned with the district's strategic plan.

Superintendent Ross was impressed by the effort that went into the strategic planning process and with the heft of the resulting document, but she was curious to see how it was implemented in the schools. In late October, she scheduled a meeting with Harry Lee Lewis, principal of the Elvis Presley Elementary School (nickname: the Kings), to discuss the improvement process of that school.

Principal Lewis explained that the SIP adopted by the staff the previous month was linked to the district goal of "Preparing students to succeed as members of a global community and global economy." The Presley School Improvement Committee had analyzed the results from the previous state assessment of third and fifth graders and concluded that word analysis was an area of weakness for students. The committee reasoned that students would not be prepared to succeed as members of a global community if they were not proficient in such an important skill. The committee recommended that the staff adopt a school improvement goal of "Improving student achievement in word analysis as indicated on the state assessment." The faculty agreed to this with little debate. Principal Lewis assured Superintendent Ross that this same process was the standard procedure in all of the district's schools.

The explanation of this improvement process troubled Superintendent Ross somewhat. She realized the state assessment wasn't administered to students until third grade, and she questioned how much impact the school's goal was having on the primary grade levels. Furthermore, she questioned whether the SIP process described to her fostered the commitment to continuous improvement she hoped to see in every school.

Superintendent Ross decided to do some informal investigating by visiting the third-grade team at Presley as its members met in their weekly meeting. She asked if they felt teachers in other grade levels were helping address the language arts goal established by Presley's School Improvement Committee. After some awkward silence, the team members admitted they did not remember the goal and asked if she could remind them of it.

Superintendent Ross did not want to generalize based upon one school, so she made arrangements to visit four other schools that week. In each, she discovered a similar situation. She was convinced that despite the board's affection for the strategic plan, it was neither impacting practice in the classroom nor contributing to a culture of continuous improvement. She knew there was little reason to believe students would achieve at higher levels until principals and teachers became much more interested in and responsible for improved results. What she did not know was what steps the district might take to foster a results orientation.

> **Reflection**
>
> How does a school or district create a results orientation among administrators and teachers—the very people who are called upon to improve results?

Part Two

Here's How

We have repeatedly listed a *results orientation* as one of the characteristics of a professional learning community. However, organizations do not focus on results: the people within them do—or they do not. There is little evidence to suggest that centralized formal strategic planning creates such an orientation. In fact, one comprehensive study of strategic planning over a thirty-year period chronicled its failure to impact results (Mintzberg, 1994).

If formal, district-led strategic planning processes do not create a results orientation, will handing the improvement process over to schools be a more effective alternative? The Consortium on Productivity in Schools (1995) answered that question with a resounding no and concluded:

> Site based management cannot overcome lack of clear goals and goal overloading. . . . Site based management does not substitute for the lack of stable, limited, and well-defined goals for schools. . . . Otherwise the agendas of site based school improvement drift into non-academic and administrative matters. (pp. 46–47)

The challenge for Superintendent Ross and for any leader who hopes to improve student achievement by creating a results orientation is to engage all members of the organization to establishing goals that, if achieved, will result in higher levels of student learning.

What Questions

What do you mean by *SMART goal*?

One of the most effective strategies for bringing district goals to life is to insist that all schools create goals that are specifically linked to district goals. But before this can be done, schools and districts must be in agreement about the meaning of the word *goal*, another of those terms that can mean many different things to different people within an organization. The

One of the most effective strategies for bringing district goals to life is to insist that all schools create goals that are specifically linked to district goals.

SMART goal acronym (O'Neill & Conzemius, 2005) provides much-needed clarity. Goals are SMART when they are:

- **Strategic** (aligned with the organization's goals) and specific

- **Measurable**

- **Attainable**

- **Results oriented**

- **Time bound** (specifying when the goal will be achieved)

What resources can you provide to assist us?

Leaders who demonstrate reciprocal accountability do more than just hope teams will be successful in developing SMART goals: they are committed to providing teams with the resources and the support that increase the likelihood that teams will be successful in establishing and achieving high-quality SMART goals. They provide clarity regarding why the work is to be done; consider what teams need in order to build shared knowledge about the work; supply teams with tools, templates, and examples to facilitate the work; establish criteria to help teams assess the quality of the work; and monitor progress of each team to intervene and assist when a team struggles.

Linking School Goals to District Goals

Assume a district has conveyed the message that its fundamental purpose is to help all students learn at high levels by adopting such simple goals as these:

- *We will help all students successfully complete every course and every grade level and demonstrate proficiency on local, state, and national assessments.*

- *We will eliminate the gaps in student achievement that are connected to race, socioeconomic status, and gender.*

- *We will increase the number of students who have access to and succeed in the most rigorous curriculum we offer.*

These broad overarching district goals can then be translated into SMART goals for each school. The school's plan should stipulate both the past level of performance and the improvement goal for the indicator being monitored. For example,

- ***Our Reality:*** *Last year, 86 percent of the grades assigned to our students were passing grades.*
  Our Goal: *This year, we will increase the percentage of passing grades to at least 93 percent.*

■ **Our Reality:** *Last year, 76 percent of our students met the proficiency standard on the state math test.*
Our Goal: *This year, we will increase the percentage of students meeting the proficiency standard on the state math test to 80 percent or higher.*

■ **Our Reality:** *Last year, 10 percent of the graduating class earned credits in advanced placement courses or the capstone course in a departmental sequence.*
Our Goal: *This year, we will increase the percentage of students earning credits in advanced placement or capstone courses in a departmental sequence to 20 percent or higher.*

Linking Team Goals to School Goals

The next critical step in this process is to ensure that each collaborative team translates one or more of the school goals into a SMART goal that drives the work of the team. As we wrote earlier, the definition of a team is "a group of people working *interdependently* to achieve a *common goal* for which members are held *mutually accountable.*" One of the most powerful strategies for building the capacity of staff to work effectively in collaborative teams is to create the conditions that require them to work together to accomplish a specific goal. The SMART Goal Worksheets (pages 164–170) provide examples of how different school goals might be translated into SMART goals for collaborative teams. A blank SMART Goal Worksheet appears on page 163. When this process is in place, a team that accomplishes its SMART goal contributes to the success of its school and its district.

One of the most powerful strategies for building the capacity of staff to work effectively in collaborative teams is to create the conditions that require them to work together to accomplish a specific goal.

Focusing on Results, not Activities

Once again, a school that defines its purpose as "High levels of learning for all students" will insist that teams include the language of learning in their goals. This is contrary to the traditional approach of writing goals that focus on evidence of what teachers will do rather than on evidence of what students will learn. Statements such as, "We will integrate technology into our course," "We will align our curriculum with the newly adopted textbook," "We will increase the use of cooperative learning activities," or "We will solicit more parent involvement" may describe worthwhile initiatives, but they do not represent goals. If the purpose of these initiatives is to increase student learning, that purpose should be explicitly stated in a goal. Effective team goals will help answer the question, "How will we know if our strategies are resulting in gains in student learning?" The goals will focus on the intended outcome rather than on the strategies to achieve the outcome.

Pursuing Both Attainable Goals and Stretch Goals

Leaders must find a balance between the attainable *goals teams feel they can achieve in the short term and* stretch *goals—goals so ambitious they could not possibly be achieved unless practices within the organization change significantly.*

When building a results-oriented culture, leaders must find a balance between the *attainable* goals teams feel they can achieve in the short term and *stretch* goals—goals so ambitious they could not possibly be achieved unless practices within the organization change significantly (Tichy, 1997). Stretch goals have also been referred to as BHAGs: Big Hairy Audacious Goals (Collins & Porras, 1997). Attainable goals are intended to document incremental progress and build momentum and self-efficacy through short-term wins. Stretch goals are intended to inspire, to capture the imagination of people within the organization, to stimulate creativity and innovation, and to serve as a unifying focal point of effort.

President John F. Kennedy announced one of the most famous stretch goals in American history when he declared in 1961 that the United States would "land a man on the moon and return him safely to earth" by the end of the decade, despite the fact that the necessary technology to achieve that goal did not exist. His pronouncement galvanized and energized the scientific community and the nation and led to the largest nonmilitary technological endeavor ever undertaken by the United States.

But merely proclaiming stretch goals does not improve an organization. In 1989, President George Bush announced Education Goals 2000, boldly proclaiming the nation would achieve such stretch goals as, "All children in America will start school ready to learn," and "United States students will be first in the world in mathematics and science achievement" by the new millennium. Neither goal was achieved because neither resulted in meaningful action.

Stretch goals are effective only if they stimulate action, if people begin to behave in new ways. Pronouncements without action are hopes, not goals. Furthermore, stretch goals must be *goals*, not mission statements. They must set specific targets rather than offer vague expressions or beliefs. Kennedy did not say, "We need to do something to strengthen the space program," or "We believe in the potential of space." He said, "We will land a man on the moon." "We believe in high levels of learning for all students" is not a stretch goal. "We will ensure all students demonstrate proficiency on the state assessment," "We will eliminate achievement gaps based on socioeconomic status," and "We will ensure the academic success of every student in every grade level" are examples of stretch goals because they are stated as targets.

If schools and districts limit themselves to the pursuit of *attainable* goals, they run the risk of never moving outside their comfort zones. Organizations are unlikely to experience dramatic improvement if they are content with creeping incrementalism—slowly inching forward over time. If the only goals educators pursue are easily attainable, the focus shifts to how good do we *have* to be rather than how good *can* we be.

On the other hand, if the only goals educators pursue are stretch goals, teachers and principals are prone to give up in hopelessness. If educators perceive goals as unrealistic to the point of being unattainable, and there are no successes to celebrate, they will be discouraged from taking action to achieve those goals.

Once again, we believe the solution to this dilemma of attainable goals versus stretch goals is found not in the Tyranny of Or but in the Genius of And. In the early stages of building a PLC, celebrating small wins is key to sustaining the effort, and attainable goals are an essential element of results-oriented small wins. Therefore, we strongly recommend that goals established by collaborative teams should be *attainable* and include short-term goals that serve as benchmarks of progress. Teams should feel reasonably confident they have the capacity to achieve their goals. They should be able to say, "If we seek and implement best practices, we have reason to believe we will achieve our team goal."

Furthermore, frequent feedback and intermittent reinforcement are two factors that help sustain the effort essential to achieving goals. A team that establishes a goal of improving student performance on a state test receives neither feedback nor reinforcement for almost a year unless it establishes some short-term goals.

Frequent feedback and intermittent reinforcement are two factors that help sustain the effort essential to achieving goals.

For example, suppose one team discovers that 23 percent of students demonstrate proficiency on a preassessment instrument it has administered at the beginning of the unit. The team then establishes a short-term goal that 90 percent of the students will demonstrate proficiency by the end of the unit. Another team reviews the results from the common assessments its members administered the previous year to determine that 64 percent of students were able to meet the established standard for writing proficiency by the end of October. That team sets a goal that 75 percent of students will meet that standard by the same date this year. In both instances, short-term goals can inform the team of progress and create a basis for celebration.

District goals, however, should be clearly linked to the purpose of learning for all students, should establish challenging targets, and should require innovation and long-term commitment if they are to be achieved. District goals should be so bold that they require the development of new capacities. The best district goals will present "adaptive challenges": challenges for which the solution is not apparent, challenges that cause us to experiment, discover, adjust, and adapt (Heifetz & Linsky, 2002).

A few district goals such as those listed in this chapter are long-term goals representing a life's work rather than a short-term project. Therefore, the district leadership should commit to these goals year after year until they are achieved. New hot topics will be touted on the professional development circuit, political leaders will come and go, and special interest groups will demand schools pay more attention to their cause. Rather than reacting to each shift in the wind by placing more initiatives on their schools, the central office staff must help buffer them from the constant turbulence so educators can stay the course.

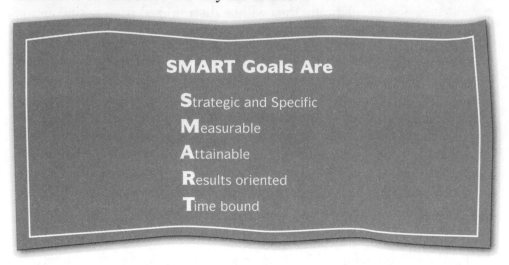

SMART Goals Are

Strategic and Specific

Measurable

Attainable

Results oriented

Time bound

SMART Goal Worksheet

School:

Team Members:

District Goal(s):

School Goal(s):

Team Name:

Team Leader:

Team SMART Goal	Strategies and Action Steps	Who Is Responsible	Target Date or Timeline	Evidence of Effectiveness

SMART Goal Worksheet: Third-Grade Team

School: George Washington Elementary   **Team Name:** Third Grade   **Team Leader:** Theresa Smith

Team Members: Ken Thomas, Joe Ramirez, Cathy Armstrong, Amy Wu

District Goal(s):

1. We will increase student achievement and close the achievement gap in all areas using a variety of indicators to document improved learning on the part of our students.

School Goal(s):

1. We will improve student achievement in language arts as measured by local, district, state, and national indicators.

Team SMART Goal	Strategies and Action Steps	Who Is Responsible	Target Date or Timeline	Evidence of Effectiveness
Our Current Reality: Last year, 85 percent of our students met or exceeded the target score of 3 on our state's writing prompt in May. **Our SMART Goal:** This year, at least 90 percent of our students will meet or exceed the target score of 3 on our state's writing prompt in May.	**Curriculum** 1. Clarify and pace essential student learning outcomes in writing using standards documents, curriculum guides, assessment blueprints and data, and the wish list of skills from the fourth-grade team.	All members of our team	October 15	Lists of essential student learning outcomes and pacing guide Increased results for all students on team, district, state, and national indicators

Team SMART Goal	Strategies and Action Steps	Who Is Responsible	Target Date or Timeline	Evidence of Effectiveness
	Assessments 2. Develop, implement, and collaboratively score grade-level formative writing prompts to:	All members of our team	October–May Checkpoints at midpoint of each grading period District benchmark assessments at end of each semester	Common writing prompts Common writing rubric Increased results for all students on team, district, state, and national indicators
	a) Frequently monitor each student's learning of essential writing outcomes			
	b) Provide students with multiple opportunities to demonstrate progress in meeting and exceeding learning targets in writing			
	c) Learn with and from each other better ways to help students become proficient writers			
	3. Provide students with writing assignments in all subject areas, and utilize a variety of instructional strategies to help students learn all essential writing skills.	All members of our team Principal Resource staff Volunteers	Daily, September–May	Intervention/enrichment schedule Student learning results
	4. Initiate individual and small-group sessions to provide additional intervention and enrichment focused on writing.	All members of our team	Daily, September–May	Intervention/enrichment schedule Student learning results
	5. Provide parents with resources and strategies to help their children succeed as writers.	All members of our team	First semester workshop: 10/20 Second semester workshop: 1/19 Newsletters End-of-grading-period conferences	Number of parents in attendance Study guides and newsletters

Team SMART Goal	Strategies and Action Steps	Who Is Responsible	Target Date or Timeline	Evidence of Effectiveness
	Staff Development 6. Develop, implement, and evaluate our team action research project in writing to improve our individual and collective ability to help our students learn to write at high levels. Use information from our common formative assessments to identify staff development needs and engage in ongoing, job-embedded staff development in the area of writing.	All members of our team	Weekly collaborative team meetings Staff development days Faculty meeting sessions Additional professional learning time by request	Common assessments Quarterly reviews Midyear progress reports End-of-year team evaluations Increased results for all students on team, district, state, and national indicators

SMART Goal Worksheet: Eighth-Grade Math

School: Thomas Jefferson Middle School   **Team Name:** Eighth-Grade Math   **Team Leader:** Chris Rauch

Team Members: Chris Carter, Dolores Layco, Mary Fischer

District Goal:

1. We will increase student achievement and close the achievement gap in all areas using a variety of indicators to document improved learning on the part of our students.

School Goal(s): We will:

1. Reduce the failure rate in our school.

2. Increase the percentage of students scoring at or above the established proficiency standard on the state assessment in all areas.

Team SMART Goal	Strategies and Action Steps	Who Is Responsible	Target Date or Timeline	Evidence of Effectiveness
Our Current Reality: Last year, 24 percent of our students failed one or more semesters of math, and 31 percent of our students were unable to meet the state proficiency standard in math.	We will align each unit of our math program with state standards, study the results of the last state assessment, identify problem areas, and develop specific strategies to address those areas in our course.	Entire team	We will complete the analysis on the teacher workday prior to the start of the year. We will review our findings prior to the start of each new unit.	Written analysis of state assessment and strategies to address weaknesses
Our SMART Goal: This year, we will reduce the percentage of failing grades to 10 percent or less and the percentage of students unable to meet state standards to no more than 15 percent.	We will develop common formative assessments and administer them every three weeks. These assessments will provide repeated opportunities for students to become familiar with the format used on the state assessment.	Entire team	Formative assessments will be created prior to the start of each unit of instruction throughout the year. They will be administered on a day designated by the team.	Student performance on team-endorsed common assessments

Team SMART Goal	Strategies and Action Steps	Who Is Responsible	Target Date or Timeline	Evidence of Effectiveness
	After each common assessment, we will identify any student who does not meet the established proficiency standard and will work with the counselor to have those students reassigned from study hall to the math tutoring center.	Members of entire team will request tutoring as their supervisory responsibility; team leader will work with the counselor after each assessment.	Assessments will be administered every three weeks. Students will be assigned to the tutoring center within one week of assessment.	Daily list of students receiving tutoring in math
	We will replace failing grades from our common assessments with the higher grade earned by students who are able to demonstrate proficiency in key skills on subsequent forms of the assessment after completing tutoring.	Entire team will create multiple forms of each assessment. Tutors will administer the assessment after a student has completed the required tutoring.	Multiple forms of an assessment will be created prior to the start of each unit of instruction. Tutors will administer the second assessment within two weeks of a student's assignment to the tutoring center.	Compilation of results from subsequent assessments
	We will examine the results of each common assessment to determine which member of the team is getting the best results on each skill, and then share ideas, methods, and materials for teaching those skills more effectively.	Each member of the team	Ongoing throughout the year each time a common assessment is administered	Analysis of findings after each common assessment is administered Decrease in the failure rate Increase in percentage of students proficient on state assessment

SMART Goal Worksheet: American Government

School: John Adams High School   **Team Name:** American Government   **Team Leader:** Tom Botimer

Team Members: Dan Hahn, Andy Bradford, Nick Larsen, Helen Harvey

District Goal(s):

1. We will increase student achievement and close the achievement gap in all areas using a variety of indicators to document improved learning on the part of our students.

2. We will provide more students with access to our most rigorous curriculum in each subject area and grade level.

School Goal(s): We will increase by at least 10 percent the number of students earning credit in:

1. Advanced placement courses

2. Capstone courses in a departmental sequence

Team SMART Goal	Strategies and Action Steps	Who Is Responsible	Target Date or Timeline	Evidence of Effectiveness
Our Current Reality: All students must complete a semester of American Government as a graduation requirement. Last year only 10 percent of the graduating class fulfilled that requirement by enrolling in advanced placement (AP) American Government.	We will make a presentation in each section of United States History, encouraging students to enroll in AP American Government and listing the advantages for doing so.	Team leader will coordinate the schedule for these presentations with the team leader for United States History. Each member of the team will assist in making these presentations and will distribute a written list of advantages created by the team.	Complete presentations by the end of January prior to students registering for their courses for next year	The presentation has been made in every United States History class.

Learning by Doing © 2006, 2010 Solution Tree Press • solution-tree.com
Visit **go.solution-tree.com/PLCbooks** to download this page.

Team SMART Goal	Strategies and Action Steps	Who Is Responsible	Target Date or Timeline	Evidence of Effectiveness
Our SMART Goal: At least 20 percent of the current junior class will enroll in and earn a score of 3, 4, or 5 on the advanced placement American Government exam by the end of next school year.	We will coordinate with the guidance department to ensure that when counselors register students for classes, they encourage any student who receives an A at the end of the first semester of United States History to enroll in AP American Government.	Team leader will attend the counselors' team meeting to enlist their support, explain advantages of the AP program, and share the team's strategies for supporting students in AP American Government.	End of first semester	Minutes of meeting
	We will advise parents of the benefits of AP American Government.	The team will draft a letter to parents of students who earn an A in United States History at the end of the semester. The letter will list the advantages of completing this course while in high school for any student planning on attending college. It will also include the team's strategy to provide students with additional support. The team will also create a flyer on the benefits of the AP program to be distributed during parent open house.	The flyer will be created for distribution at the open house in early October. The letter will be sent at the end of the first semester.	Completed documents
	We will create study groups to review material prior to the comprehensive assessments we administer every six weeks.	The team will create the common comprehensive assessments. Each member will be responsible for conducting one study group to help students review for these tests. Study groups will be held on three evenings in the week prior to the test.	Ongoing throughout the semester	Completion of common assessments and student performance on common assessments The number of students earning honor grades on the AP exam in American Government will double over last year's total.

Part Three

Here's Why

Why should educators abandon traditional strategic planning and focus instead on ensuring that each collaborative team in every school is working toward SMART goals that are specifically linked to a few school and district goals? Most simply, because there is no evidence that strategic planning leads to improved results. In his study of "great" organizations, Jim Collins (2001) was unable to discover any link between formal planning and organizational effectiveness. Jeffrey Pfeffer and Robert Sutton (2000) were even more emphatic when they concluded, "Existing research on the effectiveness of formal planning efforts is clear: Planning is essentially unrelated to organizational performance" (p. 42). In his study of strategic planning in education, Doug Reeves (2009) actually found a negative correlation between district-led formal strategic planning and improved student achievement.

There is no evidence that strategic planning leads to improved results.

Whereas effective leaders are skillful in making the complex simple, strategic planning almost inevitably makes the simple complex. The one thing most strategic plans for school districts have in common is their girth. Voluminous tomes place far too many initiatives upon schools and obscure rather than clarify priorities. The ambiguity and interchangeable use of terms adds to the confusion. How many people can assert with confidence that they can specify the differences between a *strategic goal*, a *key objective*, and a *performance outcome*? Furthermore, strategic plans often serve as a barrier to the relentless action orientation of effective organizations (Pfeffer & Sutton, 2000). Far too many school districts confuse developing or possessing a plan with taking meaningful action to ensure that something actually happens. Michael Fullan (2010) offers succinct advice to those hoping to improve their schools and districts: "Beware of fat plans" (p. 24).

The biggest factor in the ineffectiveness of formal strategic planning rests on its faulty underlying assumption: some people in organizations (the leaders) are responsible for thinking and planning, while others (the workers) are responsible for carrying out those plans. This separation of thought and action is the antithesis of a learning community, which requires widely dispersed leadership and strategic thinkers *throughout* the organization (Fullan, 2005). Asking employees to follow a five-year strategic plan chartered by others does little to generate a focus on or commitment to improved results. Engaging those employees in a process of *ongoing* continuous improvement in which they establish their own short-term goals, develop their own plans to achieve them, act on those plans, and make frequent adjustments based on their analysis of evidence is much more likely to instill a results orientation throughout the organization.

Not only do collaborative teams represent the optimum setting for the pursuit of meaningful SMART goals, but SMART goals also represent an essential tool in developing powerful collaborative teams. Teams benefit when they have a few key goals that clarify the results they seek and how each member can contribute to achieving those results (Lencioni, 2005; Schaffer & Thomson, 1998). They are more effective when they see how their goals and their efforts are linked to the larger organization (Druskat & Wolf, 2001). They are strengthened from the accomplishment and celebration of short-term wins (Collins, 2001; Katzenbach & Smith, 1993; Kotter, 1996; Kouzes & Posner, 1987). They are more committed, empowered, and motivated when they set their own targets and create their own plans to achieve them (Axelrod, 2002; Csikszentmihalyi, 1997).

In short, there is nothing more important in determining the effectiveness of a team than each member's understanding of and commitment to the achievement of results-oriented goals to which the group holds itself mutually accountable.

In short, there is nothing more important in determining the effectiveness of a team than each member's understanding of and commitment to the achievement of results-oriented goals to which the group holds itself mutually accountable. Helping teams translate long-term purpose into specific, measurable short-term goals, and then helping members develop the skills to achieve those goals, is one of the most important steps leaders can take in building the capacity of a group to function as a high-performing collaborative team (Katzenbach & Smith, 1993). Research shows that setting SMART goals is essential to achieving results (see Why Do We Need SMART Goals?).

Part Four

Assessing Your Place on the PLC Journey

Complete the PLC continuum and Where Do We Go From Here? worksheets as outlined in chapter 2.

Why Do We Need SMART Goals?

"According to research, goal setting is the single most powerful motivational tool in a leader's toolkit. Why? Because goal setting operates in ways that provide purpose, challenge, and meaning. Goals are the guideposts along the road that make a compelling vision come alive. Goals energize people. Specific, clear, challenging goals lead to greater effort and achievement than easy or vague goals do." (Blanchard, 2007, p. 150)

"Goal setting is one of the simplest and most effective organizational interventions that can be used to increase employee performance." (O'Hora & Maglieri, 2006, p. 132)

"[Schools with teachers who learn and kids who achieve] use clear, agreed-upon student achievement goals to focus and shape teacher learning." (WestEd, 2000, p. 12)

"Collegial support and professional development in schools are unlikely to have any effect on improvement of practice and performance if they are not connected to a coherent set of goals that give direction and meaning to learning and collegiality." (Elmore, 2003, p. 60)

California elementary schools that outperformed schools with similar student populations assigned a high priority to student achievement, set measurable goals for improved student achievement, and had a well-defined plan to improve achievement (Williams et al., 2006).

"Consistently higher performing high schools set explicit academic goals that are aligned with and often exceed state standards." (Dolejs, 2006, p. 1)

"Our investigations suggest it is critical to define and publish a protocol that articulates specific inquiry functions: jointly and recursively identifying appropriate and worthwhile goals for student learning; finding or developing appropriate means to assess student progress toward those goals; bringing to the table the expertise of colleagues and others who can assist in accomplishing these goals; planning, preparing, and delivering lessons; using evidence from the classroom to evaluate instruction; and, finally, reflecting on the process to determine next steps." (Gallimore et al., 2009, pp. 548–549)

The Professional Learning Communities at Work™ Continuum: Focusing on Results (Part I)

DIRECTIONS: Individually, silently, and *honestly* assess the current reality of your school's implementation of each indicator listed in the left column. Consider what evidence or anecdotes support your assessment. This form may also be used to assess district or team implementation.

We assess our effectiveness on the basis of results rather than intentions.

Indicator	Pre-Initiating	Initiating	Implementing	Developing	Sustaining
The members of each of our collaborative teams are working interdependently to achieve one or more SMART goals that align with our school goals. Each team has identified specific action steps members will take to achieve the goal and a process for monitoring progress toward the goal. The identification and pursuit of SMART goals by each collaborative team are critical elements of the school's continuous improvement process.	Goals have not been established at the district or school level. Teams are not expected to establish goals.	Teams establish goals that focus on adult activities and projects rather than student learning.	Teams have been asked to create SMART goals, but many teachers are wary of establishing goals based on improved student learning. Some attempt to articulate very narrow goals that can be accomplished despite students learning less. Others present goals that are impossible to monitor. Still others continue to offer goals based on teacher projects. There is still confusion regarding the nature of and reasons for SMART goals.	All teams have established annual SMART goals as an essential element of their collaborative team process. Teams have established processes to monitor their progress, and members work together in an effort to identify strategies for becoming more effective at achieving the team's SMART goal.	Each collaborative team of teachers has established both an annual SMART goal and a series of short-term goals to monitor their progress. They create specific action plans to achieve the goals, clarify the evidence that they will gather to assess their progress, and work together interdependently to achieve the goal. This focus on tangible evidence of results guides the work of teams and is critical to the continuous improvement process of the school. The recognition and celebration of efforts to achieve goals helps sustain the improvement process.

Where Do We Go From Here? Worksheet

Using School Improvement Goals to Drive Team Goals

Indicator of a PLC at Work	What steps or activities must be initiated to create this condition in your school?	Who will be responsible for initiating or sustaining these steps or activities?	What is a realistic timeline for each step or phase of the activity?	What will you use to assess the effectiveness of your initiative?
The members of each of our collaborative teams are working interdependently to achieve one or more SMART goals that align with our school goals. Each team has identified specific action steps members will take to achieve the goal and a process for monitoring progress toward the goal. The identification and pursuit of SMART goals by each collaborative team are critical elements of the school's continuous improvement process.				

Part Five

Tips for Moving Forward: Using Goals to Focus on Results

1 **Less is more.** Limit the number of district initiatives, and make certain the initiatives reflect the priority of high levels of learning for all students.

2 **Tie all goals to distric goals.** Require each school and each collaborative team within the school to establish a *limited* number of SMART goals that are specifically aligned with district goals.

3 **Provide templates for goal setting for every team.** The templates should reinforce the premise that the team must (1) focus on improved results rather than implementing activities and (2) clarify how the achievement of the goal will be attained, monitored, and measured.

4 **Make certain goals are team goals rather than individual goals.** Remember that an effective goal will require team members to work *interdependently* in order to achieve it. Members should be able to clarify both individual and collective responsibilities.

5 **Team goals should be established by teams rather than for teams.** Teams should be expected to create goals that align with school and district goals and to write goals that are consistent with specified parameters. However, each team should enjoy considerable autonomy in articulating its goals.

6 **Monitor work toward a goal by requiring teams to create specific products that are directly related to the goal.** Typical products include collective commitments or norms, aligned curriculum, common assessments, collective analysis of results, improvement plans, and so on.

7 **Celebrate progress.** Plan for, seek out, and celebrate small wins.

8 **Consider affective goals as well as academic goals.** The high levels of learning a school or team seeks for its students need not be limited to academic areas. Affective areas (for example, responsibility, empathy, self-efficacy, independence, and so on) are perfectly legitimate areas for establishing goals.

There is a tendency when establishing such goals, however, to be content with the implementation of new programs or the nobleness of the cause. Neither the completion of projects nor the unassailability of good intentions should substitute for goals. Teams must discipline themselves to address the question, "How will we know our students are achieving this goal?" for every goal they establish.

9   **District goals should include stretch goals.** These goals will be so challenging that people throughout the organization will be called upon to build new capacities in order to achieve them.

10   **Be wary of the complacency that can set in when a stretch goal has been achieved.** It is easy for an organization to drift into the "we have arrived" mode when it has been successful in the pursuit of a challenging goal (Collins & Porras, 1997). Combat that tendency and promote continuous improvement by celebrating the accomplishment and then creating a new stretch goal.

Part Six

Questions to Guide the Work of Your Professional Learning Community

To Assess the Commitment to a Results Orientation in Your School or District, Ask:

1. What evidence do we have that district goals are directly impacting the work of schools and collaborative teams within the school?

2. Does every collaborative team have a goal that aligns with district and school goals?

3. Are team goals SMART: Strategic and Specific, Measurable, Attainable, Results oriented, and Time bound?

4. Is there a plan in place to monitor the progress of each team? Does the plan include monitoring products created by the team as it works toward its goals?

5. Are teams provided with relevant and timely feedback regarding their progress? Remember that goals are effective motivators, but only if teams receive feedback (Kouzes & Posner, 1999).

6. Is a plan in place to identify, acknowledge, and celebrate small wins as teams make progress toward their goals?

7. Do district goals include stretch goals?

Part Seven

Dangerous Detours and Seductive Shortcuts

Beware of goals that are so narrow that they can be accomplished even if students learn less. For example, a team that establishes a SMART goal of improving student performance in the skill of capitalization could achieve that goal even if the proficiency of their students actually declines in reading comprehension or writing. Be certain to establish goals that focus on skills that are most essential in the given content or grade level.

Beware of morally impeccable goals that are impossible to monitor. A team that announces its goal is to help its students become lifelong learners has certainly established a noble goal, but unless it can identify the specific indicators it will monitor to assess students' progress as lifelong learners, they have not yet established a SMART goal.

Finally, beware of goals that do not require students to learn at higher levels. Once again, educators are accustomed to focusing on what they will do rather than the knowledge and skills that students will demonstrate. If the goal can be accomplished without students learning at higher levels (for example, "Our team will create four new common assessments"), it is not a SMART goal.

If the goal can be accomplished without students learning at higher levels (for example, "Our team will create four new common assessments"), it is not a SMART goal.

Final Thoughts

The way in which a school or district structures its planning and goal-setting process can help or hinder the adoption of the PLC concept. The most effective structures will directly impact the work and decisions of schools, the collaborative teams within the schools, and the teachers in their classrooms. Those teams and teachers must have timely access to relevant information in order to make the adjustments essential to achieving their goals. Chapter 7 describes how to provide the critical resource of timely and relevant information.

Using Relevant Information to Improve Results

Part One

The Case Study: The Reluctance to Use Information

After attending a Professional Learning Communities Institute, the school improvement committee of Gladys Knight Charter School (nickname: the Pips) unanimously resolved to use the model as the framework for improving their school. Their principal pledged her full support for the initiative. Over the summer, committee members sent supporting materials and articles on PLCs to the entire staff. When the teachers returned in August, the committee convened small-group faculty meetings to respond to any questions and concerns regarding their proposal to implement the PLC concept.

The staff's response was generally very positive. Teachers agreed it made sense to work together in collaborative teams once they were assured that work would occur during their contractual day. They acknowledged the benefits of working together to clarify what students were to learn. They agreed the school should build systematic interventions to ensure students who struggled received additional time and support for learning, and they supported the premise that common curriculum pacing was an important element in an effective intervention system.

The one aspect of the committee's proposal that met with resistance was requiring teams to develop and administer common formative assessments multiple times throughout the year in language arts and math. The committee reasoned that the results of the assessments could be used to identify students in need of additional assistance, to discover problem areas in the curriculum, and, very importantly, to help individual staff members discover strengths and weaknesses in their teaching.

Teachers raised a number of concerns regarding the use of common assessments. They expressed confidence in the competence of every teacher and argued that differences in student achievement on common assessments could be attributed to a number of factors—including the effort and ability of students—rather than to the effectiveness of the instruction. They felt any attempt to use data from common assessments to make inferences regarding the proficiency of teachers was invalid. They saw the potential for great harm: results could be used to evaluate teachers or to create winners and losers among the staff. Teachers' self-esteem could suffer. Common assessments could be a first step in a scheme to establish merit pay.

Teachers also argued that common team-developed assessments would not contribute to school improvement. They maintained that if teachers agreed to work together collaboratively to clarify essential learning and to plan effective lessons, student achievement would be certain to improve. If, as the research suggested, collaborative processes among teachers were truly linked to higher levels of student learning, teachers need only focus on the process, confident that improved results would be the inevitable consequence of their efforts. If results became the focus, they argued, teachers would pay less attention to meaningful collaboration and would merely teach to the test.

Finally, they argued that the only results that mattered in the state accountability system were the results from the state test. If teachers were to spend time on data analysis, they should focus on student performance on the state test rather than on creating another level of assessment.

Reflection

Consider the case study and the arguments presented by those who oppose the use of common assessments to monitor results. Should the committee abandon the proposal to ask each grade-level team to develop common formative assessments?

Part Two

Here's How

The very reason to engage in the PLC process is to improve results; therefore, it is incongruous to argue that the process should be inattentive to results. For too long schools have focused on processes and inputs, operating under the faulty assumption that improved learning is guaranteed if we select the right curriculum, prescribe the right teaching strategy, create the right schedule, buy the right textbook, increase graduation requirements, extend the school year, and so on. That assumption has repeatedly, consistently, and invariably proven to be incorrect. Schools only continuously improve if they switch their focus from inputs to outcomes and from activities to results.

Those who think teachers can substitute discussion about how to teach a concept at the outset of a unit for systems that ensure each teacher gets useful information on results ignore an important point: all opinions are not of equal value. Two teachers can be passionately convinced of the superiority of their respective strategies for teaching a concept. How is it possible to determine if one of those teachers has, in fact, discovered a powerful way to teach that concept? It is through the collective examination of results—tangible evidence of student learning—that teachers' dialogue moves from sharing opinions to building shared knowledge and evidenced-based decision making. Team analysis of and learning from frequent common formative assessments is an essential step on the journey to developing the capacity to function as a PLC.

What Questions

What is a *results orientation*?

A results orientation is a focus on outcomes rather than inputs or intentions. *In PLCs, members are committed to achieving desired results and are hungry for evidence that their efforts are producing the intended outcomes.*

In the previous chapter, we argued that one powerful strategy to help create a results orientation in a school is to ask the collaborative teams within it to establish SMART goals that are specifically aligned with the goals of the school and district. Results-oriented goals are *essential* to effective teams. And the capacity of teams to achieve their goals improves dramatically when members have access to feedback that informs their individual and collective practice—feedback that helps them discover what is working and what is not working in their instructional strategies.

The challenge for schools, then, is to provide each teacher with the most powerful and authentic information in a timely manner so that it can impact his or her professional practice in ways that enhance student learning. As we mentioned in chapter 3, state and provincial assessments fail to provide such feedback. Formative assessment by individual teachers in their classrooms can certainly provide timely feedback for teachers and students alike. But when a collaborative team of teachers creates and implements common formative assessments, teachers are provided with the basis of comparison that is essential for informing professional practice.

Schools have been called upon to become more "data driven"; however, this focus is misplaced because schools have never suffered from a lack of data. Every teacher who works in isolation can generate a mountain

The challenge for schools is to provide each teacher with the most powerful and authentic information in a timely manner so that it can impact his or her professional practice in ways that enhance student learning.

of data with every test he or she administers: mean, mode, median, percentage passing, percentage failing, and so on. Teachers can give their same individual assessments over a period of years, get similar results year after year, and thus have access to longitudinal data. But unless they have a basis of comparison, they cannot identify strengths and weaknesses in their teaching, and they are unable to determine if an area in which students are struggling is a function of the curriculum, their strategies, or their students.

Lack of data is not the problem. Schools typically suffer from what Robert Waterman (1987) has called the DRIP syndrome: they are data rich but information poor. Data alone will not inform a teacher's professional practice and thus cannot become a catalyst for improvement unless those data are put in context to provide a basis for comparison.

The old adage that practice makes perfect is patently false. Those who continue to engage in ineffective practices are unable to improve, much less reach perfection.

The old adage that practice makes perfect is patently false. Those who continue to engage in ineffective practices are unable to improve, much less reach perfection. A student who completes fifty math problems with the same multiplication error repeated over and over has not improved his ability to solve math problems. The golfer who hits bucket after bucket of golf balls with a major flaw in her swing does not improve her ability to make par. And a teacher who uses the same ineffective practices over and over again can work harder and harder at those practices, and still not improve learning for students. What all of the people in these examples require in order to improve are (1) feedback—the more timely, frequent, and precise, the better—and (2) ongoing support as they attempt to implement new practices.

The best way to provide powerful feedback to teachers and to turn data into information *that can improve teaching and learning* is through team-developed and team-analyzed common formative assessments. If the school in this case study, or any school, is to develop the capacity of the faculty to function as a PLC, it must create systems to ensure that each teacher:

1. Receives *frequent and timely feedback* on the performance of his or her students,

2. in meeting an *agreed-upon proficiency standard* established by the collaborative team,

3. on a *valid assessment* created by the team,

4. *in comparison to other students* in the school attempting to meet that same standard.

Finally, the school must also ensure that each teacher has the benefit of a collaborative team to turn to and learn from as he or she explores ways to improve learning for students.

Chapter 3 describes the process teams should use in developing common formative assessments and explains in detail the reasons why such assessments are vital to progressing as a PLC. The power of common formative assessments is diminished, however, if individual teachers are not provided with a basis of comparison as they examine the results for their students.

Educators seeking advice on how to create a results orientation that fosters continuous improvement will hear a consistent message from research (see pages 186–187, How Can We Create a Results Orientation and Foster Continuous Improvement?).

It has been said that collecting data is only the first step toward wisdom: sharing data is the first step toward community. If the school in this case study is to become a professional learning *community*, it must create the structures and the culture to ensure data from common formative assessments become easily accessible and openly shared among teachers who are working together interdependently toward the same SMART goal that represents higher levels of learning for their students. Every teacher should be able to ascertain how the performance of his or her students compares to all similar students taking the same assessment. Only then will individuals and teams receive the information vital to continuous improvement and a focus on results.

What resources can you provide to assist us?

School and district leaders can and should support teams in this process in two very important ways—logistically and culturally. Logistical support means that leaders must ensure that teachers receive the evidence of student learning in a timely and user-friendly manner. The process should not require educators to be data-entry clerks or statisticians. Technology is readily available to provide almost immediate feedback on selected response assessments. Some schools and districts have hired data coaches or data clerks to assist teams with the process. The goal is to present teachers with results that enable them to determine the strengths and weaknesses of their students' learning at a glance.

The use of protocols for examining student achievement data and student work can also make a significant contribution to building a team's capacity to examine evidence of student learning. In chapter 6, we discussed how team norms or collective commitments can help teams clarify how members will work together. Protocols are intended to help focus and shape the conversation as teams examine evidence of student learning and to provide a safe environment for the conversation. Protocols are designed to ensure all voices are heard on the critical issue at hand, to help members look closely at evidence of student learning, to examine success as well as failure, and to help all participants become skillful in facilitating dialogue on the right work (McDonald, Mohr, Dichter, & McDonald, 2007).

How Can We Create a Result Orientation and Foster Continuous Improvement?

PLCs *"require that [team] members reflect openly and honestly together about their own practice, intentionally seeking ways to do their work better and continually building their capacity to do so." Failure to collect, present, and analyze evidence of student learning and the reluctance to make work public are major barriers to effective professional learning communities* (Annenberg Institute for School Reform, 2005).

"One mark of schools that make headway on the achievement gap appears to be their propensity to promote and organize conversations based in evidence of student progress." (Little, 2006, p. 10)

"In our work, we help practitioners frame the next level of work by examining what they are currently doing, looking at evidence of student learning for clues about what is strongest in their practice and where they might see opportunities for improvement, [and] strengthening the capacity of colleagues to work collectively on instructional issues." (Elmore & City, 2007, p. 26)

Excellence in education requires that teachers work in collaborative teams to clarify the learning intentions and success criteria of their lessons, gather evidence of student learning, and discuss the effectiveness of their teaching based on that evidence. "Teachers [need] to share evidence about their teaching with their colleagues"; in fact, "the key question is whether teaching can shift from an immature to mature profession, from opinions to evidence." The education profession will not mature as a profession until professional dialogue focuses on evidence of student learning rather than opinions (Hattie, 2009, pp. 252, 259).

For the first two years, none of the schools in the study experienced gains in student achievement. The dramatic gains only occurred when collaborative teams focused the collaborative inquiry on "jointly and recursively identifying appropriate and worthwhile goals for student learning; finding or developing appropriate means to assess student progress toward those goals; bringing to the table the expertise of colleagues and others who can assist in accomplishing these goals; planning, preparing, and delivering lessons; using evidence from the classroom to evaluate instruction; and, finally, reflecting on the process to determine next steps" (Gallimore et al., 2009, p. 549).

"In high-poverty schools that are helping students learn at high levels, look at student achievement data" to identify which students need additional support and which need greater challenges. But this evidence of student learning is also being used to inform teacher practice. Teachers discuss why one member of the team is having success teaching a particular concept and another is not, and *"what the more successful teacher can teach the less successful teacher"* (Chenoweth, 2009, p. 41).

In schools that double student performance, teachers use results from common unit and interim assessments to help members of collaborative teams compare strategies and adopt those that are most effective. Instructional practice is out in the open, the subject of public and professional conversation, and the source of ongoing, job-embedded professional development (Odden & Archibald, 2009).

"The expansion of Professional Learning Communities (PLCs) is indicative of the increased emphasis on teacher collaboration as the means of powerful professional development. . . . PLCs are an indication of a broader trend toward professional development that is increasingly collaborative, data-driven, and peer facilitated, all with a focus on classroom practice." (Barber & Mourshed, 2009)

Here's What, So What, Now What

Bruce Wellman and Laura Lipton (2004) developed another very versatile protocol called Here's What, So What, Now What. This protocol typically takes thirty to forty-five minutes to complete and, according to Wellman and Lipton, "focuses the team's attention on a specific fact, data point, or idea (Here's What), supports and builds capacity to surface and organize prior knowledge, interpretations and perspectives (So What), and generates implications for changes in a teacher's practice (Now What)" (p. 99).

Teachers in District 96 use the Here's What, So What, Now What protocol to analyze the results of common assessments. The first five minutes of the team meeting (Here's What) are spent analyzing what happened on the assessment. Teams identify such things as which standards the students mastered and problems they encountered. The goal at this point is to identify specific trends, observations, or outcomes and to write factual, nonjudgmental statements that describe those observations. This first step takes little time if teams receive their data in an organized fashion.

The next ten minutes (So What) is spent interpreting what was discovered in the first step of the protocol. The team's discussion focuses on what may have led to the results and why. Examples of topics teachers might discuss at this point include such things as the amount of instructional time allocated to a particular topic or an analysis of a particular item to determine if the problem was one of test construction. Conclusions are written down and saved for a later date when the team may want to look at patterns of student performance over an extended period of time.

The final step in the protocol (Now What) lasts fifteen minutes and promotes data-driven decision making by challenging the team to develop a context for any changes in instruction before moving forward. Team conversations focus on applying what has been learned to instructional practice. At this point, the team may set a short-term SMART goal and engage in action research to address areas of concern.

Project Zero Protocol

Another protocol, adapted from the Collaborative Assessment Conference developed by Harvard's Project Zero, takes the following steps.

1. Team members examine evidence of student learning and/or examples of student work in silence and take notes on their observations.

2. The team leader asks, "What did you see?" Members are asked to make factual, nonevaluative statements.

3. The team leader asks, "What questions does this evidence of student learning raise for you?" Members are asked to speculate

about the thought process of students and gaps in their understanding.

4. Members discuss implications for their teaching.

5. Members establish action plans to act on their learning.

6. Members share their reactions to and assessment of the meeting. (National School Reform Faculty, 1999)

Descriptive Review

Teams can also use protocols to create a safe environment for an individual teacher to pose a problem and seek the help of his or her colleagues. For example, teams at Stevenson High School use a six-step tuning protocol called Descriptive Review as a way to support one another (adapted from Blythe, Allen, & Powell, 1999):

1. **Introduction.** A member of the team presents the results of an assessment or examples of student work to teammates (five minutes).

2. **Teacher presentation.** Members of the team review the presented work as the presenting member explains his concerns or questions. No interruptions or questions are allowed during this presentation (ten minutes).

3. **Clarifying questions.** Participants may ask clarifying questions, but again no discussion is allowed at this point (five minutes).

4. **Feedback.** The team discusses the work together, giving three kinds of feedback each in separate intervals. The presenting teacher listens and takes notes while his or her colleagues talk (ten minutes).

The feedback must directly relate to the assessment or examples of student work at hand. The three kinds of feedback include the following.

    a. Warm feedback—Positive points associated with the work

    b. Cool feedback—Questions, doubts, or possible gaps in the work

    c. Hard feedback—Challenges related to the work

5. **Reflection.** The presenting teacher responds to the feedback given by team members, highlighting new insights, seeking clarifications, and identifying changes to be made (ten minutes).

6. **Debrief.** The team leader solicits feedback regarding the team's perceptions of the process (five minutes).

Student Work Protocol

Gene Thompson-Grove (2000) has adapted the work of Eric Buchovecky to offer the following questions to help guide the collective inquiry of a collaborative team as they examine evidence of student learning:

- What did you see in the students' work that was interesting or surprising?

- What did you learn about how students think and learn? . . .

- What new perspectives did your colleagues provide?

- How can you make use of their perspectives?

- What questions about teaching and assessment did looking at students' work raise for you?

- How can you pursue these questions further?

- Are there things you would like to try in your classroom as a result of looking at the student's work?

Protocols can be a powerful tool to assist teams in their collective inquiry. Teams who use protocols have a more complete and comprehensive understanding of what students know and are able to do, develop a shared language for assessing student work and a common understanding of what quality student work looks like, and are more likely to embrace the PLC concept of collective responsibility for the success of all students (Burke, 2001). Protocols empower people throughout the organization to assess outcomes and to take action to improve them and promote a culture in which "the people who do the work are able, willing, and even eager—in consultation with their colleagues—to make changes as needed in order to make their work more effective" (McDonald et al., 2007, p. 8).

Creating Cultural Supports for Team Analysis of Evidence of Student Learning

School and district leaders must create and support a culture that uses evidence of student learning as an essential element of continuous improvement rather than a punitive tool.

School and district leaders must create and support a culture that uses evidence of student learning as an essential element of continuous improvement rather than a punitive tool. John Hattie (2009) reminds leaders that the key to effective professional dialogue based on results will be their ability "to create school, staffroom, and classroom environments where error is welcomed as a learning opportunity, where discarding incorrect knowledge and understandings is welcomed, and where participants can feel safe to learn, re-learn, and explore knowledge and understanding" (p. 239). Michael Fullan (2010) calls upon those leaders to suspend "judgmentalism" and approach poor results as problem of capacity building: "What can we do to build the capacity of this teacher or school to be more effective in what needs to be done?"

One way to undermine the effectiveness of this collaborative process is to use it to rank, rate, and assess teachers or principals. If four of the most effective teachers in the world each teach a concept to the best of their ability to similar students under similar conditions and create and administer a common assessment, one of them will rank fourth in terms of the results. If four of the most inept teachers in a horribly ineffective school create and administer a common assessment to their students, one would have the best of the bad results. The same analogy applies to ranking principals within a district on the basis of student achievement on the state assessment. The issue is not how teachers or principals rank, but rather how each teacher, each team, and each principal uses the results to get better. If they are demonstrating a commitment to seeking and implementing more effective practices, leaders should focus on supporting their efforts to become more effective. In this way, a school or district uses evidence of student learning to align with the underlying assumption of the continuous improvement philosophy: using *ourselves as benchmarks* and then working to improve upon our previous performance (Gerstner, Semerad, Doyle, & Johnston, 1995).

Conversely, those who demonstrate that they are indifferent to results and unwilling to consider changes in their practice should be dealt with more directly and assertively. We will address that issue in the next chapter.

Part Three

Here's Why

No school that purports to help all students learn can be inattentive to results. The process of becoming a PLC is designed to achieve a very specific purpose: to continuously improve the collective capacity of a group to achieve intended results. Therefore, it is incongruous to engage in elements of the process and ignore results. A focus on results:

- Is essential to organizational effectiveness

- Is essential to the effectiveness of teams

- Is essential to continuous improvement

- Serves as a powerful motivator

A Focus on Results Is Essential to Organizational Effectiveness

Whereas ineffective organizations are "activity centered, a fundamentally flawed logic that confuses ends with means, processes with outcomes" (Schaffer & Thomson, 1998, p. 191), effective organizations "create results driven improvement processes" that focus on achieving specific, measurable improvement goals (p. 193). They put aside beliefs and conventional wisdom and instead gather facts and act on evidence to make informed and intelligent decisions (Pfeffer & Sutton, 2006). They continuously improve and renew by gathering and disseminating comparative data to inform the practice of people throughout the organization (Kanter, 2004; Kotter, 1996). Leaders of these organizations are "fanatically driven, infected with an incurable desire to produce *results*" (Collins, 2001, p. 30), because results are what leadership is all about (Drucker, 1996).

The link between using evidence of results and school effectiveness has been repeatedly cited in the research (see Why Is a Results Orientation the Key to School Effectiveness?).

A Focus on Results Is Essential to Team Effectiveness

Teams that focus on results are more effective than those that center their work on activities and tasks (Katzenbach & Smith, 1993). Whereas inattention to results is characteristic of dysfunctional teams, the "ultimate measure of a great team" is the results it achieves (Lencioni, 2005, p. 69). Teams accomplish the most when they are clear and unambiguous about what they want to achieve, when they clarify how they will measure their progress, and when they create a scoreboard that helps keep them focused on results (Lencioni, 2005). When teams work together to establish measurable goals, collect and analyze data regarding their progress, and monitor and adjust their actions, they produce results that "guide, goad, and motivate groups and individuals" (Schmoker, 1999, p. 38).

A Focus on Results Is Essential to Continuous Improvement

Frederick Winslow Taylor, the father of scientific management, called upon leaders to identify the "one right way" to perform a task and then create systems to ensure that employees adhered to that specific practice. His philosophy, which provided the conceptual framework for the factory assembly line, required management to get it right and then keep it going. Public schools borrowed heavily from scientific management, calling for leaders to select the appropriate inputs and systems (curriculum, schedules, materials) and for workers (that is, teachers) to adhere to the decisions made by others. This legacy has created a tradition in which "schools are structured to reinforce continuity, not continuous improvement" (Consortium on Productivity in Schools, 1995, p. 51).

Why Is a Results Orientation the Key to School Effectiveness?

"An astonishing number of educational leaders make critical decisions about curriculum, instruction, assessment, and placement on the basis of information that is inadequate, misunderstood, misrepresented, or simply absent. Even when information is abundant and clear, I have witnessed leaders who are sincere and decent people stare directly at the information available to them, and then blithely ignore it." (Reeves, 2006, p. 95)

"Strategic leaders are worthy of the name because of their consistent linking of evidence to decision making. They respond to challenges not by scoring rhetorical points but by consistently elevating evidence over assertion." (Reeves, 2002, p. 162)

"School systems must create a culture that places value on managing by results, rather than on managing by programs." (Schlechty, 1997, p. 110)

"It is essential that leaders work to establish a culture where results are carefully assessed and actions are taken based on these assessments." (Schlechty, 2005, p. 11)

Schools committed to improving student learning need information more than ever. They must have a process that gathers authentic and relevant information and use it to identify strengths and weaknesses in a way that pushes people toward continuous improvement (Dolan, 1994).

"Teachers in gap-closing schools more frequently use data to understand the skill gaps of low-achieving students. . . . When data points to a weakness in students' academic skills, gap-closing schools are more likely to focus in on that area, making tough choices to ensure that students are immersed in what they need most." (Symonds, 2004, p. 13)

leaders of PLCs build continuous learning into the work processes of every individual and every team by working with staff to create clearly defined goals, to align activities around those goals, and to clarify measurements of progress.

In contrast, PLCs are committed to continuous improvement, an essential element of any learning organization. Members of PLCs recognize their challenge is not to get it right and keep it going, but to "get it right and make it better and better and better" (Champy, 1995, p. 27). No organization can continue to improve unless the people within it engage in ongoing learning. Therefore, leaders of PLCs build continuous learning into the work processes of every individual and every team by working with staff to create clearly defined goals, to align activities around those goals, and to clarify measurements of progress.

After devoting his career to studying the change process in schools, Michael Fullan (2008) has concluded that continuous improvement is impossible in any organization without "constant transparency," which he defines as "clear and continuous display of results, and clear and continuous access to practice (what is being done to get the results)" (p. 14). Once again, if schools and districts are to meet the challenge of becoming more effective in helping more students learn at higher levels each year, the efforts of educators must be fueled by good information that is available to them on an ongoing basis.

A Focus on Results Can Serve as a Powerful Motivator

Consider the sobering implications of the following two comprehensive research studies. The first, one of the most comprehensive analyses of factors impacting student achievement that has ever been conducted, asserts, "One of the greatest myths of teaching is that all teachers are equal. There is an appreciable amount of variability in the effectiveness of teachers" (Hattie, 2009, p. 250). The author clarifies that "the devil in the story is not the negative, criminal, and incompetent teacher, but the average, let's get through the curricula, behave, be busy, we are 'all friends in here' teacher who has no idea of the damage he or she is doing" (p. 258).

The second study, a report on the top-performing school systems in the world, concludes, "The quality of the education system cannot exceed the quality of its teachers. The only way to improve outcomes is to improve teaching" (Barber & Mourshed, 2009, p. 4). That same report emphasizes that in order to improve teaching, three things must happen:

1. The individual teacher must become aware of specific weaknesses in his or her instruction.

2. The individual teacher must become aware of more effective practices through demonstration in an authentic setting.

3. The teacher must be motivated to make the necessary changes.

We argue that the best strategy for addressing each of these prerequisites for school improvement is team analysis of the results from the common formative assessments, particularly those created by the team itself. This analysis is specifically designed to alert a teacher to weaknesses in instruction and make him or her aware of more effective practices in the most authentic of settings—similar students in the same school who are being more successful in acquiring the same knowledge and skills he or she is teaching.

Most importantly, common formative assessments address the third condition—motivating a teacher to make the necessary changes. The "central challenge" and "core problem" in every phase of any organization's improvement process is "*changing people's behavior*," that is, "what people do, and the need for significant shifts in what people do" (Kotter & Cohen, 2002, p. 2, emphasis in the original). So one of the most fundamental questions that a school or district committed to improving student achievement must address is, "What would motivate educators to make significant changes in their behavior?"

One of the most fundamental questions that a school or district committed to improving student achievement must address is, "What would motivate educators to make significant changes in their behavior?"

For decades, school districts have used the process of formal teacher evaluation to foster improvement in the professional practice of teachers despite overwhelming evidence of the ineffectiveness of that strategy. A U.S. survey revealed that three out of four teachers feel they receive absolutely no benefit from the teacher evaluation process in their school (Duffett, Farkas, Rotherham, & Silva, 2008). Another survey found that less than 1 percent of teachers were evaluated as unsatisfactory; in fact, 94 percent of teachers in districts that use multiple-leveled ratings received one of the top two ratings. That study concluded that most teacher evaluation does not recognize good teaching, leaves poor teaching unaddressed, and "does not inform decision-making in any meaningful way" (Weisberg, Sexton, Mulhem, & Keeling, 2009, p. 1).

James Popham (2009) agrees. In listing some of the biggest mistakes that have been made in education over the past fifty years, he included the focus on instruction as one of those mistakes. Robert Marzano (2009), one of the United States' leading researchers on effective teaching, agrees that focusing on the instructional practices of teachers is ineffective because none of those practices is guaranteed to work in all situations. He contends the "checklist approach" to providing teachers with feedback that is often used in teacher evaluation "probably doesn't enhance instructional expertise [and] in fact, such practice is antithetical to true reflective practice" (p. 37). An international study of teaching in mathematics concluded that "there is not one way to teach effectively, but many" (Stigler & Hiebert, 2009, p. 34).

So if we know that changes in adult behavior and practice are essential to implementing the PLC process, and we also know that supervising individual teachers to ensure they use specific instructional practices fails to bring about those changes, the question remains: what would motivate educators to make significant changes in their behavior? Popham (2009, p. 37) advises, "It is only sensible [that educators] should be focused on student learning results" to continuously improve teaching. Marzano (2009) concludes that "the ultimate criterion for successful teaching should be student knowledge gain. . . . In terms of providing teachers with feedback, the focus must always be on student learning" (p. 35). Hattie (2009) insists that improving teaching requires a collective process based on evidence of student learning. He contends that until our profession begins to be guided by evidence of student learning rather than subjective opinions, war stories, or post-hoc justification, there is little hope for significant school improvement. Their message to educators is consistent: focus not on teaching, but on evidence of student learning.

Focus not on teaching, but on evidence of student learning.

But what evidence of learning would be so persuasive that it might motivate a veteran teacher to change his or her instructional practice? Point out that similar students in the next classroom are earning better grades, and the teacher is likely to accuse his or her colleague of grade inflation or a lack of standards. Reveal that students taught by other teachers consistently score higher on the state or provincial assessment, and the teacher may argue that assessment focuses on lower-level knowledge rather than the higher-order thinking skills that he or she teaches.

Effective use of team-developed common assessments is the best strategy we know of for providing that irrefutable evidence.

These arguments are much more difficult to sustain, however, when the teacher has contributed to creating an assessment that he or she agrees is a valid instrument for gathering evidence regarding whether or not students have acquired the knowledge and skills that the teacher has identified as most essential. *The most powerful lever for changing professional practice is concrete evidence of irrefutably better results* (Elmore, 2003; Fullan, 2008; Patterson et al., 2008). As Richard Elmore (2010) writes, "Adult beliefs about what children can learn are changed by watching students do things that the adults didn't believe that they—the students—could do" (p. 8). Effective use of team-developed common assessments is the best strategy we know of for providing that irrefutable evidence.

Another powerful lever for changing behavior is the positive peer pressure and support that comes with being a member of a team. When people work in isolation, their success or failure has little or no direct and immediate bearing on others. When people work interdependently to achieve a common goal for which all members are mutually accountable, the performance of each individual directly impacts the ability of the team to achieve its goal. This interdependence and reluctance to let colleagues down can be an effective catalyst for changing behavior (Blanchard, 2007; Fullan, 2008; Lencioni, 2005; Patterson et al., 2008).

Once again, the collective analysis of evidence of student learning from multiple common assessments is ideally suited to utilize the power of positive peer pressure and support. Transparency of results makes it very difficult for people to hide or to duck their responsibility to their students or their teammates (Chenoweth, 2009; Kanter, 2004). An educator who can feign compliance or find excuses for poor results in a hierarchical system will find it increasingly problematic to remain disengaged or ignore results when the achievement of his or her students routinely prevents the team from accomplishing its goal.

In summary, consider this series of assertions:

1. The key to the ability of schools to impact student learning is the collective expertise of the educators within a school or district.

2. Improved student learning will require improved professional practice.

3. Improved professional practice will require educators to change many of their traditional practices.

4. Among the most powerful motivators for persuading educators to change their practice are (1) concrete evidence of irrefutably better results and (2) the positive peer pressure and support inherent in working interdependently with others to achieve a common goal.

5. The best strategy for utilizing these motivators and improving professional practice is engaging members of a collaborative team in the individual and collective analysis of team-developed common formative assessments on a regular basis as part of the teaching and learning process.

In schools and districts that are progressing as PLCs, teams gather and collaborate about data and use data to monitor student learning and to set SMART goals. Members of the team understand their individual roles and responsibilities and work together to achieve their targets. Finally, in PLCs, teams view data as an essential component of their process of continuous improvement. They use the results of every common assessment to identify individual students who need additional time and support for learning, to discover strengths and weaknesses in their teaching, and to inform and adjust their practice to increase the likelihood they will achieve their shared purpose: higher levels of learning for all students. They are not satisfied with taking a few half-steps on the road to becoming a PLC. They commit fully to stay the course.

In PLCs, teams view data as an essential component of their process of continuous improvement.

Once again, there is no recipe or step-by-step manual for becoming a PLC, but there are some things that *must* be done as part of the process. Using results to inform and improve practice is one of those things, and schools that are sincere in their desire to create a PLC will act accordingly. Inattention to results is antithetical to becoming a PLC.

Part Four

Assessing Your Place on the PLC Journey

Complete the PLC continuum and Where Do We Go From Here? worksheets as outlined in chapter 2.

The Professional Learning Communities at Work™ Continuum: Focusing on Results (Part II)

DIRECTIONS: Individually, silently, and *honestly* assess the current reality of your school's implementation of each indicator listed in the left column. Consider what evidence or anecdotes support your assessment. This form may also be used to assess district or team implementation.

Individuals, teams, and schools seek relevant data and information and use it to promote continuous improvement.

Indicator	Pre-Initiating	Initiating	Implementing	Developing	Sustaining
Collaborative teams of teachers regard ongoing analysis of evidence of student learning as a critical element in the teaching and learning process. Teachers are provided with frequent and timely information regarding the achievement of their students. They use that information to: ■ Respond to students who are experiencing difficulty ■ Enrich and extend the learning of students who are proficient ■ Inform and improve the individual and collective practice of members ■ Identify team professional development needs ■ Measure progress toward team goals	The only process for monitoring student learning is the individual classroom teacher and annual state, provincial, or national assessments. Assessment results are used primarily to report on student progress rather than to improve professional practice. Teachers fall into a predictable pattern: they teach, they test, they hope for the best, and then they move on to the next unit.	The district has created benchmark assessments that are administered several times throughout the year. There is often considerable lag time before teachers receive the results. Most teachers pay little attention to the results. They regard the assessment as perhaps beneficial to the district but of little use to them. Principals are encouraged to review the results of state assessments with staff, but the fact that the results aren't available until months after the assessment and the lack of specificity mean they are of little use in helping teachers improve their practice.	Teams have been asked to create and administer common formative assessments and to analyze the results together. Many teachers are reluctant to share individual teacher results and want the analysis to focus on the aggregate performance of the group. Some use the results to identify questions that caused students difficulty so they can eliminate the questions. Many teams are not yet using the analysis of results to inform or improve professional practice.	The school has created a specific process to bring teachers together multiple times throughout the year to analyze results from team-developed common assessments, district assessments, and state or provincial and national assessments. Teams use the results to identify areas of concern and to discuss strategies for improving the results.	Teachers are hungry for information on student learning. All throughout the year, each member of a collaborative team receives information that illustrates the success of his or her students in achieving an agreed-upon essential standard on team-developed common assessments he or she helped create, in comparison to all the students attempting to achieve that same standard. Teachers use the results to identify the strengths and weaknesses in their individual practice, to learn from one another, to identify areas of curriculum proving problematic for students, to improve their collective capacity to help all students learn, and to identify students in need of intervention or enrichment. They also analyze results from district, state or provincial, and national assessments and use them to validate their team assessments.

Where Do We Go From Here? Worksheet
Turning Data Into Information

Indicator of a PLC at Work	What steps or activities must be initiated to create this condition in your school?	Who will be responsible for initiating or sustaining these steps or activities?	What is a realistic timeline for each step or phase of the activity?	What will you use to assess the effectiveness of your initiative?
Collaborative teams of teachers regard ongoing analysis of evidence of student learning as a critical element in the teaching and learning process. Teachers are provided with frequent and timely information regarding the achievement of their students. They use that information to: ■ Respond to students who are experiencing difficulty ■ Enrich and extend the learning of students who are proficient ■ Inform and improve the individual and collective practice of members ■ Identify team professional development needs ■ Measure progress toward team goals				

Part Five

Tips for Moving Forward: Creating Results Orientation

1 **Provide the basis of comparison that translates data into information.** Remember that data alone will not help individuals or teams improve. They need the context of valid comparison to identify strengths and weaknesses.

2 **Use apples-to-apples comparisons.** Comparisons are most informative when conditions are similar. Schools with students from high-performing communities often take great satisfaction in "comparing" the performance of their students to state averages, but such comparisons do little to promote improvement. If a school places students into classrooms on the basis of multiple ability groups, it accomplishes little to compare the performance of students in the highest group to those in the lowest. Equivalent situations yield the most meaningful comparisons. Remember the admonition (Gerstner et al., 1995) that the comparisons most effective in promoting continuous improvement are comparisons to ourselves: what evidence do we have that we are becoming more effective?

3 **Use balanced assessments.** No single assessment source yields the comprehensive results necessary to inform and improve practice. The best strategy to gather results is to seek *balanced assessment* (National Education Association, 2003; Stiggins & DuFour, 2009). Part of that balance is between summative assessments *of* learning and formative assessments *for* learning. Summative state and provincial assessments provide an important accountability tool for schools and districts. They demonstrate how local students perform compared to others in the state or province seeking the same outcomes, and they provide a means to certify the validity of local formative assessments. Common formative assessments created within a school or district can direct teacher practice and identify students needing assistance on a timely basis. Both are important and should be utilized in a school or district assessment program.

Balanced assessment can also refer to using different types of formative assessments based upon the knowledge or skills students are called upon to demonstrate. Rather than relying exclusively on one kind of assessment—multiple-choice tests, performance-based assessments, constructed-response tests, and so on—teachers should attempt to determine the best evidence of student learning and the most effective ways to gather that evidence. Schools and teams must develop multiple ways for students to demonstrate proficiency.

 A fixation with results does not mean inattention to people. There are those who suggest an organization committed to results will be inattentive to the needs of the people within it, willing to sacrifice individuals on the altar of the bottom line. These people fall victim to the Tyranny of Or. Professional learning communities are committed to both results and relationships. They recognize that the best way to achieve the collective purpose of the group is through collaborative relationships that foster the ongoing growth and development of the people who produce the results. They recognize that the very key to school improvement is people improvement, and they commit to creating cultures that help individuals become more proficient, effective, and fulfilled by virtue of the fact that they work in that school or district.

Part Six

Questions to Guide the Work of Your Professional Learning Community

To Assess the Results Orientation of Your School or District, Ask:

1. What evidence do we have that district goals are directly impacting the work of schools and collaborative teams within schools?

2. Have we identified the evidence we must gather to determine if all students are acquiring the knowledge, skills, and dispositions we have determined are most essential? What does that evidence include?

3. Do we provide students with a variety of ways to demonstrate they are proficient? Can we identify a variety of ways in which students in our school are able to demonstrate they are proficient? What does our list include?

4. Who analyzes evidence of student learning in our school and district? What happens as a result of that analysis? What evidence can we cite that it impacts classroom practice?

5. Does our assessment program enable us to identify, on a timely basis, students who need extra time and support for learning? At what point does our systematic process enable us to identify students who require intervention?

6. Does our assessment program provide every teacher with timely and valid feedback on the extent to which his or her students are becoming proficient in comparison to other similar students in our school or district who are attempting to meet the same standard? If not, what steps must we take to provide every teacher with this timely information?

7. Do we have a balanced assessment program that includes formative and summative assessments, local and state or provincial assessments, and a variety of performance-based and written assessments?

8. Do we use evidence of student learning as part of a continuous improvement process? Is our assessment program helping us become better as a school?

9. Does our assessment program encourage or discourage student learning?

Part Seven

Dangerous Detours and Seductive Shortcuts

Beware of attempts to outsource the work of analyzing evidence of student learning. Although a central office can and should provide the resources to ensure that schools and teams receive information on student learning in a timely, easily interpreted, user-friendly format, educators in the building should not be exempt from doing their own analysis of the information. "There is no substitute for classroom-by-classroom, school-by-school analysis" by the people who are called upon to develop the improvement strategies: teachers and principals (Reeves, 2002, p. 107).

A school that is committed to helping all students acquire the most essential skills and concepts must consider the achievement of each student, skill by skill.

Don't focus on "averages" when analyzing student achievement data. A school that is committed to helping all students acquire the most essential skills and concepts must consider the achievement of each student, skill by skill. Analysis that focuses on class averages ("The average score in my class was 80 percent") can obscure the fact that many students failed to demonstrate proficiency. Indicating that an individual student achieved an overall score of 85 percent on assessment of five different skills may not reveal he was far below proficient on one of the skills. Remember, analysis must be student by student and skill by skill.

Don't engage in superficial analysis. It may be understandable that teams begin their common assessments with selected responses because they are easier to score, but the nature of your assessment should be determined on the basis of acquiring the best, most useful, most authentic information regarding student learning. Move beyond item analysis and merely tweaking the wording of questions. Dig deeper until you are able to identify which students need help with learning specific skills. Keep digging until you can identify who, if anyone, was particularly effective at teaching that skill. Learn from one another. Identify problem areas, develop an action plan to address them, and gather evidence to determine if the new strategies were more effective.

Final Thoughts

Now that we have considered the elements of a professional learning community at work in a school, let's consider the role of the central office in implementing and supporting the PLC process throughout an entire district. Chapter 8 explores that role.

Implementing the PLC Process Districtwide

Part One

The Case Study: The High Cost of Failing to Speak With One Voice

Superintendent Matt Ditka prided himself as a take charge, action-oriented leader who wanted the very best for all of the schools in the Dunning-Kruger School District. When he identified a powerful concept or program that he felt would improve the district, he was determined to do whatever was necessary to introduce it to educators in every school.

Ditka was particularly enthused about the professional learning community concept after attending an institute on the topic. He was convinced that it offered the most promising strategy for sustained and substantive improvement for the schools in his district, and he resolved to make implementation of the concept a districtwide initiative. He provided the board of education with information about PLCs and persuaded the board to adopt a goal to implement the concept throughout the district. He also was able to win board approval for funding to train the principals and teacher leaders from every school to ensure they had the knowledge, skills, and tools to bring the PLC concept to life in their schools. He purchased books on the PLC concept for each member of the central office cabinet and every principal, and he encouraged them to visit schools that had been identified as model PLCs.

Ditka charged the district's professional development department to provide the PLC training. The department created a plan to provide six days of training for the principal and five representatives of each of the district's 150 schools. Each of the training sessions was designed to build upon the knowledge and concepts presented at earlier sessions. The district's financial commitment to the initiative was extraordinary. The cost of securing 4,500 substitute teachers to cover classes for all of the staff who attended the training represented a major investment in this districtwide goal.

Superintendent Ditka directed his five area assistant superintendents to oversee implementation. Each of these administrators supervised about thirty schools, but they took very different approaches to the PLC initiative. Two of the assistant superintendents attended every day of training and huddled with principals at lunch each day to discuss their concerns and answer their questions. At the end of the training, they stipulated that all of the principals in their area were expected to address certain nondiscretionary priorities, and they clarified the indicators they would monitor to assess the progress that each school was making. From that point on, all of their meetings with principals focused on addressing and resolving PLC implementation questions.

Two other assistant superintendents were convinced that administrative mandates were ineffective in improving schools. They believed that their job was to provide educators with exposure to ideas and concepts, but to avoid top-down mandates. So they asked the principals and teacher leaders in their schools to attend the training in the hope that making them aware of the PLC concept would motivate them to act upon the concept. These assistant superintendents attended some of the training; however, they left the question of implementation to the discretion of each principal.

The last of the assistant superintendents did not attend the training, nor did she stipulate that principals were to attend. She informed her principals of the number of participants they were expected to send to each session, but she offered no other direction. Many of the principals in her area did not attend any of the training. In several instances, principals sent a different group of teachers to each of the sessions. These participants had no background on what had occurred during earlier training and no clear reason as to why they were attending.

Two years later, Superintendent Ditka had to acknowledge that the district's PLC initiative had produced very uneven results. Some of the schools had made tremendous strides, experienced significant gains in student achievement, and had energized their staffs with the positive momentum they were experiencing. Other schools had dabbled in some elements of the PLC concept but had little to show for their efforts. Still others had done virtually nothing. He was puzzled. He had clarified the goal of transforming all of the district's schools into PLCs, secured the board's support, and publicly announced the initiative to the community and to educators throughout the district. He had asked the professional development department to create a plan to provide training to representative staff from every school. He had devoted district resources to support that extensive training. Why were there such dramatic differences in the quality of implementation when all schools had been operating under the same directive, were the beneficiaries of the same plan, and provided the same level of support? Why had his effort to create the PLC concept throughout the district yielded such disappointing results?

> ### Reflection
>
> Can a central office successfully implement a substantive improvement initiative in schools throughout the district, or is school improvement something that must occur one building at a time?

Part Two

Here's How

Superintendent Ditka has done a lot of things right in this scenario. He made an effort to build shared knowledge about PLCs with his board and his administrators through articles, books, visitations, and dialogue. He secured the support of the board in articulating that the implementation of the PLC concept was a district priority. He attempted to foster a district culture that was simultaneously loose and tight by publicly articulating what was to be tight—all schools were to function as PLCs. He provided training to assist representatives from each school in implementing the concept. He directed resources to support the initiative. What went wrong? What more could he have done?

Despite his well-intentioned efforts, Superintendent Ditka had forgotten the central message of this book. Talking is not doing. Planning is not doing. Goal setting is not doing. Training is not doing. Even directing resources to support a plan is not doing. It is not until people are *doing* differently that any organization can expect different results, and this district failed to take steps to ensure that the talking, planning, and training actually resulted in action.

Talking is not doing. Planning is not doing. Goal setting is not doing. Training is not doing.

What Questions

Thus, those who hope to lead implementation of the PLC process on a districtwide basis must be prepared to address the following questions:

- What are our priorities?

- What are the specific conditions we expect to see in every school?

- What must we do to build the capacity of people throughout the organization to create these conditions?

- What indicators of progress will we monitor?

- What district practices and leadership behaviors are not aligned with the purpose and priorities we have articulated?

The challenge for Superintendent Ditka, and for any leader who hopes to improve student achievement, is to engage all members of the organization in processes to:

- Clarify priorities

- Clarify the specific conditions that must be created in each school to achieve the priorities

- Build the capacity of people throughout the organization to succeed in what they are being called upon to do

- Establish indicators of progress to be monitored carefully

- Align leadership behaviors with the articulated purpose and priorities

Establishing Clear Purpose and Priorities

It is commonplace for a district to adopt a mission statement articulating a commitment to helping all students learn. It is not unusual for a district to announce that it intends to help all students learn by transforming their schools into professional learning communities. What is very rare, however, is for district leaders to articulate exactly what they expect to see in schools that are functioning as professional learning communities.

In *Raising the Bar and Closing the Gap*, we examined three very diverse districts that had raised student achievement in every one of their schools. In every instance, the superintendent not only emphasized that the district was committed to helping all students learn by transforming schools into PLCs, but they also were very specific about the conditions they expected to see in each school. They established specific parameters and priorities for what was to occur in each school, and then provided the staff at individual schools with a degree of autonomy regarding how the school would address the priorities within the parameters. These leaders were masterful at what we have called simultaneous loose-tight leadership or the "defined autonomy" characteristic of effective district leaders (Marzano & Waters, 2009).

After taking time to build shared knowledge about the PLC concept throughout their districts, all three of the superintendents stipulated that they expected every school to:

- Organize staff into collaborative teams

- Ensure each team had created a guaranteed and viable curriculum that provided all students with access to essential knowledge and skills, regardless of the teacher to whom they were assigned

- Ensure each team had created a series of frequent common formative assessments to monitor the learning of each student on a timely basis and to inform and improve professional practice

■ Create a schoolwide plan for intervention and enrichment that guaranteed students who experienced difficulty would receive additional time and support for learning in a timely, directive, and systematic way and that those who were proficient would be given the opportunity to extend and enrich their learning

The superintendents presented a detailed rationale for their directives. Ultimately, however, they were *tight* on what they expected to see in each school at the same time that they were *loose* in terms of implementation. Each school had a significant degree of autonomy regarding how they would create the conditions, but no school could ignore the stipulation that they would address this district priority.

Limit Initiatives

Once these specific priorities were established, the superintendents pledged to protect schools from competing initiatives so educators throughout the district could focus on creating these conditions for an extended period of time. Veteran educators have become inured to the sheer volume of frequent, fragmented, and uncoordinated new projects, programs, and reforms that wash upon them in waves. They suffer from what Doug Reeves (2004) has called the "irrefutable law of initiative fatigue" (p. 59) as each new improvement scheme they are called upon to adopt saps energy, resources, and attention from those that preceded it. These highly effective superintendents avoided initiative fatigue by stipulating that building the capacity of staff to function as professional learning communities was not one of many strategies for improving student achievement but instead represented *the* district strategy for accomplishing that goal. Furthermore, they announced that they would sustain their commitment to and focus on that strategy for years to come.

These highly effective superintendents avoided initiative fatigue by stipulating that building the capacity of staff to function as professional learning communities was not one of many strategies for improving student achievement but instead represented the district strategy for accomplishing that goal.

Build Principal Capacity to Lead the PLC Process

Each of the superintendents recognized that the principal plays the pivotal role in implementing the PLC process in the school setting. They also recognized that if they were to hold principals accountable for developing their staffs into high-performing PLCs, reciprocal accountability demanded that central office leaders provide principals with the knowledge, skills, resources, and training to be successful in what they were being called upon to do.

The superintendents of these effective districts began by helping principals develop a deeper understanding of the PLC process by providing them with training, sending them to visit schools that were functioning as high-performing PLCs, and leading them in reading books and articles on the process. Second, they turned the district principals' meetings into a collaborative and collective effort to identify and resolve any implementation challenges. These meetings were now used to rehearse and role-play what principals would be called upon to do back in their buildings. For example, prior to asking teams to establish norms, a principals' meeting would be devoted to helping principals articulate a rationale for team norms and gathering the tools, templates, and resources they could use to help their teams complete this task.

Most importantly, each principal was called upon to present a progress report to the central office cabinet and to their fellow principals on how implementation was proceeding in his or her school. The presentation began with an explanation as to how the particular school had addressed the specific conditions expected of all schools. Principals were to explain how teachers had been organized into teams, how they were given time to collaborate, how the principal was monitoring the work of the teams to ensure they were creating a guaranteed curriculum and common formative assessments, how the results of the assessments were being used by teams, and how the school was providing for systematic intervention and enrichment. Principals also presented artifacts and evidence of the work of teams, a comprehensive analysis of student achievement data, and the specific strategies the school had identified to build on strengths and resolve concerns related to student achievement. The central office staff and other principals then provided suggestions to help the principal succeed. In short, these superintendents were asking principals to model what they were asking of teachers by working collaboratively with colleagues rather than independently, making student achievement data easily accessible and openly shared among the members of their team, seeking best practices, helping each other build on strengths and address weaknesses, and taking an interest in and contributing to one another's success. Thus, administrative meetings blended both pressure to hold principals accountable and support to help them meet the challenge of leading a PLC.

Monitor Progress

Each of the superintendents recognized that merely announcing new priorities, strategies, or goals does nothing to improve a school or district. They were very attentive to monitoring the progress of implementation in all of their schools and quick to respond when a school was not moving forward. The new format for principals' meetings was one very effective way to monitor implementation, as principals had to demonstrate to the central office cabinet and their peers exactly what they had done to lead the PLC process in their schools. But since the very purpose of helping schools function as PLCs was to improve results, the central office leaders also monitored progress by establishing a few results-oriented improvement goals for the district and calling upon schools and teams to establish SMART goals that aligned with the district goals.

Aligning Leadership Behavior With the District's Purpose and Priorities

One of the biggest mistakes Superintendent Ditka made in the scenario was not monitoring the work of his own central office to ensure that district leaders were modeling their own commitment to the stated purpose and priorities. Albert Schweitzer insisted, "Example isn't the main thing in influencing others, it's the only thing." In every instance of effective systemwide implementation of the PLC process we have witnessed, central office leaders visibly modeled the commitment to learning for all students, collaboration, collective inquiry, and results orientation they expected to see in other educators throughout the district. They created structures and processes to help principals and teachers function as collaborative teams. They celebrated progress and confronted individuals whose actions did not reflect the district's priorities. They recognized the need to "impose on themselves congruence between deeds and words, between behavior and professed beliefs and values" (Drucker, 1992, p. 117), because behavior inconsistent with alleged priorities would "overwhelm all other forms of communication" (Kotter, 1996, p. 90).

In every instance of effective systemwide implementation of the PLC process we have witnessed, central office leaders visibly modeled the commitment to learning for all students, collaboration, collective inquiry, and results orientation they expected to see in other educators throughout the district.

Part Three

Here's Why

The first two decades of research on how to improve student learning focused, for the most part, on the individual teacher and individual school rather than the district. More recently, research has not only focused on the role of the central office in school improvement, but has also become more specific in offering recommendations.

The Need for Central Office Leadership

After decades of studying the change process in districts, Michael Fullan (2007) has concluded that the fundamental challenge is the "too loose/too tight" dilemma. Tight, top-down leadership that dictates and micromanages every detail of the process is ineffective because it fails to generate the necessary commitment, ownership, and clarity vital to sustainable improvement. Loose, bottom-up leadership that leaves every aspect of school improvement to the discretion of each school site has proven to be even less effective (Elmore, 2003; Kruse, Seashore Louis, & Bryk, 1995; Schlechty, 2005). In fact, site-based management has been found to have a negative correlation with improved student achievement (Marzano & Waters, 2009).

Fullan (2008) concludes the solution to the too tight/too loose leadership dilemma does come from the top. Districts that create a simultaneously loose and tight culture "do not require less leadership at the top, but rather more—more of a different kind" (p. 41), leadership that fosters continuous improvement and purposeful peer interaction in the pursuit of clear priorities within specific parameters. These districts then hold school leadership teams responsible for addressing the priorities; however, they also provide the teams with both a great deal of freedom for operating within the parameters at the school site and the support to foster their success (Elmore, 2003; Marzano & Waters, 2009).

In his three decades of work examining school improvement, Larry Lezotte arrived at a similar conclusion regarding the significance of central office leadership in school improvement. The initial focus on the Effective School movement was the individual school site. Over time, however, Lezotte (2002) and his colleagues recognized that school improvement resulting in increased student achievement could only be sustained with strong district direction and support.

A synthesis of research studies on improved school districts conducted since 1990 reinforced the importance of strong district leadership. It concluded that effective district leaders established a *"clear understanding of the district and school roles"* characterized by a "balance between district control and school autonomy" (Shannon & Bylsma, 2004, p. 45, emphasis added).

The Need for Specificity

A district's simultaneous loose and tight culture will impact student and adult learning in a positive way only if the district is "tight" on the right things.

Of course, a district's simultaneous loose and tight culture will impact student and adult learning in a positive way only if the district is "tight" on the right things. A study of districts that were able to double student achievement found that those districts clarified what students were to learn, used formative assessments to monitor their learning, intervened for struggling students with extended learning time, used evidence of student learning to inform and improve their professional practice, and established collaborative relationships with widely dispersed leadership. As the authors concluded,

> It should be no surprise that one result of the multiplicity of activities was a collaborative, professional school culture—what some refer to as a "professional learning community." . . . Leaders understood that the way to attain their ambitious goals was to develop what is commonly called a "professional learning community" today. (Odden & Archibald, 2009, p. 78)

However, many district-level leaders that call for the schools to function as PLCs "lack a clear understanding of how they could engage in the work or provide the system-level supports necessary to sustain learning communities" (Annenberg Institute for School Reform, 2005, p. 6). Superintendent Ditka would have been far more effective in bringing about substantive improvement if he went beyond using the term *PLC* and instead clarified the specific expectations of the practices and processes he expected in each school. It is not imperative that district leaders use the term *professional learning community* in clarifying how schools are to operate. It is imperative, however, that when stipulating the specific conditions they expect to see in each school, those conditions reflect the practices of PLCs.

In their study of high-performing districts, Allan Odden and Sarah Archibald (2009) found central office leaders helped create the culture of professional learning community in schools throughout the district by insisting educators do what PLCs do. These leaders didn't change existing assumptions, beliefs, and expectations in order to get people to act in new ways: they got people to act in new ways in order to change assumptions, beliefs, and expectations. As organizational theorists John Kotter and Dan Cohen (2002) conclude:

> It is essential to understand a fundamental and widely misunderstood aspect of organizational change. In a change effort, culture comes last, not first. . . . A culture truly changes only when a new way of operating has been shown to succeed over some minimum period of time. . . . You can create new behaviors that reflect the desired culture. But those new behaviors will not become norms, will not take hold, until the very end of the process. (pp. 175–176)

The Need for a Common Language

But even if district leaders themselves are aware of what must be tight, they face the challenge of communicating so effectively that people all throughout the organization are clear on priorities and parameters. This will not happen unless leaders help to establish a common language with widely shared meanings of key terminology. If key terms are only vaguely understood or represent different things to people throughout the district, it will be impossible to implement the PLC concept across a district. Changing the way people talk in an organization can change they way they work (Kegan & Lahey, 2001), but only if there is a common language and clear understanding of the specific implications for *action* regarding key terms (Pfeffer & Sutton, 2000).

What Gets Monitored Gets Done

Superintendent Ditka was decisive about establishing the PLC concept in schools throughout the district, but he failed to recognize that a decision, by itself, changes nothing unless there are mechanisms in place to monitor implementation (Pfeffer & Sutton, 2000). He did nothing to monitor what the assistant superintendents were doing to support the initiative. He put no process in place to assess progress that schools were making. He established no benchmarks to clarify what was to be accomplished by when.

Once again, one of the most powerful ways leaders communicate priorities is by clarifying the indicators of progress they will track, and then creating the systems they will use to monitor those indicators on an ongoing basis (Buckingham, 2005). A key characteristic of transformational learning-centered leadership is establishing processes for monitoring priorities (Goldring, Porter, Murphy, Elliott, & Cravens, 2007), and effective districts continually monitor progress toward clearly defined goals (Marzano & Waters, 2009). Clear focus, careful monitoring, and persistence are essential to bringing about change in any organization (Fullan, 2007).

The Need to Develop the Capacity of Principals to Lead the PLC Process

One of the most consistent findings of the research on PLCs is the vital role played by the principal in implementing the PLC process at the school site (see Why Is Principal Leadership So Important?).

Given the vital importance of the principalship to the effective implementation of the PLC process, it only makes sense that district leaders would devote time and resources to developing the capacity of principals to lead the process. Initial training is certainly important, but ongoing support is even more vital. And finally, the best way to help principals learn to lead a PLC is to call upon them to do so.

A review of effective leadership development strategies concluded that the most powerful way to build the capacity of an individual to lead is not classroom training, but rather job-embedded challenges that are directly linked to the person's ongoing work, the organization's goals, and its strategies for improvement. As Gina Hernez-Broome and Richard Hughes (2004, p. 27) conclude:

> Leadership development today means providing people opportunities to learn from their work rather than taking them away from their work to learn . . . best practice organizations recognize leadership as a key component of jobs at all levels and are committed to creating leaders throughout their organizations. Increasingly, organizations have CEOs who model leadership development through a strong commitment to teach leaders internally.

Another study of best practice in developing leaders agreed that the most powerful strategy for developing leaders is providing them with meaningful experiences that integrate three components. The first is *assessment*—clarifying what the organization needs from the leader and the individual's ability to fulfill that need. The second is *challenge*—putting the individual in a situation in which he or she is challenged to accomplish something that is new to him or her and is important to the effectiveness of the organization. The third is *support*—providing the individual with the ongoing coaching and feedback necessary to meet the challenge (McCauley & Van Velsor, 2003).

Why Is Principal Leadership So Important?

"Principals are widely seen as indispensable to innovation. No reform effort, however worthy, survives a principal's indifference or opposition. When they are asked to lead projects they don't fully grasp or endorse, they are likely to be ambivalent. Central office must remember the importance of allowing time for principals to thrash out their questions as they relate to changes." (Evans, 2001, p. 202)

"Indeed, there are virtually no documented instances of troubled schools being turned around without intervention by a powerful leader. Many other factors may contribute to such turnarounds, but leadership is the catalyst." (Leithwood, Seashore Louis, Anderson, & Wahlstrom, 2004, p. 5)

We found the strongest relationships (in high-poverty/high-performing schools) were between leadership and professional community. Leadership is an important factor in shaping professional community among teachers (Mid-continent Research for Education and Learning, 2005).

"If you take the principal and other key building leaders out of the picture as a committed and skillful force for these qualities, then no successful PLC will form. The possibilities of all other forces combined (state education law and policy, standardized testing and accountability, central office staff development, parent and community pressure) to raise student achievement are fatally weakened." (Saphier, 2005, p. 38)

"Principals arguably are the most important players affecting the character and consequence of teachers' school-site professional communities. Principals are culture-makers, intentionally or not." (McLaughlin & Talbert, 2006, p. 80)

"I know of no improving school that doesn't have a principal who is good at leading improvement." (Fullan, 2007, p. 160)

"Principal leadership is an important facilitating factor in determining the level of professional community." (Goldring et al., 2007, p. 8, summarizing findings of Bryk, Camburn, & Louis, 1999)

"[Positive] outcomes are unlikely in the absence of building leadership that supports and holds teacher teams accountable for sustaining the inquiry process until they see tangible results." (Gallimore et al., 2009, p. 544)

This is precisely what effective superintendents do in developing the leadership capacity of principals. They work with principals to identify the specific skills and vital behaviors that are essential to leading the PLC process in schools. They then call upon principals to demonstrate those skills and behaviors in the context of their ongoing work in schools. They align the processes and structures of the organization to support the new skills and behaviors, engage in collective study to address challenges, construct situations that allow for deliberate practice, and provide ongoing coaching and support. They establish specific goals and expectations that stretch individuals, they use the power of positive peer pressure to challenge each individual, and they also are attentive to providing the assistance to help their people succeed. They demonstrate reciprocal accountability at its best.

Part Four

Assessing Your Place on the PLC Journey

Complete the PLC continuum and Where Do We Go From Here? worksheets as outlined in chapter 2.

The Professional Learning Communities at Work™ Continuum: Implementing a PLC Districtwide

DIRECTIONS: Individually, silently, and *honestly* assess the current reality of your school's implementation of each indicator listed in the left column. Consider what evidence or anecdotes support your assessment. This form may also be used to assess district or team implementation.

The central office leadership provides the clear parameters and priorities, ongoing support, systems for monitoring progress, and sustained focus essential to implementing the professional learning community process in schools throughout the district.

Indicator	Pre-Initiating	Initiating	Implementing	Developing	Sustaining
The district has demonstrated a sustained commitment to improving schools by developing the capacity of school personnel to function as a PLC. District leaders have been explicit about specific practices they expect to see in each school, have created processes to support principals in implementing those practices, and monitor the progress of implementation.	There is no focused and sustained districtwide process for improving schools. Improvement efforts tend to be disconnected, episodic, and piecemeal. Projects come and go, but the cultures of schools remain largely unaffected.	The district has announced that schools should operate as professional learning communities and may have articulated a rationale in support of PLCs, but the concept remains ambiguous, and educators at the school site view it as just one of many initiatives raining down upon them from the central office. Little is done to monitor implementation. Some central office leaders and principals demonstrate indifference to the initiative.	Central office leaders made a concerted effort to build shared knowledge and to establish a common language regarding the PLC process throughout the district. They have called for schools to operate as PLCs and clarified some of the specific structural changes to support teacher collaboration and systems of intervention that they expect to see in each school. They monitor the implementation of the structural changes and offer assistance to schools that seek it. Some schools move forward with effective implementation, while others merely tweak their existing structures. Professional practice is impacted in some schools and not in others.	Central office leaders have put processes in place to develop the capacity of principals to lead the PLC process in their schools, monitor implementation of the PLC process, and respond to schools that are experiencing difficulty. Building-level and central office leaders have begun to function as their own collaborative team and work interdependently to achieve common goals and identify and resolve issues that are interfering with the PLC process. Individual schools are examining ways to become more effective in the PLC process.	Administrators at all levels function as coordinated, high-performing teams characterized by a deep understanding of and commitment to the PLC process. They consider that process not as one of several improvement initiatives, but rather as *the* process by which they will continuously improve student and adult learning. They are intensely focused on student achievement data transparent among all members. They work together collaboratively to resolve problems, develop a deeper understanding of the PLC process, and learn from one another. They are committed to the collective success of the team and the individual success of each member.

Learning by Doing © 2006, 2010 Solution Tree Press • solution-tree.com
Visit **go.solution-tree.com/PLCbooks** to download this page.

Where Do We Go From Here? Worksheet
Implementing a PLC Districtwide

Indicator of a PLC at Work	What steps or activities must be initiated to create this condition in your school?	Who will be responsible for initiating or sustaining these steps or activities?	What is a realistic timeline for each step or phase of the activity?	What will you use to assess the effectiveness of your initiative?
The district has demonstrated a sustained commitment to improving schools by developing the capacity of school personnel to function as a PLC. District leaders have been explicit about specific practices they expect to see in each school, have created processes to support principals in implementing those practices, and monitor the progress of implementation.				

Part Five

Tips for Moving Forward: Implementing a Districtwide PLC Process

1 **Don't assume a common verbiage means common understanding.** The fact that people use the same term does not mean that they have a shared understanding of its meaning or its implications. Remember the advice of Jeffrey Pfeffer and Robert Sutton (2000), based on their research on high-performing organizations:

> The use of complex language hampers implementation . . . when leaders or managers don't really understand the meaning of the language they are using and its implications for action. It is hard enough to explain what a complex idea means for action when you understand it and others don't. It is impossible when you use terms that sound impressive but you don't really understand what they mean. (p. 52)

Develop formal and informal processes to determine people's interpretation of the key terms in the PLC lexicon. "Help me understand what you mean by that term" should be a phrase you use routinely in conversations with others.

2 **Don't assume that others share or understand your interpretation of what is tight.** Develop formal and informal processes to provide you with feedback on what people throughout the organization believe are the priorities. For example, at a principals' meeting, the superintendent could ask principals to write down the two or three things they believe are tight in the district. The responses should be gathered, read aloud, and discussed. How consistent are the responses?

3 **Link what is tight to board policy.** Work with the board of education to codify expectations of priorities through adoption of board policy. For example, the Blue Valley School District in Kansas specifically stipulates, "We are committed to Professional Learning Communities as the means of continuous school improvement." The board of education of Montgomery County, Maryland, adopted "guiding tenets" that specify the work of the district will be driven by the four critical questions of a PLC:

> What do students need to know and be able to do?

> How will we know when they have learned it?

What will we do when they haven't?

What will we do when they already know it?

Schaumberg District 54 in suburban Chicago has adopted a board policy that states:

> An exemplary district is a professional learning community that includes all employees working together on a variety of collaborative teams for the benefit of students . . . As a professional learning community, all employees will:
>
> - Plan/support instruction, analyze data and establish intervention and enrichment opportunities in a collaborative manner.
>
> - Commit to continuous improvement with knowledge, purpose and efficiency.
>
> - Seek appropriate resources and support.
>
> - Be dedicated to continuous learning and student achievement.
>
> - Treat everyone with courtesy, dignity, and respect, while maintaining all necessary confidences.

Of course, merely adopting policy does not ensure change in professional practice. It can, however, demonstrate a public commitment to certain expectations, and it allows leaders to serve as promoters and protectors of district policy.

 Recognize the need for specificity regarding what people throughout the organization must *do*. Telling educators to operate their schools as PLCs will almost certainly have no impact unless there is a clear understanding of the specific actions people take in a PLC. The goal is not to have educators in a district refer to their school as a PLC: the goal is to have them do what members of a PLC do. In many instances, we have seen the adoption of language substitute for meaningful action. It is far more effective to stipulate exactly what must done and then provide some latitude regarding how it is done.

 Create systems to monitor conditions that are vital to the success of a PLC. One of the most important and frequent questions effective district leaders of the PLC process ask is, "How do we know?" They identify elements they believe must be in place for the process to be effective, and then they develop specific strategies to gather ongoing evidence of the presence of those elements. We offer examples of these "how do we know" questions in part six of this chapter.

6   **Demonstrate reciprocal accountability by working with leaders throughout the organization to identify the specific support and resources staff will need in order to accomplish what they are being called to do, and then provide the necessary support and resources.** Remember that part of the responsibility of leadership is helping others develop the capacity to succeed at what they are asked to accomplish.

Part Six

Questions to Guide the Work of Your Professional Learning Community

To Assess the Commitment to Districtwide PLC Implementation, Ask:

1. How do we know if we have a common language that is widely understood throughout the district?

2. How do we know if educators throughout the district understand what must be "tight" in our organization and in each school?

3. How do we know if educators are organized into collaborative teams (not merely groups) whose members are working interdependently on the right work?

4. How do we know if each student's learning is being monitored on a frequent and timely basis and that the quality of their work is being assessed according to the same criteria?

5. How do we know if results from assessments are being used to inform and improve professional practice?

6. How do we know if every student who experiences difficulty in acquiring essential knowledge and skills will receive additional time and support for learning in a timely, directive, and systematic way?

7. How do we know what resources and support people need throughout the organization to help them succeed at what they are being called upon to do?

8. How do we know if we are providing the necessary resources and support?

9. Have we limited initiatives and sustained a collective focus in building our collective capacity to function as a professional learning community?

Part Seven

Dangerous Detours and Seductive Shortcuts

No one person can lead the PLC process at either the building or district level; effective leaders must *delegate responsibility and authority to others.*

Beware of delegating essential responsibilities. No one person can lead the PLC process at either the building or district level; effective leaders *must* delegate responsibility and authority to others. There are some things, however, that they cannot delegate. Clarifying purpose and priorities, establishing systems to monitor specific indicators of progress, ensuring steps are taken to build capacity of people to be successful, and aligning their own behavior with the priorities are among those nontransferable responsibilities.

Some leaders have interpreted the adage "What gets monitored gets done" to mean, "The more things we monitor, the more we get done." This is absolutely wrong. Clarify a few key priorities, and focus your efforts on them. Limit initiatives. Engage in what Peter Drucker (1992) has called "organizational abandonment" by periodically looking at every process, procedure, and activity and asking, "If we stopped doing this, would our organization suffer or benefit?" For example, Schaumburg District 54 surveys its principals and asks questions such as, "What tasks that are required by the central office would you recommend be simplified or eliminated to give you more time to focus on student achievement? As a district, are we effectively monitoring the right/important things? Does the central office provide a sense of coherence, speak with one voice, and help you in clarifying the important issues or send mixed messages? Please provide specific examples."

Final Thoughts

Coordination, collaboration, and interdependence between the district office and schools are essential to districtwide implementation of the PLC process. Unproductive conflict and ongoing resistance interfere with that coordination, collaboration, and interdependence. Chapter 9 considers those obstacles and offers strategies for addressing them.

Consensus and Conflict in a Professional Learning Community

Part One

The Case Study: Building Consensus and Responding to Resistance

David C. Roth, the principal of Van Halen High School (nickname: the Rockers), was annoyed. He knew how hard he had worked to build consensus for moving forward with the professional learning community concept. He provided the entire staff with research and readings on the benefits of PLCs. He sent key teacher leaders to conferences on PLCs and used those staff members as a guiding coalition to promote the concept. He encouraged interested staff to visit schools that were working as PLCs. He met with the entire faculty in small groups to listen to their concerns and answer their questions. Finally, at the end of this painstaking process, he was convinced the faculty was ready to move forward. He assigned teachers into subject-area teams and asked each team to work collaboratively to clarify the essential outcomes of their courses and to develop common assessments to monitor student proficiency.

Within a month, the sophomore English team met with Principal Roth to ask if the team could exempt one of its members from meetings. They explained that Fred made it evident he was opposed to the entire idea of collaborative teams and common assessments. Fred made no effort to contribute, and his ridicule and sarcasm were undermining the team. Principal Roth assured them he would look into the situation and attempt to remedy it.

The next day Principal Roth called Fred to his office to discuss Fred's attitude toward his colleagues and the collaborative team process. After listening to the principal's concerns, Fred expressed his unhappiness with what he felt was the heavy-handed, top-down dictate of working in teams. He rejected the idea that the staff had arrived at consensus. Not only was he opposed to the initiative, he knew many other teachers who were as well. It was fine with him if the team did not want him to participate, because he had no interest in participating. He had always been an effective teacher, and he did not need some artificial process of working with colleagues to become effective.

Principal Roth resented Fred's characterization of the decision-making process and his assertion that the staff had never arrived at consensus. As he expressed that resentment, it was evident that the emotions of both men were becoming more heated. Principal Roth decided the prudent course would be to adjourn the meeting.

Throughout the day, the principal struggled with his dilemma. On the one hand, he was not amenable to exempting Fred from the PLC process. He was wary of establishing a precedent that released overt resisters from the obligation to contribute to their collaborative teams. He was concerned that others on the staff would resent devoting time and energy to collaboration if their colleagues were able to opt out of the process. On the other hand, he knew Fred could be difficult, and he considered it unlikely that Fred could be persuaded to change his attitude.

After much deliberation, Principal Roth decided to ask the English team to continue working with Fred in the hope that his attitude would improve over time. The team was unhappy with his response.

> ### Reflection
>
> Consider Principal Roth's efforts to build consensus for an improvement process and his approach to dealing with a staff member who was unwilling to support the process. What is your reaction? Can you identify alternative strategies the principal might have used that would have been more effective?

Part Two

Here's How

In chapter 2, we offered suggestions for developing consensus: create a guiding coalition, build shared knowledge, and engage in dialogue with staff members in small groups to listen to and address concerns. Principal Roth was attentive to each of these suggestions, yet he still encountered difficulties. The problem arose, in part, because no clear, operational definition of consensus guided the decision-making process in the school. Principal Roth was certain the staff supported moving forward with the PLC concept, while Fred was equally convinced that staff members opposed the concept. Without a shared understanding, people were left to determine their own standard for consensus.

What Questions

What do you mean by *consensus*?

In our work with schools, we frequently ask a straightforward question: "How do you define *consensus* when your staff considers a proposal?" The responses we hear vary greatly within the same school. We have established a continuum of consensus based on the typical responses. Consider the following continuum, and select the point at which you feel you have reached agreement on a proposal in your own school:

We have arrived at consensus in our school when:

1. All of us can embrace the proposal.

2. All of us can endorse the proposal.

3. All of us can live with the proposal.

4. All of us can agree not to sabotage the proposal.

5. We have a majority—at least 51 percent—in support of the proposal.

The most common outcome of this survey is a staff distributed all along the continuum because members *do not have consensus on the definition of consensus.* Disagreements and allegations are inevitable when a faculty does not understand the standard that must be met in order to make a collective decision.

Actually, we advise staffs to reject all points on the five-point continuum. In our view (a view not universally shared by others), it is difficult to maintain that you have the consent of the group to move forward with a simple majority—a standard that can disregard the perspective of 49 percent of the group. On the other hand, every other point on the continuum goes beyond consensus when it calls for "all of us" to reach a level of agreement. While it is wonderful to strive for unanimity, there is a difference between unanimity and consensus. In the real world, history has proven that if *all of us* must agree before we can act, if every member of the organization can veto taking action, the organization will be subjected to constant inaction, a state of perpetual status quo that ultimately can only lead to decline. For example, in the 18th century, Poland gave each of its legislators the power to nullify any proposed legislation by shouting, "I do not allow." As Paul Krugman (2010) of the *New York Times* points out, this practice "made Poland largely ungovernable and neighboring regimes began hacking off

While it is wonderful to strive for unanimity, there is a difference between unanimity and consensus.

pieces of its territory. By 1795 Poland had disappeared, not to re-emerge for more than a century."

The definition of consensus that we prefer establishes two simple standards that must be met in order to move forward when a decision is made by consensus. A group has arrived at consensus when:

1. All points of view have not merely been heard, but actively solicited.

2. The will of the group is evident even to those who most oppose it.

This definition can, and typically does, result in moving forward with a proposal despite the fact that some members of the organization are against it. However, as Patrick Lencioni (2005) writes, "Waiting for everyone to agree intellectually on a decision is a good recipe for mediocrity, delay, and frustration" (p. 51). The insistence on unanimity conflicts with the action orientation of a PLC.

If the standards for consensus we recommend had been applied in the case study, Principal Roth and his guiding coalition would have certainly built shared knowledge and engaged in small group dialogues to address concerns. At some point, however, they would have also presented a specific proposal such as this:

> In order to create a guaranteed and viable curriculum, establish consistency in assessing student proficiency, and promote a collaborative culture, we will work together in collaborative teams that clarify essential learning by course, create common formative assessments, and analyze the results from those assessments to improve student achievement.

The staff would then be *randomly* divided into two groups. The first group would be asked to work together to create a comprehensive list of all the reasons the faculty should oppose the proposal. The second group would be called upon to create a comprehensive list of all the reasons the staff should support the proposal. At this point, personal feelings about the proposal do not to come into play. Each member of the staff is to engage in an intellectual exercise to list all the possible pros and cons regarding the specific idea under consideration.

In the next step of the process, the first group presents all the reasons they listed to oppose the suggestion. Members of the second group are asked to listen attentively until the opposed group has completed their list, and then they are invited to add to that list with other objections that might not have been identified. The process is then repeated with the proponent group announcing their comprehensive list in support of the decision, and the group responsible for listing objections invited to add to it. Participants are then encouraged to ask for clarification on any point they do not understand. If done correctly, no one will know where any member of the staff stands on the issue personally, although all points of view have been heard. The next step is to determine the will of the group. A quick and simple way to do so is to use the "fist to five" strategy. Once everyone is clear on the proposal, and all pros and cons have been offered, each person is asked to indicate a level of support, as shown in the feature box.

Fist to Five Strategy

5 Fingers: I love this proposal. I will champion it.

4 Fingers: I strongly agree with the proposal.

3 Fingers: The proposal is okay with me. I am willing to go along.

2 Fingers: I have reservations and am not yet ready to support this proposal.

1 Finger: I am opposed to this proposal.

Fist: If I had the authority, I would veto this proposal, regardless of the will of the group.

The facilitator for the process ensures that everyone understands the issue under consideration and how to express themselves through fist to five. All members of the staff are then asked to express their position simultaneously by raising their hands with the appropriate indication of support (that is, the number of fingers best expressing their level of support). Each participant is then able to look around the room to ascertain the support for the proposal. If participants do not support the proposal, or the vote is too close to determine the will of the group at a glance, the proposal does not go forward. Pilot projects may be run, more time can be taken to build shared knowledge, and in time the proposal may be presented again; however, if support is not readily apparent, the standard of consensus has not been met. On the other hand, if it is evident by looking around the room that it is the will of the group to move forward (the number of hands with three, four, and five fingers clearly outnumber those with two, one, and fists), consensus has been reached, and all staff members will be expected to honor the decision.

There are certainly variations on this format. For example, if the technology is available, staff could vote anonymously and have the tally reported instantly. If there are concerns about intimidation, an anonymous paper vote may be necessary as long as the process for counting the votes is accepted as fair by all concerned. In large schools, the vote may take place in a series of small-group staff meetings rather than one large-group meeting. In that case, it is prudent to have the teachers' association appoint a representative to attend all of the meetings in case concerns emerge about the accuracy of the reporting. But while the format may vary, one thing does not: decision making is easier, more effective, and less likely to end in disputes about process when a staff has a clear operational definition of consensus.

Decision making is easier, more effective, and less likely to end in disputes about process when a staff has a clear operational definition of consensus.

What are ways we can confront?

A faculty that has built a solid foundation for a PLC by carefully crafting consensus regarding their purpose, the school they seek to create, their collective commitments, the specific goals they will use to monitor their progress, and the strategies for achieving those goals, has not eliminated the possibility of conflict. The real strength of a PLC is determined by the response to the disagreements that inevitably occur.

Every organization will experience conflict, particularly when the organization is engaged in significant change.

Every organization will experience conflict, particularly when the organization is engaged in significant change. Every collective endeavor will include instances when people fail to honor agreed-upon priorities and collective commitments. The ultimate goal, of course, is to create a culture that is so strong and so open that members throughout the organization will use the violation as an opportunity to reinforce what is valued by bringing peer pressure to bear on the offender, saying, in effect, "That is not how we do it here." In the interim, however, it typically will be the responsibility of the leader (that is, principal or administrator) to communicate what is important and valued by demonstrating a willingness to confront when appropriate. Nothing will destroy the credibility of a leader faster than an unwillingness to address an obvious violation of what the organization contends is vital. A leader must not remain silent; he or she must be willing to act when people disregard the purpose and priorities of the organization.

It is possible to be tough-minded and adamant about protecting purpose and priorities while also being tender with people.

Confrontation does not, however, involve screaming, demeaning, or vilifying. It is possible to be tough-minded and adamant about protecting purpose and priorities while also being tender with people. One of the most helpful resources we have found for engaging in frank dialogue when "the stakes are high, opinions vary, and emotions run strong" is *Crucial Conversations* (Patterson et al., 2002, p. 3). The authors contend that skillful communicators reject the false dichotomy of the "Suckers Choice": I can either be honest and hurtful *or* be kind and withhold the truth. Instead, they search for the Genius of And—a way to be both honest *and* respectful, to say what needs to be said to the people who need to hear it without brutalizing them or causing undue offense.

Some of the strategies offered in *Crucial Conversations* for engaging in honest and respectful dialogue include:

1. Clarify what you want and what you do not want to result from the conversation before initiating it.

2. Attempt to find mutual purpose.

3. Create a safe environment for honest dialogue.

4. Use facts because "gathering facts is the homework required for crucial conversations" (p. 127).

5. Share your thought process that has led you to engage in the conversation.

6. Encourage recipients to share their facts and thought process.

Let us apply these strategies to the situation Principal Roth is facing. Prior to initiating the conversation with Fred, Principal Roth might clarify his position in his own mind: "I want all students to have the benefit of a teacher who is a member of a high-performing collaborative team. Therefore, I want Fred to honor the commitments we made as a staff to the collaborative process by making a positive contribution to his team. I do not want Fred to think we are questioning his expertise or diminishing his contribution to the school." Principal Roth would then think of how he might achieve what he wants and avoid what he does not want through a meaningful, respectful dialogue with Fred.

During the conversation with Fred, the principal could attempt to find mutual purpose: "I believe we both want a school that is committed to helping all students achieve at high levels and to providing teachers with a satisfying and fulfilling professional experience." He could ask Fred if he agrees with that assessment of their mutual purpose.

Roth could attempt to create a safe environment for dialogue by sharing facts, speaking tentatively, inviting Fred to clarify any mistakes in his thinking, and encouraging the teacher to elaborate on his own thought process: "I believe there is very compelling evidence that developing our capacity to work together collaboratively on significant issues centered in teaching and learning is vital to both raising student achievement and creating a rewarding workplace. I would be happy to share that evidence with you once again. As you know, our staff has made a commitment to work together with the colleagues on their teams, and I was wondering if that commitment is problematic for you. Here are some of the events that caused me to raise this question. I understand you frequently do not attend the meetings of your collaborative team, and that you have not made any contribution to creating common assessments. I received several complaints from students and parents that you had not taught the skills assessed on the last common test. I recognize the contribution you have made to this school over the years, and I don't want to diminish that contribution in any way. In fact, I think your teammates could benefit from your experience. So help me understand. Are my facts incorrect? Are there issues of which I am unaware? I'm very interested in hearing your perspective and your assessment of any factors that may be impacting your contribution to your collaborative team."

At this point it is important for Principal Roth to listen carefully to Fred, to make a good faith effort to understand Fred's perspective. In *Difficult Conversations*, another helpful study of how to address differences through dialogue, the authors advise, "Listening is not only the skill that lets you into the other person's world; it is the single most powerful move you can make to keep the conversation constructive" (Stone, Patton, & Heen, 2000, p. 202).

If Fred agrees with the mutual purpose but cites conditions that are impeding his ability to contribute to the team, the principal and Fred can brainstorm solutions and commit to carry out their agreed-upon plan. If Fred can express his reasons for resisting the proposal, the principal may be able to modify the context of the proposal in a way that resonates with Fred. For example, we know of a teacher who asserted he would not work with his team because he was only two years from retirement and was already getting the best results in his department. The principal acknowledged those points and complimented the teacher on the craft knowledge he had developed over the years. The principal then pointed out that all that accumulated knowledge and wisdom would walk out the door with him on his retirement day unless he shared it with his colleagues. By shifting the focus from "participate to improve" to "participate to ensure your ongoing legacy," the principal convinced the teacher to commit to contribute to his team.

It is possible, however, that Fred rejects the mutual purpose. He might say, "My primary job is to give students the opportunity to demonstrate that they have learned what I taught, and I don't need to collaborate with peers to do my job. I see your insistence on collaboration as an attempt to deprive me of my autonomy. As a professional, I have a right to determine what I will teach, the instructional strategies I deem appropriate, and how I will assess my students. If others elect to collaborate, it is their choice, but I choose not to participate."

What options might Principal Roth resort to at this point? Howard Gardner (2004) offers the following strategies for changing someone's mind.

1. **Reasoning and rational thinking.** "Doesn't it make sense that we can accomplish more by working together collaboratively rather than we can by working in isolation? If you and your colleagues are helping students acquire the same skills and knowledge, how logical is it that each of you would duplicate the work required to create lesson plans, search for supplementary materials, develop ways to integrate technology into the teaching and learning process, and construct authentic assessments? When people are engaged in the same work, isn't it more efficient for them to designate responsibilities to different members rather than replicate all that effort?"

2. **Research.** "Fred, I have shared the research with you that supports this initiative. I found it very compelling. Do you interpret the research another way? Do you have any contradictory research we could look at together?"

3. **Resonance.** "I know you believe in equity and fairness. Wouldn't it be more equitable and fair if we could assure students they will have access to the same guaranteed curriculum, no matter who their teacher is, and that their work will be assessed according to the same criteria? Shouldn't we model the equity and fairness we say is important to us?"

4. **Representational redescription.** "I have presented you with the data regarding the large numbers of our students who are not being successful. Now let me put those numbers in human terms; let me tell you some stories of the impact their failure to learn is having on their lives."

5. **Rewards and resources.** "I acknowledge this will be difficult. That is why I ask your help in identifying the resources you will need to be successful: time, training, materials, and support. Let's work together to identify the necessary resources, and I pledge I will do everything in my power to make them available."

6. **Real-world events.** "I understand you have misgivings and predict negative consequences if we implement this initiative. But let's visit some schools and districts that have done it successfully. You will hear the enthusiasm of the teachers as they explain how they and their students have benefited."

If Fred continues to refuse to participate in the process despite these efforts of persuasion, Principal Roth must resort to the seventh of Gardner's strategies:

7. **Require.** "I understand you remain unconvinced, but this is the direction in which we are going, and this is what you must do to help us get us there. I hope you will have a good experience as you work through the process, and I hope you will come to have a more positive disposition toward it, but until then, you will do it because I am directing you to do it."

If it becomes necessary to resort to the strategy of "require," Principal Roth should:

1. Continue to work with Fred in a respectful and professional manner. Losing his composure or arguing with Fred serves no one's interest.

2. Acknowledge that there are fundamental differences in their perspectives; however, those differences do not exempt Fred from participating in the collaborative process in a productive way. Principal Roth must send a clear message to Fred that the need for change is immediate and imperative.

3. Clarify the specific behaviors he requires of Fred. Admonitions such as "You need to do a better job with your team" or "You need to improve your attitude toward collaboration" do not provide Fred with the precise direction that is needed. A far more effective strategy might sound like this:

   "Fred, there are three things I need you to begin doing immediately. First, you must attend all of your team meetings. Second, you *must* honor each of the collective commitments your team has established regarding how members will fulfill their responsibilities and relate to one another. Third, you must provide me with specific evidence each week that you are (1) teaching your students the essential learning outcomes established by your team and (2) preparing your students to demonstrate their attainment of those outcomes on the common assessments created by the team. We can discuss different ways you might provide me with such evidence. To ensure that there are no misunderstandings, I will provide you with a written directive detailing these expectations."

4. Invite Fred to offer any suggestions regarding support, training, or resources he might need to comply with the directive.

5. Clarify the specific consequences that will occur if Fred ignores the directive he has been given:

    "Fred, if you disregard what I have directed you to do, I will have no choice but to consider your actions as insubordination. At that point I will suspend you without pay and take the matter to the board of education."

6. Establish strategies to monitor Fred's behavior rather than his attitude. When good-faith efforts to engage in meaningful dialogue reveal fundamental differences rather than common ground, and when attempts to participate in crucial conversations lead to impasse rather than agreement, attempts to "talk" a person into a new attitude are almost always unproductive.

7. Acknowledge and celebrate any efforts Fred may make to change his behavior.

8. Apply the specified consequences if necessary.

In *Influencer: The Power to Change Anything*, Kerry Patterson and colleagues (2008) offer remarkably similar advice for those attempting to influence others to change their perspective and their behavior. They offer recommendations in three areas—personal, social, and structural—taken from research in psychology, social psychology, and organizational theory to bring about this change.

1. Influence Personal Motivation

Patterson and colleagues contend that "*the great persuader is personal experience. . . . the mother of all cognitive map changes*" (p. 51, emphasis in the original) and "the gold standard of change" (p. 57). They call for field trips to help people see the benefits of the behavior in the real world. They also advise leaders to fight against all forms of moral disengagement such as justification ("We can't expect these kids to learn given their socioeconomic status") or displaced responsibility ("I taught it, it is their job to learn it"). Leaders should focus on human rather than statistical consequences of failure to change (for example, stories of specific students rather than last year's test results). They should present the change as a personally defining moment within a larger moral issue.

2. Enhance the Personal Ability of Others

Because one of the pressing issues in the mind of someone being asked to change is often, "Can I do it?" effective leaders build capacity by building confidence. They set aside time for deliberate practice, provide immediate feedback against a clear standard, and break mastery into several specific ministeps.

3. Harness the Power of Peer Pressure

Kerry Patterson and colleagues (2008) contend that "no resource is more powerful and accessible" than the power of peer influence and that the most effective leaders "embrace and enlist" that power rather than "denying, lamenting, or attacking it" (p. 138). Effective leaders strive to create an environment where both formal and informal leaders constantly promote behavior essential to the change and skillfully confront behaviors that are misaligned with the change.

Effective leaders strive to create an environment where both formal and informal leaders constantly promote behavior essential to the change and skillfully confront behaviors that are misaligned with the change.

4. Find Strength in Numbers

Patterson and colleagues recommend organizing people into interdependent teams in which the success or failure of the group depends upon contributions from each member. When the organizational structure requires people to work together, share ideas and materials, support one another in difficult moments, and contribute to collective goals, those people are more likely to hold each other accountable. The result is "synergy through non-voluntary interaction" (2008, p. 183).

5. Design Rewards and Demand Accountability

Effective leaders use rewards that are directly linked to vital behaviors and valued processes. They recognize and reward observable small improvement early in the change process because "even small rewards can be used to help people overcome some of the most profound and persistent problems" (Patterson et al., 2008, p. 198). However, "punishment sends a message, and so does its absence—so choose wisely" (p. 210). Failure to address those who refuse to engage in the vital behaviors sends a loud message to others that the behaviors aren't so vital after all. They recommend that punishment be preceded by a "shot across the bow"—a clear warning to an individual of what *will* happen if he or she continues with unacceptable behavior.

6. Create Structures to Support the Change and Provide Relevant Information

Patterson and colleagues argue that change in the structure and physical environment of an organization can make the right behavior easier and the wrong behavior more difficult. As they write, "Often, all that is required to make good behavior inevitable is to structure it into your daily routine" (p. 250). When the fundamental structure of the organization is the collaborative team, when time for collaboration is built in the weekly schedule, when members of a team work in close proximity to one another, they are far more likely to collaborate. Finally, Patterson and colleagues advise leaders that they can change how people feel and act by creating systems to ensure relevant and timely information is easily accessible throughout the organization.

The two different comprehensive studies on how to change people's minds offer remarkably consistent advice. Notice neither Gardner nor Patterson and colleagues suggest leaders begin the process of persuasion with "require." They do say, however, that leaders *must* be prepared to use that strategy if they are to bring about substantive change in their organizations.

Finally, leaders are always in a better position to confront when they act as the promoters and protectors of decisions, agreements, and commitments of the group. Appeals to hierarchy—"Do it because I am the boss and I said so"—may eventually become necessary on occasion, but in raising an issue initially, leaders are more effective utilizing the moral authority that comes with defending the articulated collective aspirations of the people within the organization.

Part Three

Here's Why

As we emphasized in chapter 2, research has consistently concluded that effective leaders build shared vision and a shared sense of purpose that binds people together. But unless vision and purpose result in the desired action, nothing is accomplished. So what are leaders to do when some members of the organization are opposed to taking action that is critical to moving forward? Effective leaders do not wait for unanimity, but instead build shared knowledge until they have created a "critical mass" of those willing to act—and then they move the organization forward without expecting universal support. When they do, they can expect conflict, because substantive organizational change inevitably will result in conflict.

Managing Conflict

Transforming traditional schools and districts into professional learning communities requires "disruptive change" because it requires "the system and those who work in it to do things that they have never done" (Schlechty, 2005, p. 3). Those leading the PLC process at any level must recognize that conflict is an inevitable by-product of this substantive change process (Evans, 2001; Lieberman, 1995; Louis, Kruse, & Marks, 1996). In fact, an absence of conflict suggests the changes are only superficial because "conflict and disagreements are not only inevitable but fundamental to successful change" (Fullan, 2007, p. 21).

The challenge, then, is not to eliminate or avoid conflict, because as James Champy (1995) writes: "A culture that squashes disagreement is a culture doomed to stagnate, because change always begins with disagreement. Besides, disagreement can never be squashed entirely. It gets repressed, only to emerge later as a sense of injustice, followed by apathy, resentment, and even sabotage" (p. 89). The challenge is to learn how to manage conflict productively. Effective leaders will surface the conflict, draw out and acknowledge the varying perspectives, and search for a common ground that everyone can endorse (Goleman et al., 2002). When managed well, conflict can serve as an engine of creativity and energy (Saphier, 2005), clarify priorities (Bossidy & Charan, 2002), and develop stronger teams (Lencioni, 2005).

The challenge, then, is not to eliminate or avoid conflict. . . . The challenge is to learn how to manage conflict productively.

Repeated conflict over the same issues can certainly represent a drain on an organization's time and energy, and at some point, there is a need for closure. But when educational leaders at the district or school level avoid confrontation because they favor keeping the peace over productive conflict, they can do tremendous damage to any improvement process.

Responding to Resisters

So what is an effective way to respond when conflict turns into resistance—when efforts to build shared knowledge, answer questions, use effective strategies of persuasion, and develop consensus fail to bring about the desired changes in the behavior of a few resistant staff? The most frequent question we hear as we work with educators is, "But how should we respond to the people in our organization who have bad attitudes?" Our advice is simple: don't focus on the attitude—focus on the *behavior*. There is abundant evidence from the fields of psychology, organizational development, and education that changes in attitudes follow rather than precede changes in behavior (Champy, 1995; Elmore, 2004; Fullan, 2010; Kotter, 1996; Kotter & Cohen, 2002; Pfeffer & Sutton, 2006; Reeves, 2002, 2006; Wheelis, 1973). Work that is designed to require people to *act* in new ways creates the possibility of new experiences. These new experiences, in turn, can lead to new attitudes over time.

Don't focus on the attitude—focus on the behavior.

We recognize that it is quite probable some people will *never* embrace the PLC concept, regardless of what evidence of its benefits are presented and despite the best efforts of leaders to bring them on board. Teachers who believe it is their job to teach and the students' job to learn, who are convinced that learning is a function of the aptitude of the student rather than the expertise of the teacher, who define professionalism as the autonomy to do as they please, or who take pleasure in wallowing in negativity will always find a way to dismiss the PLC concept. Principals who define their job as maintaining order and keeping the adults happy are likely to resist a concept that requires them to lead.

Many educators conclude, perhaps rightly, that there is very little hope of changing these hard-core resisters, and so they begin to ignore the resisters' repeated disregard for implementing the improvement agenda and ongoing violations of their teams' collective commitments. Such salutary neglect is always a mistake. Leaders must persist and follow through on the specific consequences they have outlined to those who continue to fail to act in accordance with what has been established as "tight." *They must keep in mind that the goal in addressing these violations is not only to bring about change in the resister, but also to communicate priorities throughout the organization.* As Kerry Patterson and his colleagues (2008) advise, "The point isn't that people need to be threatened in order to perform. The point is that if you aren't willing to go to the mat when people violate a core value. . . . that value loses it moral force in the organization. On the other hand, you do send a powerful message when you hold employees accountable" (p. 216). Unwillingness to follow through sends mixed messages about what is important and valued. In fact, Patrick Lencioni (2003) contends that if leaders don't have the courage to insist that team members fulfill their responsibilities to teammates, they are better off avoiding the idea of collaborative teams altogether.

As Robert Evans (2001) concludes, the need to confront resistance is "one of the toughest truths of change in school" (p. 276), because "confrontation forms a matching bookend with clarity and focus" (p. 288).

The responsibility to confront can create tension with a natural human emotion—the desire to develop positive relationships, particularly with our working colleagues. The good news is that a defining characteristic of successful school improvement initiatives is that relationships always improve (Fullan, 2007). The bad news is that conflict is an inevitable by-product of those initiatives, and there will be strains on relationships during the process. It is not uncommon for leaders to be vilified at the outset, despite every effort they may have taken to build consensus and to listen to and honor those who opposed the change. Even if the will of the group to go forward is evident, adamant resisters may disparage the leader and the strategies used to arrive at consensus.

In his Pulitzer Prize–winning book on leadership, James McGregor Burns (1982) offers advice to those faced with this dilemma: "No matter how strong the yearning for unanimity . . . [leaders] must settle for far less than universal affection. . . . They must accept conflict. They must be willing and able to be unloved" (p. 34). The recognition that they will not be universally loved despite their best efforts may trouble leaders initially; however, once they come to accept that truth, it can be quite liberating.

We have seen schools and districts held hostage by a few recalcitrant staff members who veto any attempt to move forward, but that situation can only occur when leaders allow it. As Jonathon Saphier (2005) wrote, "Day after day in schools across America, change initiatives, instructional improvement, and better results for children are blocked, sabotaged, or killed through silence and inaction . . . this lack of follow-through results from the avoidance or inability to face conflict openly and make it a creative source of energy among educators" (p. 37).

English philosopher Edmund Burke once observed, "The only thing necessary for the triumph of evil is for good men to do nothing." In no way do we mean to suggest that those unwilling to consider more effective ways to meet the needs of students are evil. Often they are good people who have been burned too many times by initiatives launched with enthusiasm only to be quickly abandoned. We do, however, think a paraphrase of Burke is appropriate: all that is necessary for the triumph of those who resist school improvement is for educational leaders to do nothing.

In every school that we have seen succeed as a PLC, a defining moment has occurred when a leader chose to confront rather than avoid saboteurs. We are convinced their schools' improvement efforts could not have gone forward had they ignored violations of collective commitments.

In every school that we have seen succeed as a PLC, a defining moment has occurred when a leader chose to confront rather than avoid saboteurs.

Leaders who face a scenario similar to the one described in this chapter should utilize every component of an effective change process and present the rationale for the proposed initiative using every available strategy. They must be willing to listen to concerns, seek common ground, and compromise on the details of implementation. Once they have reached a decision, however, they must be unequivocal in confronting resisters and demanding changes in behavior.

Daniel Goleman is an ardent advocate of the importance of emotional intelligence, a concept anchored, in part, in the critical significance of skillful relationship building characterized by high levels of empathy for others. Yet even Goleman (1998) advises:

> Persuasion, consensus building, and all the other arts of influence don't always do the job. Sometimes it simply comes down to using the power of one's position to get people to act. A common failing of leaders from supervisors to top executives is the failure to be *emphatically assertive* when necessary. (p. 190, emphasis added)

Part Four

Assessing Your Place on the PLC Journey

Complete the PLC continuum and Where Do We Go From Here? worksheets as outlined in chapter 2.

The Professional Learning Communities at Work™ Continuum: Responding to Conflict

DIRECTIONS: Individually, silently, and *honestly* assess the current reality of your school's implementation of each indicator listed in the left column. Consider what evidence or anecdotes support your assessment. This form may also be used to assess district or team implementation.

Indicator	Pre-Initiating	Initiating	Implementing	Developing	Sustaining
We have established processes for addressing conflict and use conflict as a tool for learning together in order to improve our school.					
Members of the staff recognize that conflict is an essential and inevitable by-product of a successful substantive change effort. They have thoughtfully and purposefully created processes to help use conflict as a tool for learning together and improving the school.	People react to conflict with classic fight-or-flight responses. Most staff members withdraw from interactions in order to avoid contact with those they find disagreeable. Others are perpetually at war in acrimonious, unproductive arguments that never seem to get resolved. Groups tend to regard each other as adversaries.	Addressing conflict is viewed as an administrative responsibility. School leaders take steps to resolve conflict as quickly as possible. The primary objective in addressing disputes is to restore the peace and return to the status quo.	Teams have established norms and collective commitments in an effort both to minimize conflict and to clarify how they will address conflict at the team level. Nonetheless, many staff members are reluctant to challenge the thinking or behavior of a colleague. If the situation becomes too disturbing, they will expect the administration to intervene.	Staff members have created processes to help identify and address the underlying issues causing conflict. They are willing to practice those processes in an effort to become more skillful in engaging in crucial conversations that seek productive resolution to conflict.	Staff members view conflict as a source of creative energy and an opportunity for building shared knowledge. They have created specific strategies for exploring one another's thinking, and they make a conscious effort to understand as well as to be understood. They seek ways to test their competing assumptions through action research and are open to examining research, data, and information that support or challenge their respective positions. They approach disagreements with high levels of trust and an assumption of good intentions on the part of all members because they know they are united by a common purpose and the collective pursuit of shared goals and priorities.

Learning by Doing © 2006, 2010 Solution Tree Press • solution-tree.com
Visit **go.solution-tree.com/PLCbooks** to download this page.

Where Do We Go From Here? Worksheet
Effective Communication

Indicator of a PLC at Work	What steps or activities must be initiated to create this condition in your school?	Who will be responsible for initiating or sustaining these steps or activities?	What is a realistic timeline for each step or phase of the activity?	What will you use to assess the effectiveness of your initiative?
Members of the staff recognize that conflict is an essential and inevitable by-product of a successful substantive change effort. They have thoughtfully and purposefully created processes to help use conflict as a tool for learning together and improving the school.				

Part Five

Tips for Moving Forward: Building Consensus and Responding to Resistance

1   **Get started and then get better.** Teach and practice skills for dealing with conflict.

2   **Walk before you run.** Ask teams to apply Peter Senge's strategies for inquiry and advocacy (presented in chapter 5) to a current issue that is not laden with emotion. For example, a team could consider, "Should we keep minutes of our team meetings?" Debrief at the end of the exercise. Ask, "What did we observe? What did we learn? How did we feel? Did we stay with the strategy? When would it be appropriate to use? How could we use it more effectively?"

3   **Include feedback in your practice process.** Ask teams to role-play a situation regarding a more volatile issue using the crucial conversation strategies we presented in this chapter. Once again, debrief at the end of the exercise.

4   **Learn from the experts.** Visit the Crucial Skills website (www. vitalsmarts.com), and click on "get free resources" to access free video clips and role-play exercises for crucial conversations.

5   **Help monitor one another.** Create cues you can use to refocus when participants seem to be resorting to fight or flight. Signal a time-out, or simply ask, "Are we moving away from dialogue?"

6   **Do your homework.** Remember that gathering facts is the prerequisite homework for any crucial conversation. What are the facts you can bring to the dialogue?

7   **Learn together.** Build shared knowledge when faced with contrasting positions. Seek agreement on what research or evidence could help lead to a more informed conclusion.

8   **Learn by doing.** Use action research to explore differences. Create strategies that allow participants to put their theories to the test.

9 **Assume positive intentions.** Recognize that conflicts are more productive when members have found common ground on major issues and approach one another with an assumption of good intentions.

10 **Be patient.** Remember that you are attempting to develop new skills that will require practice. As Patterson, Grenny, McMillan, and Switzler (2002) advise, "Don't expect perfection; aim for progress" (p. 228).

11 **Be tender with one another.**

Part Six

Questions to Guide the Work of Your Professional Learning Community

To Assess the Climate for Creating Consensus and Responding to Resistance in Your School or District, Ask:

1. What evidence do we have that district goals are directly impacting the work of schools and collaborative teams within the school?

2. Do we have an operational definition of consensus in our school? Do we know at what point in the decision-making process we will move forward with an initiative?

3. Do we have a sense of what decisions require consensus? When do we want to involve all staff in the decision-making process? Who decides who decides?

4. Should individual members of our staff be permitted to disregard agreements we have made as a staff? What is the appropriate response if they do?

5. Identify a conflict that has emerged in our school in the past. How was that conflict addressed?

6. Are we building shared knowledge and conducting action research in an effort to address conflict productively? Can we cite an example in which we resolved a difference of opinion through examining the research or conducting our own action research?

7. Describe the process we currently use to resolve conflict. What skills could we identify and practice to become more effective in this important area?

8. Do we view conflict as something to be avoided?

9. Do we expect administrators to resolve conflict or do we work together to address it in ways that improve our effectiveness?

10. Are we developing our skills to hold crucial conversations? (For free assessment tools, register at www.vitalsmarts.com.)

11. Do we have a common understanding of our purpose—learning for all—and of our priorities, our goals, and our expectations of one another that are aligned with that purpose? Does this shared understanding allow us to be open with each other? Do we operate with an assumption of the good intentions of our members?

Part Seven

Dangerous Detours and Seductive Shortcuts

Don't assign responsibility for confrontation to others. In *Crucial Conversations*, Patterson and his colleagues (2002) conclude it was not the absence of conflict that made teams effective, but rather how the team dealt with the conflict. Bad teams ignored it, letting it fester until the situation deteriorated into "fight or flight"—unproductive bickering or people not attending meetings. Good teams went to the boss and asked him or her to resolve the problem. Great teams dealt with the issue themselves, recommitting to norms or establishing new norms to address the issue.

As teams become more mature and sophisticated in the process, they should assume greater responsibility for addressing their own problems.

Principals cannot expect every team to start off as a great team. Principals will inevitably be called upon to intervene when teams experience problems, and they should not shirk that responsibility. As teams become more mature and sophisticated in the process, they should assume greater responsibility for addressing their own problems.

Another example of deflecting responsibility to others is a leader who addresses an issue with a member of the staff but explains that he or she is doing someone else's bidding. For example, the principal who advises a teacher of the need for change because "the central office wants you to do this" is abdicating responsibility and undermining a systematic effort.

Don't use blanket announcements to deal with individual problems. Ineffective leaders will sometimes seek to avoid personal confrontation by sending out general admonitions regarding inappropriate behavior. Not only does this typically fail to impact the inappropriate behavior, but it also is offensive to those who are not acting in that way.

Reflection

Educational leaders who make a good-faith effort to implement every suggestion presented in the preceding chapters will nevertheless confront a brutal fact: leading a substantive change process, one that impacts the very culture of the organization, is a complex and often bewildering endeavor. Chapter 10 examines what we have come to understand about the change process in schools and school districts.

The Complex Challenge of Creating Professional Learning Communities

John Gardner (1988) once observed that "the impulse of most leaders is much the same today as it was a thousand years ago: accept the system as it is and lead it" (p. 24). Those who hope to serve in any leadership capacity in building PLCs must overcome that impulse. They must help people break free of the thicket of precedent, the tangle of unquestioned assumptions, and the trap of comfortable complacency. Their task is not only to help people throughout the organization acquire the knowledge and skills to solve the intractable challenges of today, but also to develop the collective capacity and confidence to tackle the unforeseen challenges that will emerge in the future. No program, no textbook, no curriculum, no technology will be sufficient to meet this challenge. Educators will remain the most important resource in the battle to provide every child with a quality education, and thus leaders must commit to creating the conditions in which those educators can continue to grow and learn as professionals.

We use the term *leaders* here in an inclusive sense that goes far beyond administrators. Throughout this book we have referenced many leadership roles for teachers: as members of a guiding coalition, participants on task forces, team leaders, and informal leaders who exert their authority through their expertise and character rather than their position. We also include, of course, those who are in formal positions of leadership: superintendents, principals, department chairpeople, district coordinators, and so on. Widely dispersed leadership is essential in building and sustaining PLCs, and it is important that individuals at all levels lead effectively.

Widely dispersed leadership is essential in building and sustaining PLCs, and it is important that individuals at all levels lead effectively.

We acknowledge that the challenge of leading effectively is formidable. Most efforts to improve schools tinker at the edge of existing practice. A new program may be added, but everything else in the structure and culture of the school remains much the same. But as Andy Hargreaves (2004) observed, "A professional learning community is an ethos that infuses every single aspect of a school's operation. When a school becomes a professional learning community, everything in the school looks different than before" (p. 48).

There is a corollary to Hargreaves' observation that becoming a PLC "changes everything": it also changes everyone. Every educator—every teacher, counselor, principal, central office staff member, and superintendent—will be called upon to redefine his or her role and responsibilities. People comfortable working in isolation will be asked to work collaboratively. People accustomed to hoarding authority will be asked to share it. People who have operated under certain assumptions their entire careers will be asked to change them.

The goal of second-order change is to modify the very culture of the organization and the assumptions, expectations, habits, roles, relationships, and norms that make up that culture. Transforming schools into PLCs demands second-order change.

In their comprehensive study of school leadership, Marzano, Waters, and McNulty (2005) distinguish between first-order and second-order change. The former is incremental, representing the next step on an established path and operating within existing paradigms. The change can be implemented by utilizing the existing knowledge and skills of the staff. The goal of first-order change is to help us get better at what we are already doing. Second-order change, however, is a dramatic departure from the expected and familiar. The goal of second-order change is to modify the very culture of the organization and the assumptions, expectations, habits, roles, relationships, and norms that make up that culture. Transforming schools into PLCs demands second-order change, and engaging in second-order change is particularly problematic.

Finally, what we advocate in this book is not a program, but an *ongoing, never-ending* process specifically designed to change the very culture of schools and districts. Educators are accustomed to a predictable cycle of initiatives with short life spans, launched with fanfare and promises, only to be buffeted by confusion, concerns, criticisms, and complaints, until ultimately drowning in despair. Educators are very familiar with *initiating* change, but the idea of a process that continues forever is foreign to them.

There is only one conclusion that can be drawn about a transformation that changes everything, changes everyone, represents a departure from the familiar, demands the acquisition of new skills, and continues forever: this transformation requires substantive change—real change—and *real change is real hard!*

On pages 249–251, we offer a brief review of the significant cultural shifts we have referenced in this book.

Cultural Shifts in a Professional Learning Community

A Shift in Fundamental Purpose

From a focus on teaching . . .	to collaboration
From emphasis on what was taught . . .	to a fixation on what students learned
From coverage of content . . .	to demonstration of proficiency
From providing individual teachers with curriculum documents such as state standards and curriculum guides . . .	to engaging collaborative teams in building shared knowledge regarding essential curriculum

A Shift in Use of Assessments

From infrequent summative assessments . . .	to frequent common formative assessments
From assessments to determine which students failed to learn by the deadline . . .	to assessments to identify students who need additional time and support
From assessments used to reward and punish students . . .	to assessments used to inform and motivate students
From assessing many things infrequently . . .	to assessing a few things frequently
From individual teacher assessments . . .	to assessments developed jointly by collaborative teams
From each teacher determining the criteria to be used in assessing student work . . .	to collaborative teams clarifying the criteria and ensuring consistency among team members when assessing student work
From an over-reliance on one kind of assessment . . .	to balanced assessments
From focusing on average scores . . .	to monitoring each student's proficiency in every essential skill

A Shift in the Response When Students Don't Learn

From individual teachers determining the appropriate response . . .	to a systematic response that ensures support for every student
From fixed time and support for learning . . .	to time and support for learning as variables
From remediation . . .	to intervention
From invitational support outside of the school day . . .	to directed (that is, required) support occurring during the school day
From one opportunity to demonstrate learning . . .	to multiple opportunities to demonstrate learning

A Shift in the Work of Teachers

From isolation . . .	to collaboration
From each teacher clarifying what students must learn . . .	to collaborative teams building shared knowledge and understanding about essential learning
From each teacher assigning priority to different learning standards . . .	to collaborative teams establishing the priority of respective learning standards
From each teacher determining the pacing of the curriculum . . .	to collaborative teams of teachers agreeing on common pacing
From individual teachers attempting to discover ways to improve results . . .	to collaborative teams of teachers helping each other improve
From privatization of practice . . .	to open sharing of practice
From decisions made on the basis of individual preferences . . .	to decisions made collectively by building shared knowledge of best practice
From "collaboration lite" on matters unrelated to student achievement . . .	to collaboration explicitly focused on issues and questions that most impact student achievement
From an assumption that these are "my kids, those are your kids". . .	to an assumption that these are "our kids"

A Shift in Focus

From an external focus on issues outside of the school . . .	to an internal focus on steps the staff can take to improve the school
From a focus on inputs . . .	to a focus on results
From goals related to completion of project and activities . . .	to SMART goals demanding evidence of student learning
From teachers gathering data from their individually constructed tests in order to assign grades . . .	to collaborative teams acquiring information from common assessments in order to (1) inform their individual and collective practice and (2) respond to students who need additional time and support

A Shift in School Culture

From independence . . .	to interdependence
From a language of complaint . . .	to a language of commitment
From long-term strategic planning . . .	to planning for short-term wins
From infrequent generic recognition . . .	to frequent specific recognition and a culture of celebration that creates many winners

A Shift in Professional Development

From external training (workshops and courses) . . .	to job-embedded learning
From the expectation that learning occurs infrequently (on the few days devoted to professional development) . . .	to an expectation that learning is ongoing and occurs as part of routine work practice
From presentations to entire faculties . . .	to team-based action research
From learning by listening . . .	to learning by doing
From learning individually through courses and workshops . . .	to learning collectively by working together
From assessing impact on the basis of teacher satisfaction ("did you like it?") . . .	to assessing impact on the basis of evidence of improved student learning
From short-term exposure to multiple concepts and practices . . .	to sustained commitment to limited focused initiatives

Confronting the Brutal Facts of Substantive Change

It is disingenuous to suggest that the transformation will be easy or to present it with a rosy optimism that obscures the inevitable turmoil ahead.

Those who hope to transform their schools and districts into PLCs should heed the advice of Jim Collins (2001): "You absolutely cannot make a series of good decisions without first confronting the brutal facts" (p. 70). The first and most brutal fact that must be confronted in creating PLCs is that the task is not merely challenging; it is daunting. It is disingenuous to suggest that the transformation will be easy or to present it with a rosy optimism that obscures the inevitable turmoil ahead.

The recommendations we present throughout this book are grounded in solid research from a number of different fields. We can point to a growing number of schools and districts throughout North America who have successfully implemented the recommendations. And as we stated at the outset, the most frequent reaction of those who attend our workshops is, "This just makes sense." But the fact that a concept is backed by research, evidence, and logic does not mean those who are called upon to abandon the comfort and security of their known practices will embrace and implement it. The response to any significant change is typically not logical; it is emotional. In examining the psychology of change, Robert Evans (2001) found that even when change is recognized as positive, it is accompanied by a sense of loss and causes a kind of bereavement. We are more prone to protect the assumptions that have guided us than to re-examine them because those assumptions have provided us with a sense of identity; they have helped us make sense of our world. Therefore, we are likely to react defensively if our assumptions are called into question. Change also challenges our competence. When we are called upon to develop new proficiencies (for example, to become a contributing member of a collaborative team), we are likely to feel the anxiety that accompanies moving outside our comfort zone. Change creates confusion. The clarity and predictability of the status quo are replaced by uncertainty. Change can open old wounds and rekindle lingering resentment from those who committed to previous innovations only to see them abandoned or from those whose own calls for change about which they cared deeply were ignored by others (Evans, 2001).

Finally and inescapably, as we stressed in the last chapter, substantive change creates conflict. When schools are engaged in second-order change, staff members may perceive that the culture of their school has been weakened, their opinions are not valued, and that the stability and order of the school have been undermined (Marzano et al., 2005). When people are called upon to do differently, it is inevitable that they question why and challenge both the need for and the specifics of the change. It serves no purpose to ignore, obscure, or brush aside these brutal facts. Those who hope to help their schools and districts become PLCs will embrace them, respect them, and most importantly, address them. Recognition of the harsh realities must be a part of any implementation plan.

We want to stress, however, that acknowledging the difficulty of the challenge is no excuse for either procrastination or for merely tweaking existing practices. We concur with the late Ted Sizer's (1991) conclusion that a slow, gradual, incremental approach to school improvement is unlikely to bring about the significant transformation our schools and districts require. We need to act, and we need to act in substantive ways.

The Need for Leadership

The current emphasis on shared decision making, dispersed leadership, staff empowerment, collaboration, and collegiality has tended to obscure another harsh reality about substantive change: it demands the sustained attention, energy, and effort of school and district leaders. The idea of bottom-up reform is great, but it is unrealistic to assume that one day a group of educators gathered together in the faculty lounge will suddenly begin to re-examine the basic assumptions, beliefs, and practices that constitute the culture of their school. Major change almost never begins from the bottom (Evans, 2001). There are examples of departments or grade-level teams who operate according to the PLC concept in a school that does not, but we know of no instances in which a *schoolwide* PLC was created and sustained without effective leadership from the principal. We know of no successful *districtwide* implementation without the sustained focus of the superintendent. Some responsibilities simply cannot be delegated. At the school level, it is the principal who creates the conditions that allow the PLC concept to flourish (McLaughlin & Talbert, 2001), and districtwide implementation will require the leadership of the superintendent.

School and district leaders cannot passively wait for substantive change to "bubble up." They must understand that deep reform will require support *and* pressure. There is a tendency in education to regard support as inherently positive and pressure as intrinsically negative. We have seen educators ask, "Will you support me?" as a litmus test for their leaders, assuming a "good" leader will assure them of unwavering support. Effective leaders, however, will not support ineffective practice, cruel comments, or deliberate violations of collective commitments. In those instances, support would be no virtue.

We have also heard from educators who oppose an improvement initiative, regardless of its merits, for one reason: it came from the administration. They expect us to be appalled at the disclosure of a top-down initiative. But top-down leadership has its place, or as Michael Fullan (2010) succinctly puts it, "It's okay to be assertive" (p. 30). Effective change processes demand both pressure and support and leaders at both the district and building level must be willing to kick-start the improvement process and exert top-down pressure when needed.

If leaders allow participation in PLC processes to be optional, they doom the initiative to failure. Piloting a program with interested staff can be a

A slow, gradual, incremental approach to school improvement is unlikely to bring about the significant transformation our schools and districts require. We need to act, and we need to act in substantive ways.

We know of no instances in which a schoolwide PLC was created and sustained without effective leadership from the principal. We know of no successful districtwide implementation without the sustained focus of the superintendent.

valuable way to build shared knowledge regarding its effectiveness, but substantive change that transforms a culture will ultimately require more than an invitation. As Evans (2001) wrote, "If innovation is merely offered as a suggestion or left as a voluntary initiative, it generally fails. . . . It is insufficient simply to wait for changes in belief to produce changes in behavior; one must insist on some of the latter as a way to foster some of the former" (p. 244). The challenging of deep assumptions inherent in changing the culture of a school or district requires leaders to assert their influence, to get and hold people's attention. In short, leaders must be willing to lead.

When Jim Collins (2001) set out to determine what distinguished "great" companies from those that were less effective, he made a conscious decision to exclude leadership as a factor because he felt it was simplistic to attribute the success or failure of an organization to its leaders. The empirical evidence, however, brought him to an inescapable conclusion: every great company was characterized by effective leadership. Furthermore, Collins found that those leaders were not charismatic, flamboyant personalities, but rather self-effacing individuals with a ferocious resolve to make their organizations great and a fanatical fixation on results. Their goal was to build the capacity of their organizations to be successful long after they had retired.

Collins argues that his findings apply not only to the private sector but to other organizations as well—including schools and school districts. We believe he is right, particularly on the significance of leadership. Leaders do not empower others by disempowering themselves. Self-directed teams and highly autonomous schools characterized by shared decision making are important targets toward which to strive. In fact, one of the reasons for becoming a PLC is to lessen the dependency on individual leaders and to build the capacity of staff to sustain a strong culture despite changes in leadership. But these laudable conditions simply cannot occur without key leaders assuming personal responsibility for initiating the process. One of the great ironies in education is that it takes strong and effective educational leaders to create truly empowered people who are capable of sustaining improvement after the leader has gone.

Advice for Leading a PLC Initiative

If, as we have argued thus far, (1) implementing the PLC concept is complex and challenging, and (2) it is impossible to meet that challenge without the advocacy and attention of effective leaders, then it is important to explore the most promising leadership strategies. We offer the following insights.

Link the Change Initiative to Current Practices and Assumptions When Possible

Educators are more inclined to support what is presented as evolution rather than revolution. Therefore, leaders should, if possible, attempt to connect an innovation to existing practices and principles. In effect, they should show that the proposal represents a natural next step in the school's ongoing effort to improve results for students. They should be certain to honor rather than demean past efforts and paradigms. The message should be, "We did then what we knew how to do. Now that we know better, we can do better."

The message should be, "We did then what we knew how to do. Now that we know better, we can do better."

Focus First on the "Why" of Change, Then Focus on the "How"

One of the most effective strategies for linking substantive change to the past is demonstrating how the change will advance the articulated purpose of the school. As mentioned previously, virtually all schools and districts have written "mission" statements that solemnly assert the intention to have a profound and positive impact on the lives of the students they serve. In effect, those statements declare that the school is committed to serving a moral purpose. Leaders should return to that purpose; provide evidence that current practices, although well intentioned, are failing to achieve it; and clarify how the proposed change will enhance the school's ability to achieve its purpose. Fullan (2001) lists "moral purpose" as a critical element in his framework for effective leadership. He argues that leadership, if it is to be effective, must "have an explicit 'making-a-difference' sense of purpose . . . and ultimately be assessed by the extent to which it awakens people's intrinsic commitment, which is none other than the mobilizing of everyone's sense of moral purpose" (pp. 19–20).

"Good leaders lead from something deep in the heart" (Bolman & Deal, 1996, p. 5), and we have found the most effective leaders of PLCs publicly and repeatedly cite their commitment to an overarching purpose. It might be eliminating the achievement gap, breaking the cycle of poverty, responding to the individual needs of each student, expanding access to opportunities, or promoting excellence and equity. This direct appeal to collective purpose calls upon a staff to unite in order to achieve a higher end. Staff may be anxious to hear a detailed explanation of "How?" (knowing the devil is in the details), but leaders should start with and repeatedly return to "Why?" They should create a story with a teachable point of view—a succinct explanation of the school or district's purpose and how the initiative is advancing that purpose—and they should repeat that story with boorish redundancy.

We have found the most effective leaders of PLCs publicly and repeatedly cite their commitment to an overarching purpose. . . . This direct appeal to collective purpose calls upon a staff to unite in order to achieve a higher end.

Align Actions With Words

Articulating a mission or purpose does nothing to close the knowing-doing gap unless people act upon that mission. Leaders establish personal credibility far more readily by what they do than by what they say. Expressions of commitment to strong moral purpose only generate cynicism if the commitment is not manifested through behavior. If leaders are to be believed, they must establish their personal integrity, and "integrity requires action. . . . Authentic leaders embody character in action: they don't just say, they do" (Evans, 2001, p. 90).

Unfocused and undirected action, however, detracts from rather than enhances the clarity and coherence of a leader's communication. Clarity demands focused, sustained attention and consistent direction over time. Building the capacity of staff to work as a PLC represents a *major* initiative, and effective leaders will do everything in their power to protect the staff from other intrusions on their time and energy (Marzano et al., 2005). They will model a fundamental premise of effective leadership: "The main thing is to keep the main thing the main thing" (Covey, 1994).

Be Flexible on Implementation but Firm on the Essence of the Initiative

This is merely another way to call upon leaders to demonstrate loose *and* tight leadership (see chapter 3). There are typically multiple ways to solve a given problem, and leaders should be open to exploring alternative strategies for implementation. An unwillingness to consider alternative strategies or to amend timelines for implementation will impede rather than enhance the PLC journey. Leaders must be willing to listen and to adapt. There will be battles to fight, but drawing a line in the sand regarding the specifics of implementation is typically the wrong battle.

On the other hand, leaders must hold firm to the core principles that underlie the PLC concept if the concept is to take root. Imagine a principal who presents her staff with all the evidence in support of PLCs and how the concept is aligned with the school's commitment to high levels of learning for all students. She paints a portrait of a school in which the entire staff works collaboratively to clarify the knowledge, skills, and dispositions each student must acquire in each grade level and unit; to monitor the learning of each student on a timely basis; and to create systematic interventions to ensure students receive additional time and support for learning. She describes teachers working together to examine multiple sources of evidence of student learning and using that evidence as part of a process of continuous improvement. After much dialogue, the faculty achieves consensus to work to create such a school.

As the initiative moves forward, however, staff members begin to propose compromises to expedite the process: "Couldn't we simply use the questions from the textbook to monitor student learning instead of working together to create common assessments?" "Can't an individual teacher opt out of the collaborative team meetings as long as he is getting good results?" "Shouldn't students who fail to demonstrate proficiency suffer the consequences rather than being provided additional opportunities to learn?" "Aren't systematic interventions 'enabling' students?" "Do we really need to examine student achievement data?" Questions like these do not represent issues of implementation or timelines. They get to the very heart of PLC concept. We are convinced that the most common cause of the demise of PLC initiatives is not the result of a single cataclysmic event, but rather repeated compromises regarding the fundamental premises of PLCs. There is no one fatal blow: PLCs die from a thousand small wounds.

One of the most common small wounds inflicted on a PLC initiative occurs with protestation of the lack of time to implement PLC concepts. We have made the point repeatedly that the process does take time, and we have emphasized that staff members should be provided with time to work at the process during their contractual day and within their contractual year. We recognize the significance of time, but leaders cannot accept scarcity of time as justification for not moving forward. The best thinking in time management boils down to a single principle: "organize and execute around priorities" (Covey, 1989, p. 149). A principal who alleges she is too busy doing her job to work on building a PLC must be reminded that the very essence of her job is to create the conditions in which a PLC will flourish. A teacher who contends he is too busy teaching to work with colleagues to clarify what students must learn, the methods to be used in monitoring student learning, and the strategies to be implemented when students struggle must be told such work is critical to the effective teaching process. A counselor who professes she is too busy writing college recommendations to monitor the academic and emotional well-being of her students must be told to redefine her role and her priorities. In each case, a sincere attempt can be made to explore options for removing less essential tasks from the staff member's duties in order to address the issue of time, but the work of building a PLC should never be considered an "add on." No one who has worked in schools for any length of time would question whether educators work hard. They do. The challenge for leaders and the key to the success of a school is to ensure they are doing the *right* work (Elmore, 2003). The priority work of effective schools, and the educators within them, is building the collective capacity to function as a PLC.

Disperse Leadership

We have stressed that leadership is essential to successful implementation of PLCs; however, leadership is not a solo act. In studying thousands of cases of effective leadership, James Kouzes and Barry Posner (2003) could not find a single example of extraordinary achievement that occurred without the active involvement and support of many people. As they wrote:

> We've yet to find a single instance in which one talented person—leader or individual contributor—accounted for most, let alone 100 percent, of the success. Throughout the years, leaders from all professions, from all economic sectors, and from around the globe continue to tell us, "You can't do it alone." Leadership . . . is a team performance. . . . The winning strategies will be based on the "we not I" philosophy. Collaboration is a social imperative. Without it people can't get extraordinary things done in organizations. (p. 20)

We are convinced that the most common cause of the demise of PLC initiatives is not the result of a single cataclysmic event, but rather repeated compromises regarding the fundamental premises of PLCs.

In his study, Collins (2001) found ineffective organizations tended to operate under the model of one genius leader with lots of helpers. The leaders of effective companies, on the other hand, created a powerful leadership team that energized the improvement effort. Furthermore, the creation of that team came early in the process—often preceding the specific improvement initiative—as leaders focused on getting the "right people on the bus" (p. 41).

Another comprehensive study discovered building a guiding coalition was "an essential part of the early stages" of leading a change process (Kotter, 1998). Members of the coalition committed to working together interdependently in order to achieve a collective purpose and common goal for which they were mutually accountable.

The significance of widely dispersed leadership has been stressed in the educational research as well. A comprehensive study of the principalship concluded that responsibilities of the position are so diverse and demanding that no single person could possibly fulfill them. Creating a leadership team is essential to effective leadership at the school level (Marzano et al., 2005). Almost everyone who has examined how to improve schools has endorsed this call for shared, widely distributed leadership (see Why Do We Need Widely Distributed Leadership?).

As one study of professional learning communities concluded, "The message is unequivocal: sustaining the impact of improvement requires the leadership capability of many rather than a few" (Bezzina, 2006, p. 164). Michael Fullan (2005) was right when he concluded that the real measure of an educational leader is not merely student achievement scores but how many leaders he or she has developed to carry on the work *after* his or her departure.

Embrace the Premise of "Ready, Fire, Aim"

As we stressed in chapter 9, however, leaders cannot wait for unanimity before moving forward with an improvement process. Throughout this book we have offered advice in building consensus, conducting crucial conversations, using the art of persuasion, and implementing strategies to enlist resisters in the initiative. A leader can execute flawlessly every step we have proposed and still experience both overt and covert resistance. This situation does not represent failure on the part of the leader; it represents the reality of substantive change.

We have seen principals who respond to this reality by ignoring the willingness and readiness of a staff to implement PLC processes in order to devote their effort and energy to convincing a few holdouts of the worthiness of the initiative. In these instances, instead of using shared decision making and participatory processes as a springboard to action, they allow participation to become a quagmire that prevents action.

Why Do We Need Widely Distributed Leadership?

We now understand that instructional leadership in effective schools "will be broadened and viewed as a dispersed concept that includes teachers. This is in keeping with the teacher empowerment concept; it recognizes that a principal cannot be the only leader in a complex organization like a school. With the democratization of organizations, especially schools, the leadership function becomes one of creating a community of shared values" (Lezotte, 1991).

"[Principals of the most effective schools] were at the center rather than at the top of their school's organization. To facilitate consensus building and collective effort, they shared power. . . . Their actions encouraged teacher leadership and. . . . nurtured decision making by teachers." (Newmann & Associates, 1996, pp. 292, 258)

"Rather than focusing on the character traits and actions of individual leaders—in the heroic American tradition of charismatic leadership—we will increasingly have to focus on the distribution of leadership." (Elmore, 2006, p. 42)

"It is only through participatory leadership that one is likely to create the level and type of commitments necessary to sustain disruptive innovations." (Schlechty, 2005, pp. 12–13)

"Strong learning communities develop when principals learn to relinquish a measure of control and help others participate in building leadership throughout the school." (McLaughlin & Talbert, 2006, p. 81)

Shared leadership is based on the concept of the school as a community of learners and recognition of the fact that the principal can't do it alone (Hallinger, 2007).

Remember that effective leaders are *action oriented*. Fullan (2010) refers to this orientation as "ready, fire, aim" and urges leaders to remember the following:

1. To get anywhere, you have to *do* something (a bias for action).

2. In doing something you have to focus on skills (building collective capacity).

3. Acquisition of skills requires *clarity*.

4. Clarity results in ownership.

5. Doing this together with others generates *shared* ownership.

6. Persist no matter what. Resilience is your best friend. (p. 32)

Expect to Make Mistakes and Learn From Them

Setbacks should be viewed as opportunities to begin again, this time with the benefit of greater insight and experience.

Murphy's Law promises, "If anything can go wrong, it will." In reflecting on the problem of school change, psychologist Seymour Sarason (1996) concluded Murphy was an optimist and Murphy's Law was a "gross underestimation" (p. 339). Leaders should approach the change process honestly and advise staff that it is unrealistic to expect flawless execution in initial efforts to implement complex concepts. The best-laid plans and noblest of efforts will typically fall short of the desired results, at least initially. Staff must be assured that these setbacks are simply a natural part of the learning process rather than a failure of will or skill. Rather than being branded as failures, setbacks should be viewed as opportunities to begin again, this time with the benefit of greater insight and experience.

If our earliest efforts in technology were regarded as final products rather than first drafts, we would all still be driving model Ts and computers would be stored in warehouses rather than sitting on our laps. Similarly, there is no reason to believe first efforts to transform a school will lead to spectacular results. Resilient leaders will celebrate effort, learning, and progress even when things do not go well, but they will also immediately start to think about how they can make the situation better (Goleman, 1998). Their resilience allows them to accept criticism, acknowledge setbacks, and welcome recommendations for alternative strategies for achieving shared purpose at the same time they remain optimistic about the final outcome. They keep the faith.

Learn by Doing

One of the most common traps that prevent organizations from closing the knowing-doing gap is reliance upon learning by training rather than learning by doing. As Pfeffer and Sutton (2000) conclude, "The answer to the knowing-doing problem is deceptively simple: *embed more of the process of acquiring new knowledge in the actual doing of the task* and less in the formal training programs that are frequently ineffective. If you do it, then you will know it" (p. 27, emphasis added).

The learning by doing characterized by an action orientation is a critical factor in both organizations in general and educational organizations in particular (Bennis, 1997; Block, 2003; Collins & Porras, 1997; Elmore, 2003). Yet we have seen schools devote years of training to becoming a PLC according to elaborate strategic plans. The first year may be devoted to helping staff learn to work in teams through training in consensus building, conflict resolution, and norm writing. The second year may be devoted to examining and rewriting curriculum. In the third year, teachers are trained in writing good assessments; in the fourth, staff learn how to analyze data from assessments; and so on.

Meanwhile, as these schools and districts are *preparing* to become a PLC, other schools roll up their sleeves and dig into the work of PLCs. They learn by doing, and they build community by doing the work together (Fullan, 2001; McLaughlin & Talbert, 2001). As questions arise, appropriate training is provided to help staff resolve the questions as part of their ongoing process. The schools and districts with this action orientation make the most progress on the PLC journey.

We are more convinced than ever that schools develop as PLCs when their staffs actually work *at the process rather than train for the process.*

When we wrote *Professional Learning Communities at Work*™, we made a conscious decision to emphasize *work* in order to stress the importance of an action orientation. We didn't refer to "PLCs at training," "PLCs at study," "PLCs at reading," or "PLCs at staff development." Now that we have had the opportunity to work with school systems throughout North America, we are more convinced than ever that schools develop as PLCs when their staffs actually *work* at the process rather than train for the process.

Pfeffer and Sutton (2000) contend that most organizations already have all the knowledge they need to improve—they do not simply implement what they already know. What those organizations typically require to move forward is more will than skill. As Peter Block (2003) wrote, "We deny ourselves action when we keep looking for more and more information to ensure greater certainty as a condition for moving on" (p. 42). Those who hope to lead PLCs should stop waiting for more training, more knowledge, and more skills, and instead create the conditions that enable staff members to learn by doing.

Keep Hope Alive

Even the most powerful vision of a better future will inspire people to act only if they have a strong sense of self-efficacy, the belief that they can create their future through their own purposeful actions. Fostering this self-efficacy by helping people believe in themselves is one of a leader's highest duties (Gardner, 1988). This responsibility is particularly important in building a PLC because the concept rests upon the premise that the best way to improve the school or district is by developing the people within it. Leaders of PLCs must consistently communicate, through their words and actions, their conviction that the people in their school or district are capable of accomplishing great things through their collective efforts. Conventional wisdom asks if people in an organization believe in their leaders. While that question is significant, the question, "Do the leaders believe in their people?" may be even more relevant to the successful implementation of PLC processes.

Leaders must not only personally keep the faith; they must also foster hope, optimism, and a sense of collective efficacy throughout the organization.

We are arguing here that leaders must not only personally keep the faith; they must also foster hope, optimism, and a sense of collective efficacy throughout the organization. Effective leaders do not engender this confidence by ignoring or denying problems and challenges. They do, however, convey their conviction that those problems and challenges are temporary and can be solved once they gather more information and build greater collective capacity by getting to work and doing something (Kanter, 2004). They do not succumb to a defeatist attitude when confronted with setbacks, but motivate themselves, break down formidable tasks into smaller steps, and seek out different ways of achieving their objectives.

Most importantly, optimism and self-efficacy are not simply innate; they can be learned, and the leader is in the key position to teach those emotions. Psychologist Daniel Goleman and his colleagues (2002) concluded that the passion, energy, enthusiasm, and self-efficacy of the leader are contagious, invigorating people throughout the organization. Fullan (2001) also found that the most effective leaders conveyed an optimism, confidence, and determination to persevere that were infectious. A comprehensive review of the research on the principalship found that principals, for better or worse, set the emotional tone of their building, and that one of the most significant responsibilities of the principal was "portraying a positive attitude about the ability of the staff to accomplish substantive things" (Marzano et al., 2005, p. 56).

Communicating confidence and hopefulness in good times is important in any organization, but demonstrating confidence and hopefulness in trying times is imperative.

Cynics, pessimists, and those who do not believe in the ability of their colleagues make poor leaders. Communicating confidence and hopefulness in good times is important in any organization, but demonstrating confidence and hopefulness in trying times is imperative. This imperativeness is only heightened in schools where the collective efficacy of a staff is a better predictor of student success than the socioeconomic status of the students (Goddard, Hoy, & Hoy, 1994). For the sake of their students, teachers need to believe that their collective efforts can make a difference.

During our workshops, we sometimes ask participants which students they would prefer in their classrooms next fall. The first class is comprised entirely of students who exhibit what psychologist Carol Dweck (2006) has termed a "fixed mindset"—that is, the students believe that their achievement in the course will be based solely on their innate ability and that their effort will have little bearing on their success. The second class is comprised of students who exhibit a "growth mindset." They believe that their achievement will be determined primarily by their effort. Invariably, the entire workshop group opts for students who believe in effort-based ability, students who are convinced that "smart is not something you just are; smart is something you can get" (Efficacy Institute, 2005). Educators have good reason to make that choice, given the well-established link between a student's sense of self-efficacy and his or her academic achievement. The next question we pose is, "If we want students to believe in effort-based achievement, aren't we obligated to model the principle of effort-based achievement ourselves? Shouldn't we demonstrate a core belief that our collective efforts as a staff can have a tremendous impact on the learning of our students?" Optimism burns brightest in those who believe in their ability to impact the future.

The good news is that their belief in their ability to make a difference in the lives of students continues to be the single most powerful factor cited by those entering the teaching profession. The most striking finding in a non-partisan national survey of new teachers was their passion for teaching—a passion fueled by their fervent desire to make a difference for their students. Teaching was a conscious choice for them, a response to a calling. Only 12 percent indicated that they fell into the profession by chance, and the zeal of the new teachers for their work far exceeded their contemporaries who entered the private sector (Farkas, Johnson, Foleno, Duffett, & Foley, 2000).

The bad news, however, is that most of those same enthusiastic teachers soon discovered that they were ill equipped to deal with issues such as classroom management, inspiring unmotivated students, and meeting the needs of struggling students. Within a short period of time, almost 75 percent doubted whether the efforts of a staff could transform a low-performing school. They attributed problems they were encountering to circumstances beyond their control and questioned their ability to make things better. When pressed for what they might do to improve their situation, they proposed finding a school with more motivated students and more supportive parents as their best alternative. In a very short time, the passion and fervor of these new teachers and their desire to make a difference gave way to a collective sense of resignation and helplessness (Farkas et al., 2000).

A study (Johnson & Kardos, 2007) of how to retain new teachers found that traditional school cultures only exacerbated this loss of self-efficacy among new teachers. In these "veteran-oriented cultures," workplace norms were set by veteran teachers who protected individual autonomy at the expense of professional interaction. Schools with novice-oriented culture, where the values and work modes were established by a predominantly novice faculty, were no better. In both settings, inexperienced teachers were unable to benefit from the accumulated wisdom of veteran staff because there was little professional interchange between the two groups. Schools that provided a new teacher with an individual mentor did no better at improving the teacher's job satisfaction or retention rate.

The study did find, however, that schools with "integrated professional cultures," cultures that structured ongoing professional exchanges among teachers of various experience levels, offered the inclusion and support that led to higher levels of satisfaction, retention, and self-efficacy among new teachers. These cultures are grounded in the belief that

> students are best served when teachers assist each other and share responsibility for their students' learning as well as their own. . . . structures are in place that further facilitate teacher interaction and reinforce interdependence. Schools with integrated professional cultures explicitly value teachers' professional growth and renewal [that] benefit both new teachers and their veteran colleagues. New teachers are supported in their efforts to teach their students well, veteran teachers are continually renewing themselves, and the entire faculty is united in its pursuit of student success and school improvement. (Johnson & Kardos, 2007, pp.159–160)

Professional learning communities set out to restore and increase the passion of teachers by not only reminding them of the moral purpose of their work, but also by creating the conditions that allow them to do that work successfully.

It should be evident that the culture these researchers describe is the culture of a PLC. Professional learning communities set out to restore and increase the passion of teachers by not only reminding them of the moral purpose of their work, but also by creating the conditions that allow them to do that work successfully. The focus is on making a positive difference in the lives of kids rather than on raising test scores. There is constant emphasis that the staff must work collectively, as a community, if they are to meet the needs of students because they cannot adequately respond to students if they work in isolation. Leaders provide constant reminders of the impact teachers and teams are having on the lives of students. They make heroes of staff members by weaving a never-ending story of committed people who touch both the minds and hearts of their students.

Those who regard these direct appeals to emotions as too "touchy-feely" for the "bottom-line" mentality that should drive results-oriented schools are mistaken. Daniel Goleman and colleagues (2002) present a compelling argument that "great leadership works through the emotions" (p. 3). Educators hunger for evidence that they are successful in their work, that they are part of a significant collective endeavor, and that their efforts are making a positive difference in the lives of the students they serve. Professional learning communities are specifically designed to address these emotional needs, and that is precisely why the PLC concept offers the most promising strategy for sustained and substantive school improvement.

Those who have succeeded in developing PLCs attest to the energy and enthusiasm—the joy—generated by committed people working together, sharing ideas, and accomplishing goals they value. Fullan (2001) found that once teachers begin to experience the benefits of a PLC, "they literally can't get enough of it" (p. 99). In her study of schools characterized by shared purpose, collaborative teams, data-driven decisions, and job-embedded learning, Joan Richardson (2004) found faculties infused with passion and benefiting from powerful, positive relationships.

High school faculties are notorious for their recalcitrance, but in their study of high schools, Milbrey McLaughlin and Joan Talbert (2001) found that even teachers at the high school level were energized and renewed by the power of working in PLCs: "In collaborative professional communities teachers experience careers marked by collective accomplishments and a sense of continuing professional growth" (p. 91).

Particularly striking in McLaughlin and Talbert's study were the sharply differing perspectives and attitudes of teachers in two different departments *in the same school*—departments that were close in physical proximity but miles apart in terms of their cultures. The English department was organized into collaborative teams, while social studies teachers worked in isolation. English teachers raved about their relationship with their colleagues, while social studies teachers complained bitterly about others in their department. English teachers attacked problems collectively. Social studies teachers worried alone. English teachers were uniformly positive regarding their students, describing them as "excellent," "bright," and "cooperative." They responded to students who experienced academic difficulties by assigning them to an "intensive care" list to receive additional support. Social studies teachers considered the same students unmotivated and apathetic and offered no response to students who struggled.

Creating the culture of a PLC is indeed hard work; however, what is the alternative? Teaching in isolation in traditional schools is also very hard work, and the teachers in the social studies department in the McLaughlin and Talbert study were feeling worn down by the demands being placed upon them. The choice facing educators is not, "Shall we do the easy work of maintaining traditional schools or the difficult work of creating a PLC?" The real issue is to assess honestly which kind of hard work offers the greatest hope for success for students and for professional satisfaction for educators. We have always worked hard. Will we now choose to work smart? The path to school improvement has never been clearer. We know what to do, but will we demonstrate the discipline to do it? Will we close the knowing-doing gap by taking purposeful action because, at long last, we acknowledge that "to *know* and not to *do* is really not to know" (Covey, 2002, p. xiv)?

We have always worked hard. Will we now choose to work smart?

And will we act with the sense of urgency the situation demands? The words Martin Luther King, Jr., used in 1967 to describe a different desperate situation ring true for educators today:

> We are confronted with the fierce urgency of now. In this unfolding conundrum of life and history there is such a thing as being too late. Procrastination is still the thief of time. We must move past indecision to action. Now let us begin. The choice is ours, and though we may prefer it otherwise, we must choose in this crucial moment of human history. (p. 163)

Many who work through this handbook will endorse this call for action, will agree that something needs to be done, and then will wait for someone else to do it. There is a natural tendency to assign responsibility for improving schools to others. We have heard principals say, "I hope the central office heard your message and is prepared to do something about it," ignoring the fact that individual schools have become powerful PLCs without support from the central office. We have heard teachers say, "I sure hope the principal will take responsibility for implementing what you advocate," ignoring the fact that individual departments and grade-level teams have become islands representing powerful PLCs in schools that seem indifferent to the concept. Perhaps, as Michael Fullan (2005) argues, the effort to create PLCs should be a trilevel effort involving the state or province, the district, and the individual school and community working in consort. But Fullan also warns it is a fundamental mistake to assume the system must change before we do. As he writes, "Each of us *is* the system" (p. 222), and therefore each of us must recognize his or her personal and individual responsibility to promote the PLC concept. Here is the brutal fact: the most common reason for failure to close the knowing-doing gap is not conflict with others, but conflict from within. We fail to do what we recognize we should do simply because it is easier to continue an unquestionably ineffective or bad practice than it is to adopt a new one. The ultimate challenge is not to manage others; the challenge is to manage ourselves and to demonstrate, day-by-day, the self-discipline to "put first things first" (Covey, 1989, p. 148)

Final Thoughts

This book has attempted to address some of the structural and cultural challenges of schooling that prevent schools and districts from making progress as professional learning communities. We have attempted to draw upon research from organizational development, education, leadership, psychology, and sociology to suggest alternative strategies for dealing with those challenges. We have attempted to give you the preliminary awareness, knowledge, and tools to help you begin the PLC journey—*but you will only develop your skill and capacity to build a PLC by engaging in the work.* You must learn by doing.

We have attempted to give you the preliminary awareness, knowledge, and tools to help you begin the PLC journey—but you will only develop your skill and capacity to build a PLC by engaging in the work.

Thus, we have not presented you with a "how to" book. The history, cultures, and contexts of each school and district are unique and must be considered in the improvement process. Furthermore, challenges to education will arise in the coming years that we could not possibly anticipate when we wrote this book. We remain convinced, however, that when educators learn to clarify their priorities, to assess the current reality of their situation, to work together, and to build continuous improvement into the very fabric of their collective work, they create conditions for the ongoing learning and self-efficacy essential to solving whatever problems they confront. We hope every school or district that begins the PLC journey will come to believe deeply in and, more importantly, act upon the advice attributed to Ralph Waldo Emerson: "What lies behind us and what lies ahead of us are insignificant compared to what lies within us."

References and Resources

Ainsworth, L. (2007). Common formative assessments: The centerpiece of an integrated standards-based assessment system. In D. Reeves (Ed.), *Ahead of the curve: The power of assessment to transform teaching and learning* (pp. 79–102). Bloomington, IN: Solution Tree Press.

Ainsworth, L., & Viegut, D. (2006). *Common formative assessments: An essential part of the integrated whole.* Thousand Oaks, CA: Corwin Press.

Amabile, T., & Kramer, S. (2010). What really motivates workers: Understanding the power of progress. *Harvard Business Review, 88*(1), 44–45.

Annenberg Institute for School Reform. (2005). *Professional learning communities: Professional development strategies that improve instruction.* Accessed at www .annenberginstitute.org/pdf/ProfLearning.pdf on January 18, 2010.

Autry, J. (2001). *The servant leader: How to build a creative team, develop great morale, and improve bottom-line performance.* New York: Three Rivers Press.

Axelrod, R. (2002). *Terms of engagement: Changing the way we change organizations.* San Francisco: Berrett-Koehler.

Barber, M., & Mourshed, M. (2007). *How the world's best school systems come out on top.* Accessed at www.mckinsey.com/App_Media/Reports?SSO/Worlds_School_Systems_ Final.pdf on January 1, 2010.

Barber, M., & Mourshed, M. (2009). *Shaping the future: How good education systems can become great in the decade ahead. Report on the International Education Roundtable.* Accessed at www.mckinsey.com/locations/southeastasia/knowledge/Education_ Roundtable.pdf on January 1, 2010.

Bardwick, J. M. (1996). Peacetime management and wartime leadership. In F. Hesselbein, M. Goldsmith, & R. Beckhard (Eds.), *The leader of the future: New visions, strategies and practices for the next era* (pp. 131–140). San Francisco: Jossey-Bass.

Bennis, W. (1997). *Organizing genius: The secrets of creative collaboration.* Cambridge, MA: Perseus Books.

Bezzina, C. (2006). The road less traveled: Professional learning communities in secondary schools. *Theory Into Practice, 45*(2), 159–167.

Black, P., Harrison, C., Lee, C., Marsh, B., & Wiliam, D. (2004). Working inside the black box: Assessment for learning in the classroom. *Phi Delta Kappan, 86*(1), 9–19.

Black, P., & Wiliam, D. (1998). The formative purpose: Assessment must first promote learning. In M. Wilson (Ed.), *Towards coherence between classroom assessment and accountability (103rd Yearbook of the National Society for the Study of Education,* pp. 20–50). Chicago: University of Chicago Press for the National Society for the Study of Education.

Blanchard, K. (2007). *Leading at a higher level: Blanchard on leadership and creating high performing organizations.* Upper Saddle River, NJ: Prentice Hall.

Block, P. (2003). *The answer to how is yes: Acting on what matters.* San Francisco: Berrett-Koehler.

Blythe, T., Allen, D., & Powell, B. (1999). *Looking together at student work.* New York: Teachers College Press.

Bolman, L. G., & Deal, T. E. (1996). *Leading with soul: An uncommon journey of spirit.* San Francisco: Jossey-Bass.

Bolman, L. G., & Deal, T. E. (2000). *Escape from cluelessness: A guide for the organizationally challenged.* New York: AMACOM.

Bossidy, L., & Charan, R. (2002). *Execution: The discipline of getting things done.* New York: Crown Business.

Brophy, J. E. (2004). *Motivating students to learn* (2nd ed.). Mahwah, NJ: Lawrence Erlbaum.

Bryk, A., Camburn, E., & Louis, K. S. (1999, December). Professional community in Chicago elementary schools; Facilitating factors and organizational consequences. *Educational Administration Quarterly, 35,* 751–781.

Buckingham, M. (2005). *The one thing you need to know . . . about great managing, great leading and sustained individual success.* New York: Free Press.

Buffum, A., Mattos, M., & Weber, C. (2008). *Pyramid response to intervention: RTI, professional learning communities, and how to respond when kids don't learn.* Bloomington, IN: Solution Tree Press.

Burke, P. (2001). *Turning points: Looking collaboratively at student and teacher work.* Boston: Center for Collaborative Education. Accessed at www.turningpts.org/pdf/LASW.pdf on January 10, 2010.

Burns, J. M. (1982). *Leadership.* New York: Harper Perennial Classics.

Bushaw, W., & McNee, J. (2009). Americans speak out: The 41st annual Phi Delta Kappa/Gallup Poll of the public's attitudes toward public schools. *Phi Delta Kappan, 91*(1), 9–23.

Carroll, T. (2009). The next generation of learning teams. *Phi Delta Kappan, 91*(2), 8–13.

Champy, J. (1995). *Reengineering management: The mandate for new leadership.* New York: HarperCollins.

Chenoweth, K. (2009). It can be done, it's being done, and here's how. *Phi Delta Kappan, 91*(1), 38–43.

Childress, S., Doyle, D., & Thomas, D. (2009). *Leading for equity: The pursuit of excellence in the Montgomery County public schools.* Boston: Harvard Education Press.

Chokshi, S., & Fernandez, C. (2004, March). Challenges to importing Japanese lesson study: Concerns, misconceptions, and nuances. *Phi Delta Kappan, 85*(7), 520–525.

Christman, J., Neild, R., Sulkley, K., Blanc, S., Liu, R., Mitchell, C., et al. (2009). *Making the most of interim assessment data: Lessons from Philadelphia.* Accessed at http://pdf.researchforaction.org/rfapdf/publication/pdf_file/558/Christman_J_Making_the_Most_of_Interim_Assessment_Data.pdf on January 10, 2010.

Collins, J. (1996, Summer). Aligning action and values. *Leader to Leader, 1,* 19–24.

Collins, J. (2001). *Good to great: Why some companies make the leap . . . and others don't.* New York: Harper Business.

Collins, J., & Porras, J. (1997). *Built to last: Successful habits of visionary companies.* New York: Harper Business.

Consortium on Productivity in Schools. (1995). *Using what we have to get the schools we need.* New York: Teachers College Press.

Cotton, K. (2000). *The schooling practices that matter most.* Alexandria, VA: Association for Supervision and Curriculum Development.

Council of Chief School Officers. (2002). *Expecting success: A study of five high-performing, high-poverty schools.* Washington, DC: Author.

Covey, S. (1989). *The seven habits of highly effective people: Powerful lessons in personal change.* New York: Fireside.

Covey, S. (1994). *First things first: To live, to love, to learn, to leave a legacy.* New York: Fireside.

Covey, S. (1996). Three roles of the leader in the new paradigm. In F. Hesselbein, M. Goldsmith, & R. Beckhard (Eds.), *The leader of the future: New visions, strategies and practices for the next era* (pp.149–160). San Francisco: Jossey-Bass.

Covey, S. (2002). Introduction. In K. Patterson, J. Grenny, R. McMillan, & A. Switzler, *Crucial conversations: Tools for talking when stakes are high* (pp. xi–xiv). New York: McGraw-Hill.

Covey, S. (2006). *The speed of trust: The one thing that changes everything*. New York: Free Press.

Csikszentmihalyi, M. (1997). *Finding flow: The psychology of engagement with everyday life*. New York: Basic Books.

Darling-Hammond, L. (1996). What matters most: A competent teacher for every child. *Phi Delta Kappan, 78*(3), 193–200.

Darling-Hammond, L., Wei, R., Andree, A., Richardson, N., & Orphanos, S. (2009). *Professional learning in the learning profession: A status report on teacher development in the United States and abroad*. Oxford, OH: National Staff Development Council.

Deal, T. E., & Key, M. K. (1998). *Corporate celebration: Play, purpose and profit at work*. San Francisco: Berrett-Koehler.

Deal, T. E., & Peterson, K. D. (1999). *Shaping school culture: The heart of leadership*. San Francisco: Jossey-Bass.

Dolan, P. (1994). *Restructuring our schools: A primer on systemic change*. Kansas City: Systems and Organizations.

Dolejs, C. (2006). *Report on key practices and policies of consistently higher performing high schools*. Accessed at www.betterhighschools.org/docs/ReportOfKeyPracticesand Policies_10–31–06.pdf on January 10, 2010.

Drucker, P. (1992). *Managing for the future: The 1990s and beyond*. New York: Truman Talley Books.

Drucker, P. (1996). Not enough generals were killed. In F. Hesselbein, M. Goldsmith, & R. Beckhard (Eds.), *The leader of the future: New visions, strategies and practices for the next era* (pp. xi–xvi). San Francisco: Jossey-Bass.

Druskat, V., & Wolf, S. (2001). Group emotional intelligence and its influence on group effectiveness. In C. Cherniss & D. Goleman (Eds.), *The emotionally intelligent workplace: How to select for, measure, and improve emotional intelligence in individuals, groups, and organizations* (pp. 132–158). San Francisco: Jossey-Bass.

Duffett, A., Farkas, S., Rotherham, A. J., & Silva, E. (2008). *Waiting to be won over: Teachers speak on the profession, unions, and reform*. Washington, DC: Education Sector.

DuFour, R. (2003). *Through new eyes: Examining the culture of your school* [video]. Bloomington, IN: Solution Tree Press.

DuFour, R., DuFour, R., Eaker, R., & Karhanek, G. (2010). *Raising the bar and closing the gap: Whatever it takes*. Bloomington, IN: Solution Tree Press.

DuFour, R., & Eaker, R. (1998). *Professional learning communities at work: Best practices for enhancing student achievement*. Bloomington, IN: Solution Tree Press.

Dweck, C. (2006). *Mindset: The new psychology of success*. New York: Ballantine Books.

Eastwood, K., & Seashore-Louis, K. (1992). Restructuring that lasts: Managing the performance dip. *Journal of School Leadership, 2*(2), 213–224.

Efficacy Institute. (2005). *About us*. Accessed at www.efficacy.org/AboutUs/tabid/221/ Default.aspx on January 10, 2010.

Elmore, R. (2000). *Building a new structure for school leadership*. Accessed at http:// citeseerx.ist.psu.edu/viewdoc/download?doi=10.1.1.103.7688&rep=rep1&type=pdf on January 20, 2010.

Elmore, R. (2003). *Knowing the right thing to do: School improvement and performance-based accountability*. Washington, DC: NGA Center for Best Practices.

Elmore, R. (2006). *School reform from the inside out: Policy, practice, and performance*. Boston: Harvard Educational Press.

Elmore, R. (2010). "I used to think . . . and now I think . . ." *Harvard Education Letter, 26*(1), 7–8.

Elmore, R., & City, E. (2007). The road to school improvement. *Harvard Education Newsletter, 23*(3). Accessed at www.hepg.org/hel/article/229#home on January 15, 2010.

Evans, R. (2001). *The human side of school change: Reform, resistance and the real-life problems of innovation.* San Francisco: Jossey-Bass.

Farkas, S., Johnson, J., Foleno, T., Duffett, A., & Foley, P. (2000). *A sense of calling: Who teaches and why. A report from Public Agenda.* New York: Public Agenda.

Fullan, M. (1993). *Change forces.* London: Falmer Press.

Fullan, M. (2001). *Leading in a culture of change.* San Francisco: Jossey-Bass.

Fullan, M. (2005). *Leadership and sustainability: System thinkers in action.* San Francisco: Corwin Press.

Fullan, M. (2007). *The new meaning of educational change* (4th ed.). New York: Teachers College Press.

Fullan, M. (2008). *The six secrets of change: What the best organizations do to help their organizations survive and thrive.* San Francisco: Jossey-Bass.

Fullan, M. (2010). *Motion leadership: The skinny on becoming change savvy.* Thousand Oaks, CA: Corwin Press.

Fulton, K., Yoon, I., & Lee, C. (2005). *Induction into learning communities: National Commission on Teaching and America's Future.* Accessed at www.nctaf.org/documents/ NCTAF_Induction_Paper_2005.pdf on January 10, 2010.

Gallimore, R., Ermeling, B., Saunders, W., & Goldenberg, C. (2009). Moving the learning of teaching closer to practice: Teacher education implications of school-based inquiry teams. *Elementary School Journal, 109*(5), 537–551.

Gardner, H. (2004). *Changing minds: The art and science of changing our own and other people's minds.* Boston: Harvard Business School Press.

Gardner, J. (1988). *Leadership: An overview.* Washington, DC: Independent Sector.

Garmston, R. (2007). Results-oriented agendas transform meetings into valuable collaborative events. *Journal of Staff Development, 28*(2), 55–56.

Garmston, R., & Wellman, B. (1999). *The adaptive school: A sourcebook for developing collaborative groups.* Norwood, MA: Christopher-Gorden.

Georgiades, W., Fuentes, E., & Snyder, K. (1983). *A meta-analysis of productive school cultures.* Houston: University of Texas.

Gerstner, L., Semerad, R., Doyle, D., & Johnston, W. (1995). *Reinventing education: Entrepreneurship in America's public schools.* New York: Penguin Books.

Goddard, R., Hoy, W., & Hoy, A. (1994). Collective efficacy beliefs: Theoretical developments, empirical evidence, and future directions. *Educational Researcher, 33*(3), 3–13.

Goldberg, M., & Cross, C. (2005). Time out. *Edutopia.* Accessed at http://email.e-mailnetworks .com/ct/ct.php?t=1018842&c=561784071&m=m&type=3 on August 18, 2005.

Goldring, E., Porter, A., Murphy, J., Elliott, S., & Cravens, X. (2007). *Assessing learning-centered leadership: Connections to research, professional standards, and current practices.* Accessed at www.wallacefoundation.org/NR/rdonlyres/2D4629AE-6592– 4FDD-9206-D23A2B19EAC5/0/AssessingLearningCenteredLeadership.pdf on March 14, 2008.

Goldsmith, M. (1996). Ask, learn, follow up, and grow. In F. Hesselbein, M. Goldsmith, & R. Beckhard (Eds.), *The leader of the future: New visions, strategies and practices for the next era* (pp. 227–240). San Francisco: Jossey-Bass.

Goleman, D. (1998). *Working with emotional intelligence.* New York: Bantam Books.

Goleman, D., Boyatzis, R., & McKee, A. (2002). *Primal leadership: Learning to lead with emotional intelligence.* Boston: Harvard Business School Press.

Good, T. L., & Brophy, J. E. (2002). *Looking in classrooms* (9th ed.). Boston: Allyn & Bacon.

Hall, G., & Hord, S. (1987). *Change in schools: Facilitating the process*. Albany: State University of New York Press.

Hallinger, P. (2007, August 13). *Leadership for learning*. Presentation at annual conference of Australian Council for Educational Research, Melbourne, Australia.

Hamel, G. (2002). *Leading the revolution: How to thrive in turbulent times by making innovation a way of life*. Boston: Harvard Business School Press.

Handy, C. (1995). Managing the dream. In S. Chawla & J. Renesch (Eds.), *Learning organizations: Developing cultures for tomorrow's workplace* (pp. 45–56). New York: Productivity Press.

Handy, C. (1996). The new language of organizing and its implications for leaders. In F. Hesselbein, M. Goldsmith, & R. Beckhard (Eds.), *The leader of the future: New visions, strategies and practices for the next era* (pp. 3–10). San Francisco: Jossey-Bass.

Hargreaves, A. (2004). Broader purpose calls for higher understanding: An interview with Andy Hargreaves. *Journal of Staff Development, 25*(2), 46–50.

Hattie, J. (2009). *Visible learning: A synthesis of over 800 meta-analyses relating to student achievement*. New York: Routledge.

Haycock, K. (1998). Good teaching matters . . . a lot. *Thinking K–16, 3*(2), 1–14.

Heifetz, R. A., & Linsky, M. (2002). *Leadership on the line: Staying alive through the dangers of leading*. Boston: Harvard Business Press.

Hernez-Broome, G., & Hughes, R. (2004). Leadership development: Past, present, and future. *Human Resource Planning, 27*(1), 24–32.

Heskett, J. L., & Schlesinger, L. A. (1996). Leaders who shape and keep performance-oriented culture. In F. Hesselbein, M. Goldsmith, & R. Beckhard (Eds.), *The leader of the future: New visions, strategies and practices for the next era* (pp. 111–120). San Francisco: Jossey-Bass.

Hirsch, E. D. (1996). *The schools we need and why we don't have them*. New York: Doubleday.

Hord, S., Rutherford, W. L., Huling-Austin, L., & Hall, G. (1987). *Taking charge of change*. Alexandria, VA: Association for Supervision and Curriculum Development.

Interstate School Leaders Licensure Consortium. (1996). *Standards for school leaders*. Washington, DC: Council of Chief State School Officers.

Jacobs, H. H. (2001). New trends in curriculum: An interview with Heidi Hayes Jacobs. *Independent School, 61*(1), 18–24.

Johnston, J. (1995). Climate: Building a culture of achievement. *Schools in the Middle, 5*(2), 10–15.

Johnson, S. M., & Kardos, S. M. (2007). Professional culture and the promise of colleagues. In S. M. Johnson, *Finders and keepers: Helping new teachers survive and thrive in our schools* (139–166). San Francisco: Jossey-Bass.

Kanold, T. (2006). The continuous improvement wheel of a professional learning community. *Journal of Staff Development, 27*(2), 16–21.

Kanter, R. M. (1999, Summer). The enduring skills of change leaders. *Leader to Leader*. Accessed at www.leadertoleader.org/knowledgecenter/L2L/summer99/kanter.html on January 10, 2010.

Kanter, R. M. (2004). *Confidence: How winning streaks and losing streaks begin and end*. New York: Three Rivers Press.

Kanter, R. M. (2005, Winter). How leaders gain (and lose) confidence. *Leader to Leader, 35*, 21–27.

Katzenbach, J. R., & Smith, D. K. (1993). *The wisdom of teams: Creating the high-performance organization*. Boston: Harvard Business School Press.

Kegan, R., & Lahey, L. (2001). *How the way we talk can change the way we work: Seven languages for transformation*. San Francisco: Jossey-Bass.

Kendall, J., & Marzano, R. J. (2000). *Content knowledge: A compendium of standards and benchmarks for K–12 education* (3rd ed.). Alexandria, VA: Association for Supervision and Curriculum Development.

King, M. L., Jr. (1967, April 4). Beyond Vietnam: Address delivered to the clergy and laymen concerned about Vietnam. In C. Carson & K. Shepherd (Eds.), *A call to conscience: Landmark speeches of Dr. Martin Luther King, Jr.* (pp. 133–164). New York: Warner Books.

Kotter, J. P. (1996). *Leading change.* Boston: Harvard Business School.

Kotter, J. P. (1998, Fall). Winning at change. *Leader to Leader, 10,* 27–33.

Kotter, J. P., & Cohen, D. S. (2002). *The heart of change: Real-life stories of how people change their organizations.* Boston: Harvard Business School Press.

Kouzes, J., & Posner, B. (1987). *The leadership challenge: How to get extraordinary things done in organizations.* San Francisco: Jossey-Bass.

Kouzes, J. M., & Posner, B. Z. (1996). Seven lessons for leading the voyage to the future. In F. Hesselbein, M. Goldsmith, & R. Beckhard (Eds.), *The leader of the future: New visions, strategies and practices for the next era* (pp. 99–110). San Francisco: Jossey-Bass.

Kouzes, J. M., & Posner, B. Z. (1999). *Encouraging the heart: A leader's guide to rewarding and recognizing others.* San Francisco: Jossey-Bass.

Kouzes, J., & Posner, B. (2003, Spring). Challenge is the opportunity for greatness. *Leader to Leader, 28,* 16–23.

Kouzes, J., & Posner, B. (2006). *A leader's legacy.* San Francisco: Jossey-Bass.

Krugman, P. (2010, February 8). America is not yet lost. *New York Times.* Accessed at www.nytimes.com/2010/02/08/opinion/08krugman.html?scp=3&sq=Polish%20I%20do%20not%20allow&st=cse on February 28, 2010.

Kruse, S., Seashore Louis, K., & Bryk, A. (1995). *Building professional learning community in schools.* Madison, WI: Center for School Organization and Restructuring.

Leithwood, K., Seashore Louis, K., Anderson, S., & Wahlstrom, K. (2004). *How leadership influences student learning.* New York: Wallace Foundation.

Lencioni, P. (2003, Summer). The trouble with teamwork. *Leader to Leader, 29,* 35–40.

Lencioni, P. (2005). *Overcoming the five dysfunctions of a team: A field guide for leaders, managers, and facilitators.* San Francisco: Jossey-Bass.

Lezotte, L. (1991). *Correlates of effective schools: The first and second generation.* Okemos, MI: Effective Schools Products. Accessed at www.effectiveschools.com/Correlates.pdf on January 6, 2006.

Lezotte, L. (2002). *Revolutionary and evolutionary: The effective schools movement.* Accessed at www.effectiveschools.com/images/stories/RevEv.pdf on January 10, 2010.

Lezotte, L. (2005). More effective schools: Professional learning communities in action. In R. DuFour, R. Eaker, & R. DuFour (Eds.), *On common ground: The power of professional learning communities* (pp. 177–191). Bloomington, IN: Solution Tree Press.

Lickona, T., & Davidson, M. (2005). *Smart and good high schools: Integrating excellence and ethics for success in school, work, and beyond.* Cortland, NY: Center for the 4th and 5th R's (Respect and Responsibility) and Washington, DC: Character Education Partnership.

Lieberman, A. (1995). Restructuring schools: The dynamics of changing practice, structure, and culture. In A. Lieberman (Ed.), *The work of restructuring schools: Building from the ground up* (pp. 1–17). New York: Teachers College Press.

Little, J. (1990). The persistence of privacy: Autonomy and initiative in teachers' professional relations. *Teachers College Record, 91*(4), 509–536.

Little, J. (2006). *Professional community and professional development in the learning-centered school.* Washington, DC: National Education Association. Accessed at www.nea.org/assets/docs/mf_pdreport.pdf on January 18, 2010.

Lortie, D. (1975). *Schoolteacher: A sociological study*. Chicago: University of Chicago Press.

Louis, K. S., Kruse, S. D., & Marks, H. M. (1996). *Schoolwide professional community*. In F. Newmann & Associates, *Authentic achievement: Restructuring schools for intellectual quality* (pp. 179–204). San Francisco: Jossey-Bass.

Louis, K., & Leithwood, K. (2009). *Learning from districts' efforts to improve student achievement*. New York: Wallace Foundation.

Marzano, R. J. (2003). *What works in schools: Translating research into action*. Alexandria, VA: Association for Supervision and Curriculum Development.

Marzano, R. J. (2006). *Classroom assessment and grading that work*. Alexandria, VA: Association for Supervision and Curriculum Development.

Marzano, R. J. (2009). Setting the record straight on "high-yield" strategies. *Phi Delta Kappan, 91*(1), 30–37.

Marzano, R. J., & Waters, T. (2009). *District leadership that works: Striking the right balance*. Bloomington, IN: Solution Tree Press.

Marzano, R. J., Waters, T., & McNulty, B. A. (2005). *School leadership that works: From research to results*. Alexandria, VA: Association for Supervision and Curriculum Development.

Maurer, R. (2010). *How to create a vision (or compelling goal) statement*. Accessed at www.beyondresistance.com/pdf_files/5x3_5x8.pdf on January 1, 2010.

Maxwell, J. (1995). *Developing the leaders around you: How to help others reach their full potential*. Nashville: Thomas Nelson.

McCauley, C., & Van Velsor, E. (2003). *The Center for Creative Leadership handbook of leadership development*. San Francisco: Jossey-Bass.

McDonald, J., Mohr, N, Dichter, A., & McDonald, E. (2007). *The power of protocols: An educator's guide to better practice* (2nd ed.). New York: Teachers College Press.

McLaughlin, M., & Talbert, J. (2001). *Professional communities and the work of high school teaching*. Chicago: University of Chicago Press.

McLaughlin, M., & Talbert, J. (2006). *Building school-based teacher learning communities: Professional strategies to improve student achievement*. New York: Teachers College Press.

Mid-continent Research For Education and Learning. (2005). *High needs schools: What does it take to beat the odds?* Aurora, CO: Author.

Mintzberg, H. (1994). *The rise and fall of strategic planning*. New York: Free Press.

Mintzberg, H. (2005). *Managers not MBAs: A hard look at the soft practice of Managing and Management Development*. San Francisco: Berrett-Koehler.

Naisbitt, J., & Aburdene, P. (1985). *Reinventing the corporation*. New York: Warner Books.

Nanus, B. (1992). *Visionary leadership*. San Francisco: Jossey-Bass.

National Center on Response to Intervention. (2008, May 12). *What is response to intervention* [webinar]. Accessed at www.rti4success.org/index.php?option=com_content&task=blogcategory&id=22&Itemid=79 on January 18, 2010.

National Commission on Teaching and America's Future. (2003). *No dream denied: A pledge to America's children*. Washington, DC: Author.

National Education Association. (2003). *NEA's Keys initiative*. Accessed at www.nea.org/schoolquality/index.html on January 6, 2006.

National School Reform Faculty. (1999). *The Collaborative Assessment Conference: Overview*. Accessed at www.nsrfharmony.org/protocol/doc/cac.pdf on January 10, 2009.

National Staff Development Council. (1999, August/September). Developing norms. *Tools for Schools, 3*(1) 3–5.

National Staff Development Council. (2006). *Collaboration skills*. Accessed at www.nsdc.org/standards/collaborationskills.cfm on January 21, 2010.

Newmann, F., & Associates. (1996). *Authentic achievement: Restructuring schools for intellectual quality.* San Francisco: Jossey-Bass.

Newmann, F., & Wehlage, G. (1995). *Successful school restructuring: A report to the public and educators by the center for restructuring schools.* Madison: University of Wisconsin.

Newmann, F., & Wehlage, G. (1996). Restructuring for authentic student achievement. In F. Newmann & Associates, *Authentic achievement: Restructuring schools for intellectual quality* (pp. 286–301). San Francisco: Jossey-Bass.

Odden, A. (2009). We know how to turn school around—We just haven't done it. *Education Week, 29*(14), 22–23.

Odden, A. R., & Archibald, S. J. (2009). *Doubling student performance . . . and finding the resources to do it.* Thousand Oaks, CA: Corwin Press.

O'Hora, D., & Maglieri, K. (2006). Goal statements and goal-directed behavior: A relational frame account of goal setting in organizations. *Journal of Organizational Behavior Management, 26*(1), 131–170.

O'Neill, J., & Conzemius, A. (2005). *The power of SMART goals: Using goals to improve student learning.* Bloomington, IN: Solution Tree Press.

Patterson, K., Grenny, J., Maxfield, D., McMillan, R., & Switzler, A. (2008). *Influencer: The power to change anything.* New York: McGraw-Hill.

Patterson, K., Grenny, J., McMillan, R., & Switzler, A. (2002). *Crucial conversations: Tools for talking when stakes are high.* New York: McGraw-Hill.

Perkins, D. (2003). *King Arthur's roundtable.* New York: Wiley.

Peters, T. (1987). *Thriving on chaos: A handbook for a management revolution.* New York: Knopf.

Peters, T., & Austin, N. (1985). *A passion for excellence: The leadership difference.* New York: Random House.

Pfeffer, J., & Sutton, R. (2000). *The knowing-doing gap: How smart companies turn knowledge into action.* Boston: Harvard Business School Press.

Pfeffer, J., & Sutton, R. (2006). *Hard facts, dangerous half-truths & total nonsense: Profiting from evidence-based management.* Boston: Harvard Business School Press.

Pinchot, G., & Pinchot, E. (1993). *The end of bureaucracy and the rise of the intelligent organization.* San Francisco: Berrett-Koehler.

Popham, W. J. (2004). Curriculum matters. *American School Board Journal, 191*(11), 30–33.

Popham, W. J. (2008). *Transformative assessment.* Alexandria, VA: Association for Supervision and Curriculum Development.

Popham, W. J. (2009). Curriculum mistakes to avoid. *American School Board Journal, 196*(11), 36–38.

President's Commission on Excellence in Special Education. (2002). *A new era: Revitalizing special education for children and their families.* Accessed at www2.ed.gov/inits/commissionsboards/whspecialeducation/index.html on April 1, 2010.

Purkey, S., & Smith, M. (1983). Effective schools: A review. *Elementary School Journal, 83*(4), 427–452.

Reeves, D. B. (2000). *Accountability in action: A blueprint for learning organizations.* Denver, CO: Advanced Learning Press.

Reeves, D. B. (2002). *The leader's guide to standards: A blueprint for educational equity and excellence.* San Francisco: John Wiley & Sons.

Reeves, D. B. (2004). *Accountability for learning: How teachers and school leaders can take charge.* Alexandria, VA: Association for Supervision and Curriculum Development.

Reeves, D. (2005). Putting it all together: Standards, assessment, and accountability in successful professional learning communities. In R. DuFour, R. Eaker, & R. DuFour,

On common ground: The power of professional learning communities (pp. 45–63). Bloomington, IN: Solution Tree Press.

Reeves, D. B. (2006). *The learning leader: How to focus school improvement for better results*. Alexandria, VA: Association for Supervision and Curriculum Development.

Reeves, D. B. (2009). *Leading change in your school: How to conquer myths, build commitment, and get results*. Alexandria, VA: Association for Supervision and Curriculum Development.

Reeves, D. B. (in press). *Assessing 21st century skills*. Bloomington, IN: Solution Tree Press.

Richardson, J. (2004). *From the inside out: Learning from the positive deviance in your organization*. Oxford, OH: National Staff Development Council.

Saphier, J. (2005). *John Adams' promise: How to have good schools for all our children, not just for some*. Acton, MA: Research for Better Teaching.

Saphier, J., King, M., & D'Auria, J. (2006). 3 strands form strong school culture. *Journal of Staff Development, 27*(3), 51–59.

Sarason, S. (1996). *Revisiting the culture of the school and the problem of change*. New York: Teachers College Press.

Schaffer, R., & Thomson, H. (1998). Successful change programs begin with results. In *Harvard Business Review on Change* (pp. 189–214). Boston: Harvard Business School Press.

Schein, E. (1996). Leadership and organizational culture. In F. Hesselbein, M. Goldsmith, & R. Beckhard (Eds.), *The leader of the future: New visions, strategies and practices for the next era* (pp. 59–70). San Francisco: Jossey-Bass.

Schlechty, P. (1990). *Schools for the 21st century*. San Francisco: Jossey-Bass.

Schlechty, P. (1997). *Inventing better schools: An action plan for educational reform*. San Francisco: Jossey-Bass.

Schlechty, P. (2005). *Creating the capacity to support innovation* (occasional paper no. 2). Accessed at www.schlechtycenter.org/tools-for-change on January 10, 2010.

Schmoker, M. (1999). *Results: The key to continuous school improvement* (2nd ed.). Alexandria, VA: Association for Supervision and Curriculum Development.

Schmoker, M. (2004a). Learning communities at the crossroads: A response to Joyce and Cook. *Phi Delta Kappan, 86*(1), 84–89.

Schmoker, M. (2004b). Start here for improving teaching. *School Administrator, 61*(10), 48.

Schmoker, M. (2006). *Results now: How we can achieve unprecedented improvement in teaching and learning*. Alexandria, VA: Association for Supervision and Curriculum Development.

Senge, P., Kleiner, A., Roberts, C., Ross, R., & Smith, B. (1994). *The fifth discipline fieldbook: Strategies and tools for building a learning organization*. New York: Doubleday/Currency.

Sergiovanni, T. (2005). *Strengthening the heartbeat: Leading and learning together in schools*. San Francisco: Jossey-Bass.

Shannon, G., & Bylsma, P. (2004). *Characteristics of improved school districts: Themes from research*. Olympia, WA: Office of the Superintendent of Instruction.

Sizer, T. (1991). No pain, no gain. *Educational Leadership, 48*(8), 32–34.

Southern Regional Education Board. (2000). *Things that matter most in improving student learning*. Atlanta, GA: Southwest Regional Education Board.

Sparks, D. (2007). *Leading for results: Transforming, teaching, learning and relationships in schools*. Thousand Oaks, CA: Corwin Press.

Stevenson, H., & Stigler, J. (1992). *The learning gap: Why our schools are failing and what we can learn from Japanese and Chinese education*. New York: Simon & Simon.

Stiggins, R. (2004). New assessment beliefs for a new school mission. *Phi Delta Kappan, 86*(1), 22–27.

Stiggins, R. (2005). Assessment FOR learning: Building a culture of confident learners. In R. DuFour, R. Eaker, & R. DuFour (Eds.), *On common ground: The power of professional learning communities* (pp. 65–83). Bloomington, IN: Solution Tree Press.

Stiggins, R., & DuFour, R. (2009). Maximizing the power of formative assessments. *Phi Delta Kappan, 90*(9), 640–644.

Stigler, J., & Hiebert, J. (2009). Closing the teaching gap. *Phi Delta Kappan, 91*(3), 32–37.

Stone, D., Patton, B., & Heen, S. (2000). *Difficult conversations: How to discuss what matters most.* New York: Penguin Books.

Symonds, K. (2004). *Perspectives on the gaps: Fostering the academic success of minority and low-income students.* Naperville, IL: North Central Regional Educational Laboratory.

Thompson, J. (1995). The renaissance of learning in business. In S. Chawla & J. Renesch (Eds.), *Learning organizations: Developing cultures for tomorrow's workplace* (pp. 85–100). New York: Productivity Press.

Thompson-Grove, G. (2000). *National school reform faculty.* Accessed at www.nsrfharmony .org/protocol/doc/atlas_ifsw.pdf on January 10, 2010.

Tichy, N. (1997). *The leadership engine: How winning companies build leaders at every level.* New York: Harper Business.

Ulrich, D. (1996). Credibility x capability. In F. Hesselbein, M. Goldsmith, & R. Beckhard (Eds.), *The leader of the future: New visions, strategies and practices for the next era* (pp. 209–220). San Francisco: Jossey-Bass.

Waterman, R. (1987). *The renewal factor: How the best get and keep the competitive edge.* New York: Bantam Books.

Weisberg, D., Sexton, S., Mulhem, J., & Keeling, D. (2009). *The widget effect: Our national failure to recognize differences in teacher effectiveness.* Accessed at http://widgeteffect .org/downloads/thewidgeteffect_execsummary.pdf on January 10, 2010.

Wellman, B., & Lipton, L. (2004). *Data-driven dialogue: A facilitator's guide to collaborative inquiry.* Sherman, CT: Mira Via.

WestEd. (2000). *Teachers who learn, kids who achieve: a look at schools with model professional development.* San Francisco: Author.

Wheatley, M. (1999). Goodbye command and control. In F. Hesselbein & P. M. Cohen (Eds.), *Leader to leader: Enduring insights from the Drucker Foundation's award-winning journal* (pp. 151–162). San Francisco: Jossey-Bass.

Wheelis, A. (1973). *How people change.* New York: Harper & Row.

Wiliam, D., & Thompson, M. (2007). Integrating assessment with learning: What will it take to make it work? In C. A. Dwyer (Ed.), *The future of assessment: Shaping teaching and learning* (pp. 53–84). Mahwah, NJ: Lawrence Erlbaum.

Williams, T., Perry, M., Studler, C., Brazil, N., Kirst, M., Haertel, E., et al. (2006). *Similar students, different results: Why do some schools do better?* Mountain View, CA: EdSource.

Wright, S., Horn, S., & Sanders, W. (1997). Teacher and classroom context effects on student achievement: Implications for teacher evaluation. *Journal of Personnel Evaluation in Education, 11,* 57–67.

Index

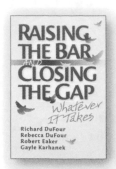

Raising the Bar and Closing the Gap
Whatever It Takes
Richard DuFour, Rebecca DuFour, Robert Eaker, and Gayle Karhanek
This sequel to the best-selling *Whatever It Takes: How Professional Learning Communities Respond When Kids Don't Learn* expands on original ideas and presses further with new insights. Foundational concepts combine with real-life examples of schools throughout North America that have gone from traditional cultures to PLCs. **BKF378**

Leadership in Professional Learning Communities at Work™
Learning by Doing
Featuring Richard DuFour, Rebecca DuFour, Robert Eaker, and Thomas Many
Watch leaders in action within a professional learning community. This short program for PLC leaders uses unscripted interviews and footage from schools to illustrate the role of effective leadership, particularly from the principal, in embedding PLC practices and values in a school. **DVF024**

Collaborative Teams in Professional Learning Communities at Work™
Learning by Doing
Featuring Richard DuFour, Rebecca DuFour, Robert Eaker, and Thomas Many
This video shows exactly what collaborative teams do. Aligned with the best-selling book *Learning by Doing,* it features unscripted footage of collaboration in action. Learn how teams organize, interact, and find time to meet; what products they produce; and more. **DVF023**

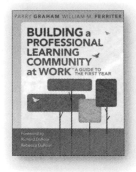

Building a Professional Learning Community at Work™
A Guide to the First Year
Parry Graham and William M. Ferriter
Foreword by Richard DuFour and Rebecca DuFour
This play-by-play guide to implementing PLC concepts uses a story to focus each chapter. The authors analyze the story, highlighting good decisions and mistakes. They offer research behind best practice and wrap up each chapter with practical recommendations and tools. **BKF273**

On Common Ground: The Power of Professional Learning Communities
Edited by Richard DuFour, Robert Eaker, and Rebecca DuFour
Examine a colorful cross-section of educators' experiences with PLCs. This collection of insights and stories from practitioners throughout North America highlights the benefits of PLCs and offers unique angles of approach to a variety of school improvement challenges. **BKF180**

Solution Tree | Press *a division of* Solution Tree

Visit solution-tree.com or call 800.733.6786 to order.